THE THEORY OF MONEY AND FINANCE

Related titles from The Macmillan Press

R. W. Evans and G. H. Makepeace: MONETARY THEORY, INSTITUTIONS AND PRACTICE

C. A. E. Goodhart: MONEY, INFORMATION AND UNCERTAINTY

Brian Morgan: MONETARISTS AND KEYNESIANS

J. Ribaud: THE MECHANICS OF MONEY

THE THEORY OF MONEY AND FINANCE

RICHARD COGHLAN

First published 1980 by
THE MACMILLAN PRESS LTD
London and Basingstoke
Associated companies in Delhi Dublin
Hong Kong Johannesburg Lagos Melbourne
New York Singapore and Tokyo

Printed in Great Britain by
J. W. Arrowsmith Ltd, Bristol BS3 2NT

British Library Cataloguing in Publication Data

Coghlan, Richard
The theory of money and finance
1. Money
I. Title
332.4'01 HG221

ISBN 0-333-25643-3
ISBN 0-333-25644-1 Pbk

To Wynrhys

CONTENTS

PREFACE

This is a practical book, or that at least is its intention. It introduces the concept of *money* and deals comprehensively with the basic monetary theory required for an undergraduate course on money or macroeconomics. There is also, however, detailed discussion of empirical work in the area of monetary economics, and emphasis is placed on the problems encountered in giving practical expression to abstract theory. In this context it is particularly necessary to distinguish clearly between the various possible definitions of money. While this is likely to prove crucial to the role money is to play in the economy, it is very poorly dealt with in the literature, and more usually money is presented as an homogeneous commodity, implying that it makes no difference to, say, the specification of a demand for money function which definition is employed.

An introduction to flow-of-funds accounting, and the operation, and significance, of financial markets and institutions is also provided. It is hoped that this will help the student to relate his economic theory to the published data and to existing financial institutions. Often, theory is presented in a completely abstract manner and little attempt is made to introduce the student to the raw data which will form a basic material input to any practical application of economics.

The financial institutions, and the financial flows they generate, are generally not dealt with in any detail, and yet they are fundamental to an understanding of the role of money, and are anyway important in their own right. The economy, and the financial markets and institutions, develop together, and any study of the growth of output requires an explanation of how the increasing financing requirements are accommodated.

Finally, the process of money-supply creation is dealt with in some detail. This is in two parts. The first, Chapter 9, deals with the standard money multiplier approach and the criticisms that have been raised against it, in particular the debate surrounding the 'New View'. The second part, Chapter 10, develops an argument in terms of the lending activities of banks to explain the process of money creation. This provides a dynamic, disequilibrium, framework which justifies a direct relationship between the supply of money and income/expenditure markets. There have already been some interesting empirical studies which have attempted to explain the importance of money within disequilibrium models, and the number of such studies is increasing.

This book is primarily intended for students following a second- or third-year course in monetary or macroeconomics, and who have already become familiar with elementary economic theory. It should, however, also have a wider use. It should prove useful for courses dealing with financial analysis and portfolio choice, providing a link with the operation of financial institutions and the role of money and finance in the economy. In addition, much of the book should be accessible to those working in a financial market environment.

The practical approach adopted, and the requirements of modern applied economics, have required the occasional inclusion of a few econometric and statistical terms. These need not cause concern to those unfamiliar with the terminology, and it should be possible to follow the presentation without necessarily understanding the detailed derivation.

Much of the material included in this book was originally written up in separate papers, and, at that stage, benefited from discussions with colleagues both inside the Bank of England and elsewhere. In particular I would like to thank Charles Goodhart for his perceptive comments. In addition I am most grateful to Michael Artis and Brian Hilliard, who have read the book in its complete form and whose comments and suggestions have been invaluable. The Bank of England were generous enough to provide facilities for drawing the many diagrams included in the book, and I am indebted to Amy Crosby, and all those involved, for their splendid work. Finally, I would like to thank my family, who have provided support and inspiration during the long evenings and weekends that I have been locked away in my study.

RICHARD COGHLAN

ACKNOWLEDGEMENTS

The author and publishers wish to thank the following, who have kindly given permission for the use of copyright material:

Bank of England, for a table from *Quarterly Bulletin* (June 1970).

Federal Reserve Bank of St Louis, for tables from *Review* (April 1970).

Gower Press, for a table from *Financial Services Review 1972–73.*

Lloyds Bank Ltd, for two charts from *Lloyds Bank Review* (July 1978).

London Business School, for a table from *Economic Outlook 1977–80.*

North-Holland Publishing Company, Amsterdam, for a table from *Review of Economics and Statistics* (November 1966).

1. THE FUNCTIONS OF MONEY

In defining the role played by money we need first to draw the distinction between the institutional arrangements that facilitate the employment of a single commodity (or small group of commodities) as a means of payment for all other commodities, and the commodity that actually serves that function. The former may be termed 'the institution of money' while the latter is 'the money commodity'.

We begin by examining the need for the institution of money, and the role it plays in the economic system. This is done by contrasting the organisation and operation of markets under alternative barter exchange systems with a monetary economy. In this way the existence of money is shown to depend critically upon *uncertainty*. Having thus established the institutional foundation of money, the next stage is to take a closer look at the essential characteristics of this institution and the physical commodity that bears that title.

Economics is about scarcity. Elementary courses in microeconomics demonstrate the advantages of trade resulting from the existence of different tastes, endowments and skills which thereby permits the division of labour and specialisation in production, and consequently the attainment of a higher welfare function. The problems involved in this trade, however, are often assumed away.

The most obvious example of this is in the basic Walrasian general-equilibrium model. In such models Pareto optimality is attainable through specialisation and trade, and money has no role to play. Exchanges in this system take place by means of barter – that is, a series of bilateral pairwise exchanges requiring a double coincidence of wants and endowments at particular points in time. Admittedly, it is a very sophisticated barter system, taking place in a formal market, and controlled at the centre by an auctioneer. In this market perfect knowledge exists of all relative prices and the creditworthiness of all participants over all times. There is no risk and no uncertainty, and the cost of transactions is zero, i.e. the auctioneer is not paid and information is costless. General equilibrium is established and all relative prices determined once all excess demands have been eliminated (see, for example, Hahn, 1973).

It is a beautifully simple model which permits analysis of the interaction between markets and individuals. In this way it enables us to get away from the partial analysis of isolated activities where it is assumed that there are no repercussions on the rest of the economy, and no feedbacks to the particular market being considered. It therefore has an analytical value when we are concerned with the abstract theory of choice, but, because of the unrealistic nature of the assumptions, it is an approach that has little practical value for considering the policy decisions that have to be taken in the real economy, or for analysing the problems that are likely to arise in such an economy.

In the real world uncertainty exists to a very high degree, and mainly because of this transactions costs are high. These transactions costs exclude the cost of transport and storage which may affect relative prices but not the cost of concluding a particular deal. Transactions costs are real costs absorbed in making transactions and arise out of the time and effort required to obtain information regarding relative prices, the qualities of various commodities offered in exchange, how values may change over time, the creditworthiness of buyers (or sellers), and so on. In a world of perfect certainty this information would be freely available to everyone and transactions costs would not exist.

As economies develop a high degree of specialisation and trade, and the production process lengthens, so time becomes an important factor in the production and exchange of goods and services. The separation of production and use, and the delay between the purchase of inputs and sale of output, brings with it increased uncertainty about the future availability and price of, and markets for, goods and services. This uncertainty can be reduced by employing money in transactions, and it is probably fair to say that the institution of money is a prerequisite to the technological developments described above.

Inflation will tend to reduce the information content of fiat money. The information content of money does not imply that money provides information on the quality of goods exchanged, or individual probity, etc., but rather that people will generally have much greater knowledge about the quality and durability of money than they will about the credit or goods that might otherwise be offered in exchange. This situation may be changed in periods of very rapid and accelerating inflation. The extent to which people are prepared to maintain their use of a rapidly devaluing currency is some indication of the degree of uncertainty involved in barter transactions and the information content of an established monetary mechanism. This is illustrated by the example of many South American countries which have had very high rates of inflation for long periods, and the recent experience of many Western countries, including the United Kingdom. Probably the best example is the hyperinflationary experience of Germany in the 1920s which has been documented by Bresciani-Turroni (1937).

The Development from Barter to a Monetary Economy

As a starting-point it is possible to imagine two extremes, neither of which requires the use or existence of money:

(i) A state in which uncertainty and mistrust are so high that no trade takes place and each person, or self-contained group, makes or steals all its own requirements. Money is not required if the division of labour and distribution of goods is regulated by convention or power. This is most likely to be the case only within relatively small groups, when such groups may be thought to share the same welfare function. An obvious example is the operation of the family unit, but there are plenty of others; the internal functioning of a monastery or commune, and even certain exchanges between small communities and friends.

(ii) At the other extreme is the costless, certain trade of a Walrasian general-equilibrium system, within which each individual (or group) can trade up to the point where he maximises his welfare.

Both are extremes and both are unrealistic descriptions of existing national economies. However, by tracing out a path from one towards the other we can see the part played by money.

(1) In a complete barter system with no specialised means of payment, for any exchange to take place it is necessary for the person wishing to sell a commodity to find someone else who wants this particular commodity, at that particular time, and who will offer in exchange the very thing desired by the vendor, i.e. it must be an *effective* demand. This, naturally, will be very difficult to achieve. If we restrict trade to direct barter, i.e. a market system in which the only goods exchanged are those desired for their use value, there is no reason why any form of recognisable equilibrium should be achieved. It will generally be impossible for each economic unit to complete all the transactions desired, and as a result all excess demands will not be eliminated.

(2) Only with the introduction of indirect barter do we approach a market economy and the possibility of achieving a general equilibrium. With this system people hold goods which are desired solely for their value in exchange rather than for their immediate use.

Suppose, for example, person 1 wishes to exchange good *A* for good *F* but that the only other person who wants *A* is person 2, who will give good *B* in exchange. The first person then has to arrange a series of exchanges until he eventually arrives at the desired exchange. It is therefore possible to establish the following *exchange chain*:

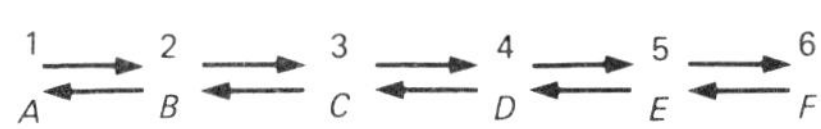

The problems and costs involved are enormous. Having arranged the exchanges person 1 then has the risk that the promised exchanges will in fact take place as planned and that he will be left with a commodity which is not wanted for its own sake. He could, for example, get to 4 in the chain only to find that 5 had decided he would like F himself and has already made the exchange with 6. In addition the quantities and qualities of the goods must be acceptable to each of the parties in the exchange. This method of trading requires each transactor to have a great deal of knowledge regarding not only his own subjective preferences but also those of the people with whom he is dealing, the true nature of the goods traded, and the trustworthiness of the various transactors.

For the moment we are excluding transportation and storage costs involved in each link in the chain, but still it is obvious that trade will not be as great as it might otherwise be. If it is assumed that transactions costs are directly proportional to the number of transactions required, it becomes possible to think of them as a *tax on trade*. So the development towards a monetary economy, and the monetary economy itself, can be seen as attempts to reduce this tax.

(3) An improvement on the previous system of indirect barter would be to bring the transactors together in an organised market, such as a fairground. Costs would be reduced since it would now be much easier to find a partner to a desired exchange. It would not, however, in general reduce the high number of transactions required. Naturally enough such a system may be called 'fairground barter'.

(4) The next step to be taken is to move to a system of trading-post barter. Search costs will be further reduced if trading-posts are set up for trade between particular pairs of commodities. Such a system should at the same time result in an improvement in information regarding market exchange rates, leading, presumably, to a uniform rate of exchange between any two commodities. Even so, the system will still require $\frac{1}{2}n(n-1)$ trading-posts[1] for n commodities. In an economy with only 1000 commodities there would still be 499,500 trading-posts and rates of exchange. So far the number of links in the exchange chain has not altered, but the search costs, and degree of uncertainty, have been reduced.

(5) Finally, we arrive at a monetary economy. If there were a single commodity (or piece of paper) that would be accepted by all traders in *complete and final settlement of debts*, this would

greatly facilitate exchange, reducing search costs *and* the number of transactions required to obtain a desired commodity. In such an economy only $n-1$ rates of exchange will be required; there will be only a single exchange rate for each of $n-1$ commodities in terms of the nth which has general acceptability.

Returning to the original exchange chain considered it can be seen that the previous five exchanges required for person 1 eventually to exchange A for F has been reduced to only two.

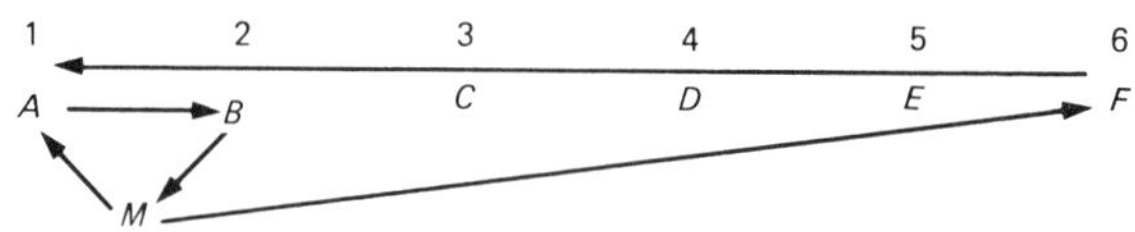

In exchange for A, 2 now gives 1 a commodity called M which is also acceptable to 6 in exchange for F. As a result, any two exchanges will only require two transactions. Since this commodity, M, has, by definition, general acceptability the degree of uncertainty is greatly reduced. Arguments along these lines have been employed by Hicks (1967), Clower (1969) and Brunner and Meltzer (1971), among others.

The foregoing argument may be formalised by defining two separate kinds of costs associated with trade:

(1) *Transactions costs* (C_t). These are the costs involved in search and bargaining. Such costs are assumed to vary directly with the number of transactions undertaken in any one time period, and are not related to the size of the transaction. These are the 'taxation' costs referred to above. The less frequently you trade, the lower the transaction cost. For example, if you could go forever without trading, this cost would be zero. Transactions costs are therefore lower the greater the interval between transactions. This interval is referred to as the *transactions period*, T:

$$C_t = f(T), \qquad f_T < 0$$

(2) *Waiting costs* (C_w). These are the costs which result from not trading. These are objective in the sense of costs of storage and home production, and subjective in the sense of not

consuming or owning what you would rather have. Such waiting costs obviously vary directly with the length of the transactions period:

$$C_w = g(T), \qquad g_T > 0$$

These two types of cost are combined in a single two-dimensional diagram in Figure 1.1. C represents the vertical summation of the two separate cost schedules. At the lowest point on this curve marginal transactions costs are equal to marginal waiting costs, so that T_o represents the *optimal transactions period.* Any variation from this period, given the cost schedules, will increase the total cost, i.e. it will add more to one cost than it subtracts from the other.

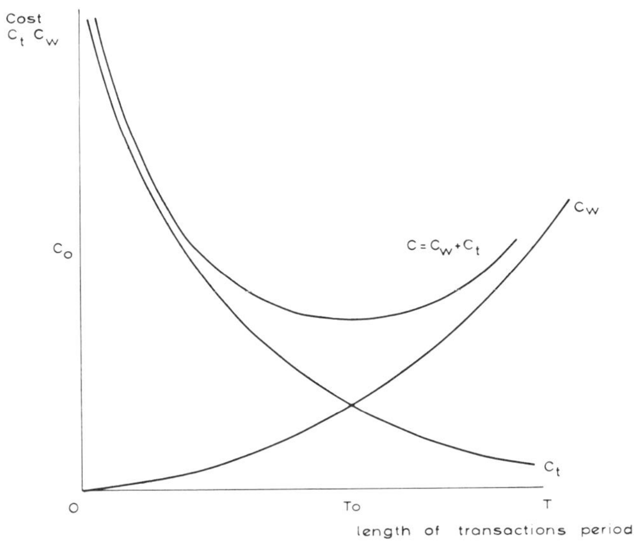

Figure 1.1 The Costs of Trade

We can now employ this framework to look at the effect of organised markets on trade. The organisation of markets, and the eventual institution of money itself, will reduce transactions costs but leave waiting costs largely unaffected. The transactions cost curve will therefore move progressively to the left, and the total cost curve will move down and to the left. This movement is summarised in Figure 1.2. As a result total trading costs are reduced, with the result that the transactions period is shortened and people trade more frequently.

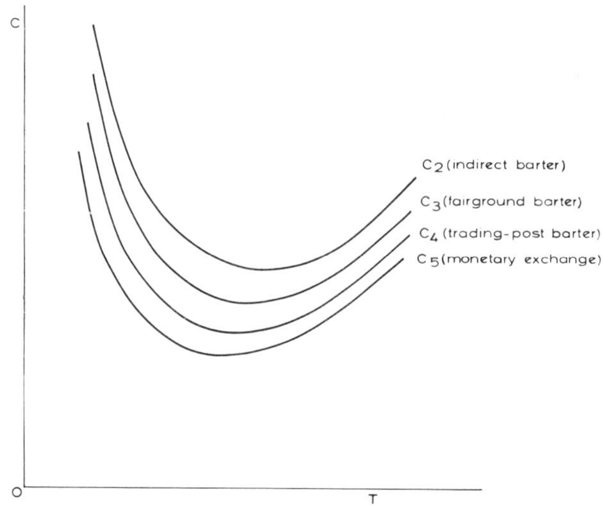

Figure 1.2 The Gains from Market Organisation

An obvious prerequisite for the existence of money is that there is some trading activity. The importance of money resides in its information content reducing the uncertainty implicit in specialisation and trade. The monetary mechanism can be seen as lifting a technological barrier to trade: it is enabling, not determining, trade. But that is not to say that money is not important, since a similar statement could be made about any technological advance. In facilitating trade and specialisation money plays a fundamental role.

Because production and exchange take place over periods of time there is obviously a temporal aspect to any monetary economy. In the certain, costless, general-equilibrium world we have already discussed, the future may be collapsed to the present, and all present and future decisions can be made at a single point in time. In a more realistic setting money may be seen as the essential link between the present and the future in an uncertain world.

So far we have discussed the advantages of a monetary economy in terms of the resultant reduction in uncertainty and the transactions period. But this is not the complete story. The adoption of a monetary system will lead to increases in efficiency and, consequently, in the level of economic activity. These gains result from the nature of the market organisation and are independent of the actual monetary commodity in use.[2] They may be summarised under the following three headings:

(i) improvements in efficiency resulting from the increased ability to take advantage of specialisation and division of labour in production and exchange;

(ii) the release of resources previously engaged in the process of bartering and gathering information; and

(iii) a general reduction in uncertainty should improve expectations of the future and encourage producers and consumers to adopt a more optimistic and expansionary approach.

The introduction of money can therefore be seen to result in improvements in economic efficiency which will be reflected in both demand and supply relationships.

The Characteristics of Money

Having established the advantages of a monetary economy, we turn now to a discussion of the distinguishing characteristics of money. (At the moment we are still concerned with an abstract concept, though we shall define below the necessary characteristics of any commodity that is to perform this function.)

Money is generally defined to have three functions, i.e. to serve as:

(i) a means of payment,
(ii) a unit of account, and
(iii) a store of value.

Money will need to be a store of value given that it bridges the gap between payments and receipts; the temporal aspect of the monetary mechanism has already been referred to above. It is, however, by no means the only, or even the best, store of value. There are many other assets which will act as a store of value, and which in many cases will yield a positive return as well.

Because money acts as the means of payment it is naturally convenient that it should also serve as the unit of account. The direction of causation is, however, clearly established, and, furthermore, there may well be exceptions. The guinea in the United Kingdom, for example, continued to be employed as a unit of account long after it ceased to be an acceptable means of payment. This is then not even a necessary characteristic of money.

The fundamental distinguishing characteristic of money is that it is the means of payment, which means that it is *generally acceptable in final settlement of all debts to the satisfaction of both parties.* The definition of money as a means of payment places it in a narrower category than a means of exchange. With a simple means of exchange, e.g. a mortgage, hire purchase, trade credit, etc., a claim remains to be discharged – it is only at this point that the means of payment comes in. It also implies *general acceptability*, which is not required by a means of exchange (see Shackle, 1971).

In recent years there has been a sharp increase in the availability and use of credit cards. These cards make credit more accessible to the individual, with a bank providing information on the creditworthiness of the purchaser and accepting the risks involved. The bank in effect makes a loan to an individual for the purchase of goods and services, and the risk of default remains until that loan has been repaid. Moreover, credit cards are not acceptable in all shops, and the size of transactions is anyway restricted. Credit cards do not provide a substitute for money. Someone, in this case a bank, has got to pay the vendor, and a debt has been created which has still to be settled through a monetary exchange. Credit cards, and other financial claims, play an important role in facilitating exchange in any developed economy, but they still require the prior existence of the institution of money. This topic will be returned to when we come to consider financial markets and institutions later.

If there is to be some particular commodity, or piece of paper, that is to perform the function of a means of payment, it must possess certain physical characteristics. These may be listed as follows:

(i) *Durability*. This is obviously related to the fact that the temporal aspect of a monetary economy requires money to act as a store of value.

(ii) *Homogeneity*. Money that is in some sense worth less than other money will tend to circulate more quickly, with the good money being withdrawn from circulation. This is an example of what has become known as *Gresham's Law*, after Sir Thomas Gresham (adviser to Queen Elizabeth I), who observed these effects following a debasing of the coinage. To take a more parochial example, if cows are accepted as a means of payment, at a known rate of exchange, people will be more likely to eat the fat cows and trade with the thin ones. Additionally, uncertainty will not be minimised if there are a great variety of commodities, varying in type and quality, circulating as money.

(iii) *Recognisability*. It is no good offering money in settlement of a debt if it is not recognised, and accepted as such. This is part of the requirement that money be 'generally acceptable'.

(iv) *Divisibility*. There are many different types and sizes of transaction to be conducted. An efficient monetary commodity must obviously be highly divisible to accommodate these needs. In this respect cows are unlikely to serve very well.

(v) *Portability*. Unless all trade is restricted to a single small area the means of payment has to be transported. The easier and more cheaply this can be done, the more efficient the monetary commodity.

(vi) *Stable demand and supply conditions*. These are necessary to prevent wild fluctuations in the value of money, i.e. in the general price level.

Bearing these characteristics in mind we can trace the (typical) development of money in the so-called 'advanced' countries. For an interesting, but uncomplicated, introduction to the historical development of money, see Morgan (1965), and also Cameron (1967). The first type of money to develop generally embodies a high intrinsic value. This is necessary because of the absence of any strong centralised authority and the high degree of uncertainty and mistrust that is likely to exist. As economic organisation improves and states come into existence, the monetary commodity becomes formalised through the minting of coins. These coins, however, retain their intrinsic value, i.e. the metal from which they are made is equivalent to their face value. This is still necessary if there are many weak states in existence and the technology does not exist to protect the currency against forgery.

There also arose a debate between the 'metalists', who believed that currency obtained its value purely by virtue of the intrinsic value of the metal from which it was made, and the 'cartelists', who claimed that its value resided essentially in the power of the issuing authority. This debate, however, misses the point, for, as we argued above, money requires social acceptability. If the central authority is weak and forgery easy then a high intrinsic value is necessary. If, on the other hand, there is a strong government and technology and supervision are such that counterfeiting can be made very difficult, it is likely that the intrinsic value of the currency can be greatly reduced. A powerful central authority can itself improve the social acceptability of the currency it issues by insisting that all transactions with the rest of the economy are conducted via this currency.

This possibility for reducing the inherent value of the currency introduces *seignorage* gains for the government, in its position as producer of the currency. This is the difference between the production cost of the money and its value in exchange. From what has just been said above, it should be clear that the degree of seignorage obviously depends upon the power of the issuing authority and the state of printing technology.

Modern currencies have an extremely high seignorage content, which must make the printing of money an attractive alternative to governments having to borrow at high interest rates. The reason for the obvious restraint (although there are those who would argue that far too little restraint has been shown) must be the fear of the inflation, and consequent loss of authority, that would result. There are those, although decreasing in number, who believe money cannot have any effect on prices or output. Presumably if that were true, the national debt (the outstanding indebtedness of the central government) should be liquidated immediately. In this book we shall be adopting a rather more positive view of money without necessarily going to the other extreme of expecting money to be the sole influence on the economy.

Nothing so far has been said about an operational definition of money, i.e. money actually in use. This we shall leave until we come to examine the demand for money.

Money is the first and most fundamental financial innovation in any economy, but money alone will not permit great specialisation in production and risk-taking. What money will allow is the establishment of financial debts and claims which enables the transmission of funds within the economy. As a consequence of this development, there is a role for financial intermediaries to play in improving the transmission of funds, and reducing risks generally. This may also result in an improvement of the monetary mechanism itself, for example the establishment of banks providing a payments mechanism, but also other financial institutions providing different, and necessary, financial services. The importance of these developments provides justification for the attention we shall be giving to this process and the gains that result therefrom. So far it has been the institution of money rather than any particular definition which has been under discussion. The question of which liabilities of the banking sector should be defined as money is discussed later at some length. For the moment we turn to the role money plays in a macroeconomic model.

2. MONEY IN MACROECONOMIC MODELS

This chapter places money within the context of a basic model of the macro economy. It begins by outlining the classical quantity theory and goes on to develop the *IS/LM* paradigm which replaced it as the basic organising framework. Emphasis is placed on the financial aspects of the *IS/LM* model, and there is an introduction to the 'crowding-out' debate. The main weaknesses of this approach are also considered. Finally, the external side of the economy is added to this simple framework in order to see how this affects the money supply, and the policy options, and operations, of the central authorities.

Although there are a number of substantial criticisms of the *IS/LM* model, it still represents the core of most intermediate macroeconomic courses. These criticisms are fully recognised in the chapter, but the approach still provides a reasonable introduction within which to illustrate an important role for money and finance. It is argued below, for example, that it is useful to think of the *IS* schedule as the demand for finance and the *LM* schedule as the supply of finance. In addition the model provides a point of reference with other economics courses, and with the dynamic approach developed in Chapter 10.

The Quantity Theory of Money

This is the simplest and earliest model to emphasise the importance of money. It can be broadly dated as starting with John Locke (1691) and David Hume (1752), and is associated particularly with the latter.

These writers set out to break the direct association between money and wealth, and in the spirit of the new liberalism of the time emphasised the automatic adjustment process of both external flows and the price level. The suggestion is therefore that money serves simply as an oil to lubricate the economic machine. Any positive effects on trade and industry were thought to be short term and would not last; in the long run only prices would change. Hume (1752), for example, stated that, 'In my opinion, it is only in this interval or intermediary situation between the acquisition of money and the rise in prices, that the increasing quantity of gold and silver is favourable to industry.' The interval between an increase in the quantity of money and the full effect on prices is considered to be very long, and a *reduction* in the supply of money to be very destructive to trade. Therefore, while on the basis of comparative statics[1] the quantity of money is unimportant except for prices, a dynamic analysis reveals that it plays a vital role. Hume did expect the rate of interest to change, in the opposite direction to the change in the money supply, but the link between expenditure and the rate of interest was missing. The quantity of money was expected to affect activity and prices directly.

The quantity theory, so-called, then passed through many stages and eventually received universal popularity through the work of Irving Fisher (1913) in the early part of this century. Fisher set out the 'equation of exchange' (really an identity):

$$PT = MV + M'V' \tag{2.1}$$

where P = prices, T = volume of transactions, M = currency – primary money, M' = bank deposit money, V = currency transactions velocity, and V' = deposit transaction velocity.

Theoretical content was given to this model by making P the dependent variable, and the main exogenous influence, but by no means the only possible one, a change in the currency base. Such an exogenous change increases prices directly but also increases the nominal rate of interest and reduces the real rate, where the real rate is the return on real assets, and with perfect information and markets should be equal to the nominal rate less the expected rate of inflation (see also the final section of Chapter 4). Consequently borrowing and lending increase and the resultant credit creation adds to the price rise. In this model the market rate of interest moves in the same direction as the quantity of money and both direct and indirect consequences of any change in the money supply are recognised.

During the process of adjustment both the transactions volume and the velocity of circulation are likely to change. However, equilibrium will be achieved with these stabilising around their old values, and prices rising approximately proportionately to the rise in the money supply. It is this equilibrium conclusion that has attracted most of the attention and has led to the equation of exchange being generally presented as:

$$MV \equiv PY \tag{2.2}$$

where M = the stock of money, V = the velocity of circulation of this stock, i.e. the number of times each unit is employed during the period chosen, P = the price level (index), and Y = the current *flow* of real income/output measured at constant prices.

Apart from the more obvious changes that have been made, it is important to recognise that transactions have been replaced by income. This change has been made for essentially practical reasons since no measure of transactions is available. It is therefore necessary to assume that income and transactions are closely related.

In the form presented, the expression is a mere tautology, so in order to give it theoretical content the following assumptions are made:

(i) Output is fixed at the full-employment level.

(ii) The supply of money is controlled directly by the monetary authorities and decisions regarding the level are taken independently of the rest of the economy, i.e. it is exogenously determined.

(iii) Velocity is fixed in the short to medium term by legal and commercial institutions, and by history and custom. It can be allowed to change but it must be independent of any of the other components in the equation of exchange. V therefore takes on very much the characteristics of a fixed technical coefficient of production, i.e. a certain amount of money is required per unit of transactions, or output. This is determined by the structure of industry, the degree of integration, the efficiency of the payments mechanism, e.g. the sophistication of the financial system, particularly the banking sector, and finally the regularity and timing of payments.

The Cambridge version of this theory was set out explicitly in terms of the quantity of money required to finance the value of transactions. The relationship was therefore put forward more as a demand for money equation, and was based on individual motives for holding money, though these were not analysed at all closely:

$$M = kPY \tag{2.3}$$

where $k = 1/V$.

In such a system money is neutral, a veil serving only to obscure the operation of real forces. It leads directly to what has become known as the *classical dichotomy*:

(i) Money only determines the aggregate price level.
(ii) The interest rate, income and employment are determined by the real forces of productivity and thrift.

Keynes and the *IS*/*LM* Model

Keynes, in *The General Theory* (1936), set up just such a simple, stylised, 'classical' model which he then rejected on the grounds that:

(i) Real income was not fixed at its full-employment level. Writing in the early 1930s he needed no sophisticated econometric techniques to provide evidence for this assertion. In this model changes in the money supply would have real output effects and not simply price effects. The actual effect depends on the elasticity of response of output and prices to changes in the supply of money (see Keynes, 1936, ch. 21); and this relationship will change with the degree of unemployment. Furthermore, the interest rate is the channel through which money is expected to have its influence on output.

(ii) Velocity was no longer considered constant but would itself be a function of the rate of interest and the degree of uncertainty (see Chapter 4 on the demand for money).

The model Keynes set up to replace the classic model has been summarised and popularised in static form by Hicks (1937) and Hansen (1953). This so-called '*IS/LM* model' greatly simplified the analysis by reducing the system to its barest essentials so that the whole thing could be described within a two-dimensional framework. This is both its strength and its weakness. In the first place it helped popularise the Keynesian model and made it easily available and understandable to students of economics. On the other hand, it completely abstracted from the dynamics of the model and as a result has recently come under heavy attack for ignoring the importance of uncertainty and the inelasticity of expectations (Leijonhufvud, 1968; Clower, 1965).

In developing the *IS/LM* model it is worth bearing in mind Keynes's caveat that it is not the intention 'to provide a machine, or method of blind manipulation, which will furnish an infallible answer, but to provide ourselves with an organised and orderly method of thinking out particular problems' (*The General Theory*, 1936, p. 297). All income/expenditure variables are measured in real terms:

$$Y \equiv C + I + G \qquad \text{Equilibrium condition in the goods market} \quad (2.4)$$

$$C = c_0 + c_1(Y - T) \qquad \text{Consumption function} \quad (2.5)$$

$$I = A - ar \qquad \text{Investment function} \quad (2.6)$$

$$\frac{M^d}{P} = e_1 Y - e_2 r \qquad \text{Money demand (real)} \quad (2.7)$$

$$M^s = M \qquad \text{Money supply (nominal)}$$

$$\frac{M^d}{P} = \frac{M^s}{P} \qquad \text{Equilibrium condition in the money market} \quad (2.8)$$

$$G = G \qquad \text{Government expenditure}$$

$$T = T \qquad \text{Government income}$$

where

Y = national income.

C = aggregate consumption. This can more usefully be thought of as the total of private-sector expenditures which are functionally related to income.

I = aggregate investment, or more generally, all those private-sector expenditures which are not functionally related to income – in this case assumed to be partly exogenous (reflecting business expectations) and partly a function of the rate of interest.

G = total public-sector expenditures, assumed to be exogenous.

T = tax income – assumed to include all income to the public sector. While T is obviously a function of income, we shall be assuming that the authorities set the budget deficit as their fiscal policy, taking into account the predicted level of income on the tax yield. We therefore assume that T is exogenously determined; this is probably as valid an assumption as that relating to G.

r = the long-term interest rate. Given the aggregative nature of the model it is necessary to maintain the usual macroeconomic assumption that all interest rates move in reasonable conformity, so that they may all be adequately summarised by a single rate – generally taken to be the rate on long-term government bonds. Abstracting from the problem of inflationary expectations, this can be thought of as both the nominal and real rate of interest.

M^d = liquidity preference, or the nominal demand for money. As will become clear, given the assumptions of the model, this is the obverse of the willingness to part with liquidity in order to finance expenditure, either directly or indirectly through the financial system.

M^s = the nominal money supply – assumed to be exogenously determined by the authorities.

P = the price level.

G, T and M^s are assumed to be exogenous, and all income/expenditure variables are measured at constant prices.[2]

This model is generally presented along sectoral lines, i.e. consumption and saving is done by the personal sector and investment by the company sector, though the division is really being made on functional grounds. All of what is defined as 'investment' by companies, fixed capital formation in national income accounts, is put into I, and all current expenditure by the personal sector into C. This leaves personal-sector expenditure on durable goods and fixed capital formation, houses, etc. The former is usually allocated to C and the latter to I. And, of course, all income is assumed to accrue to the personal sector.

The important thing to note is that saving and investment decisions are not directly related, any indirect connection between them depending on the relative interest-elasticities of the investment and demand for money schedules. The separation of saving and investment was fundamental to Keynes's approach, a factor on which he laid great emphasis, and which presumably led to the development of the 45° line diagram (see below).

Income in this model is *real* income, and in order to avoid extensive complications we shall assume output responses up to full employment and price changes only after that point has been reached. It is assumed that the existence of unemployed resources does not lead to a fall in prices, or in inflationary circumstances to a decline in the rate of price change.

The IS schedule depicts equilibrium in the goods market and is obtained by substituting equations (2.5) and (2.6) into identity (2.4):

$$r = \frac{1}{a}[A + c_0 - (1 - c_1)Y - c_1 T + G], \quad IS \text{ schedule} \tag{2.9}$$

The LM schedule is obtained by substituting (2.8) into (2.7):

$$r = \frac{1}{e_2}\left[e_1 Y - \frac{M}{P}\right], \quad LM \text{ schedule} \tag{2.10}$$

Both of these schedules define r as a function of Y, and they can therefore be combined in order to produce the familiar Hicks–Hansen diagram shown in Figure 2.1.

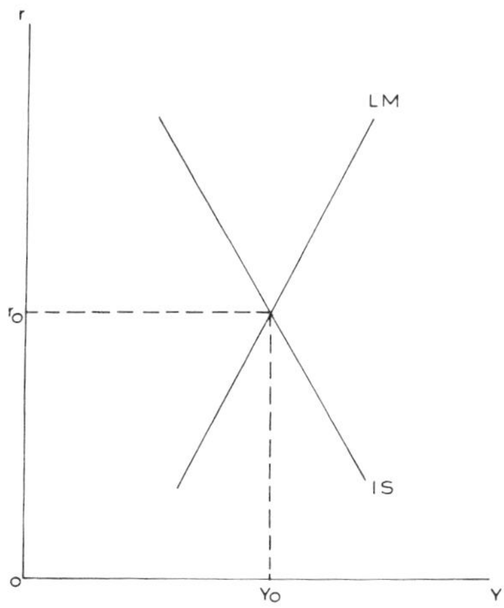

Figure 2.1 *IS/LM* Diagram

Given expectations, uncertainty and government behaviour this model then determines the interest rate and the level of income. There will be a unique solution as long as the various exogenous variables are truly exogenous and the parameters of the system are fixed. There are only three important behavioural relationships contained in the model:

(i) consumption function;
(ii) investment function;
(iii) demand for money.

How important money will be depends on the *relative* interest-elasticities of the investment schedule and the demand for money schedule. The simplest Keynesian model, and the one through which most economic students are still introduced to macroeconomics, is that embodied in the so-called '45° line diagram' (see Figure 2.2). This model makes the decisions to save and to invest completely independent, and as a consequence money has no role to play. Private consumption expenditure (and imports and taxes) are made linear functions of income, leaving government expenditure, private-sector capital expenditure (and exports) to be exogenously determined. Therefore all withdrawals are independent of all injections, and income can only change if one of the exogenous variables change. Furthermore, whatever happens is independent of the rate of interest, the supply of money or financial conditions generally.

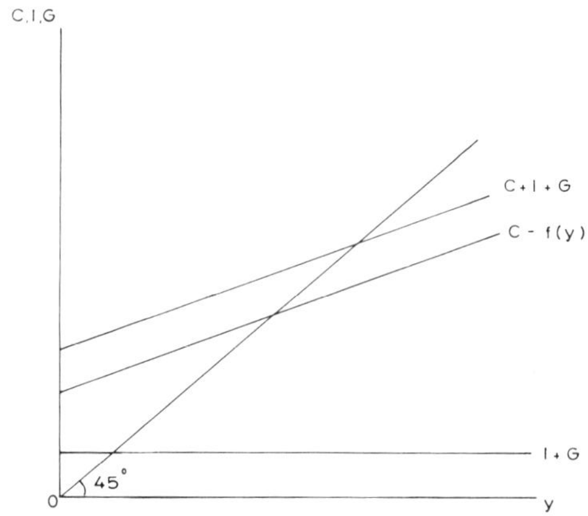

Figure 2.2 Keynesian 45° Line Diagram
Note: the 45° line represents points of equilibrium (equality) between aggregate income and expenditure.

The only financial behaviour that can possibly justify this model is if it is assumed that finance is automatically available upon demand. Either the supply of money or the demand for money must be infinitely interest-elastic. There is no possibility for an independent monetary policy operating through market forces. What we are left with is a simple mechanical multiplier process relating income to the exogenous variables. The implications for the *IS*/*LM* model are shown in Figure 2.3.

In such a model a change in autonomous expenditures will therefore have a full multiplier effect on income, i.e.

$$Y = \frac{1}{1 - c_1} [A + c_0 - c_1 T + G] \tag{2.11}$$

From such a model it is possible to derive, for example,

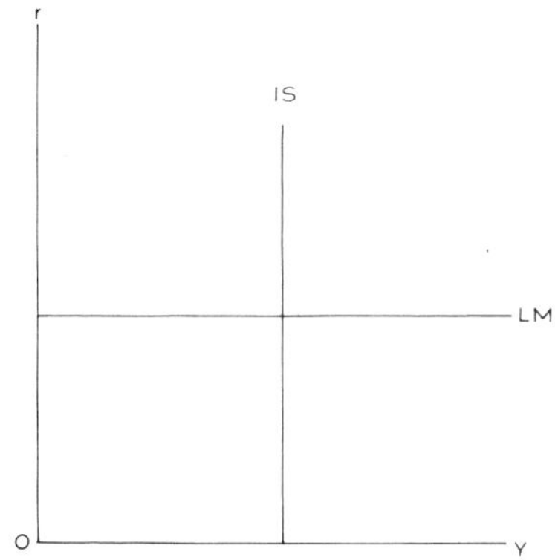

Figure 2.3 The Extreme Keynesian Model

balanced budget multipliers. A reduction in the propensity to consume, i.e. an increase in the propensity to save, will be reflected in a fall in the level of income, and it will not matter at all in what form these savings are held. The model implies that investment is completely interest-inelastic and the demand for money is infinitely interest-elastic. Keynes, however, did not abstract from the financial side. He established a simplified general-equilibrium model requiring simultaneous equilibrium in both 'real' and 'financial' markets.

The exact opposite of this model is the simple quantity theory model in which investment is assumed to be infinitely interest-elastic, and the demand for money is completely interest-inelastic (see Figure 2.4). In this case we can write real income only in terms of the real money supply:

$$Y = \frac{1}{e_1}\left(\frac{M}{P}\right) \tag{2.12}$$

If real income is assumed fixed at the full-employment level, then it makes more sense to rewrite this as:

$$P = \frac{1}{e_1}\left(\frac{M}{Y}\right) \tag{2.13}$$

so that changes in the money supply have their total effect on the price level. Either way money is all that matters. It makes no

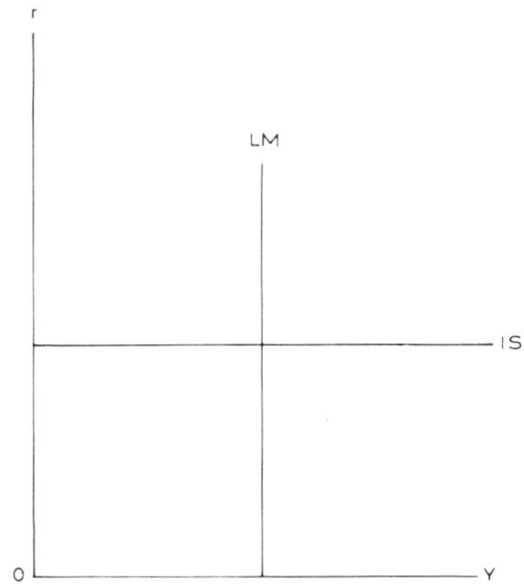

Figure 2.4 The Extreme Quantity Theory Model

difference whether income is spent on current consumption or saved, the flexibility of the financial system ensures that it all ends up on expenditure.

It might help to clarify the argument so far if we take the reduced form of the series of equations and identities with which we started. In equilibrium there can only be one rate of interest at which point the *IS* schedule must equal the *LM* schedule:

$$\frac{1}{a}\left[A+c_0-(1-c_1)Y-c_1T+G\right]=\frac{1}{e_2}\left[e_1Y-\frac{M}{P}\right] \tag{2.14}$$

Gathering the income terms on the left-hand side gives

$$\left[\frac{(1-c_1)}{a}+\frac{e_1}{e_2}\right]Y=\frac{A+c_0+G-c_1T}{a}+\frac{M/P}{e_2}$$

which simplifies to

$$Y=\frac{A+c_0+G-c_1T}{1-c_1+\dfrac{ae_1}{e_2}}+\frac{M/P}{\dfrac{e_2(1-c_1)}{a}+e_1}$$

or

$$Y = \frac{e_2(A + c_0 + G - c_1 T)}{e_2(1 - c_1) + ae_1} + \frac{aM/P}{e_2(1 - c_1) + ae_1} \tag{2.15}$$

The two expressions on the right-hand side of (2.15) can be interpreted as, respectively, autonomous expenditure and money multipliers. It is possible now to consider the previous extreme models within this unified framework.

Keynesian. Investment is insensitive to the rate of interest, i.e.

$$\frac{\partial I}{\partial r} \simeq 0 = a$$

The real demand for money is infinitely sensitive to the rate of interest, i.e.

$$\frac{\partial (M^d/P)}{\partial r} \simeq \infty = e_2$$

Classical Quantity Theory. Investment is infinitely sensitive to the rate of interest, i.e.

$$\frac{\partial I}{\partial r} \simeq \infty = a$$

The real demand for money is insensitive to the rate of interest, i.e.

$$\frac{\partial (M^d/P)}{\partial r} \simeq 0 = e_2$$

Substituting these values into the equation above reduces it to the multiplier expressions previously obtained: equations (2.11) and (2.12).

In between these two extremes, the higher is e_2 relative to a, i.e. the greater the interest-elasticity of the demand for money as compared with the interest-elasticity of investment, the greater the effect of autonomous expenditures on income compared with the effect of a change in the supply of money – and vice versa. If both schedules are highly interest-sensitive, then any exogenous change will have its major impact on income, and if both are highly insensitive to interest changes, the major effect will be on the interest rate. What is important in determining the effectiveness of monetary policy is not the absolute interest sensitivity of the demand for money, but rather its sensitivity *relative* to that of investment.

The 'traditional' Keynesian view that prevailed over most of the post-war period, and is still accepted by many economists, is that

(i) investment is highly insensitive to changes in the rate of interest, and
(ii) the demand for money is virtually infinitely interest-elastic.

This was the conclusion of the Radcliffe Committee reporting in 1959. It could find no real evidence that investment expenditure was interest-elastic and the verbal evidence of the businessmen interviewed supported this view. At the same time it believed that the financial system was so highly developed, and the substitutes for money so many and so close, that a change in the quantity of money would not change the rate of interest very much (Radcliffe Report, 1959, para. 392, p. 133); and even went so far as to claim that 'we cannot find any reason for supposing, or any experience in monetary history indicating that there is any limit to the velocity of circulation' (Radcliffe Report, 1959, para. 391, p. 133). This grand statement is a rather extreme overstatement indicating that the economy could function quite adequately on a single pound!

The more recent Keynesian view sees changes in the money supply as working with a ripple effect along the asset spectrum, arranged according to liquidity. So a change in the supply of money may have quite a large impact at the short end, but this effect will diminish greatly by the time it reaches the long end and will thus have little effect on real assets. The process runs from money through other capital-safe assets, treasury bills, etc., short bonds, medium bonds and long bonds, equities, eventually to reach real capital assets. It is assumed that substitutability is only really good with neighbouring assets; the effect is therefore shoved along, but with diminishing vigour.

At the same time it has been recognised that 'investment' in this model should not be restricted to the capital expenditure of incorporated businesses but should include all purchases not required for current consumption. Taking this broad view of investment some interest sensitivity has been identified by empirical studies, but it is generally recognised that a great deal of work remains to be done in this area. Such work lies outside the scope of this book, and its neglect should in no way be interpreted as an indication of unimportance.

To the extent that the monetarist view can be adequately summarised within the *IS/LM* framework the relative sizes of the elasticities expected would be rather different. The monetarists would certainly accept the broad view of investment expenditure, with the expectation that it would be highly interest-elastic. Furthermore, the demand for money is not considered to be very interest-elastic; in fact quite the opposite is assumed. The effect of a change in the supply of money is not expected to work its way through a liquidity spectrum as in the Keynesian proposal. Instead, money is seen as a unique asset which is highly substitutable with all other assets, real and financial, and is therefore no particular substitute with any one of them. This does, however, raise the question of the relevance of this model. Most of the large scale macroeconomic models that have been developed have been disaggregated versions of the *IS/LM* model. Disaggregation is intended, among other things, to help identify the detailed transmission mechanism whereby money has its effect on the economy. This is supposed to be through a limited range of financial rates of return, and occasionally quantitative restrictions on the availability of credit. The alternative attempt by monetarists to identify direct effects of money on income and prices is generally characterised as a 'black box' approach in that it fails to identify the transmission mechanism through which money has its effect. This work is briefly surveyed in Chapter 3, and it will then be argued that this criticism may not be quite as obvious as it may at first appear.

Criticisms of the *IS/LM* Model

A problem with the *IS/LM* model is that it is really only applicable to the very short run. In particular it abstracts from the effects of changes in the capital stock and the wealth of the private sector. In the model as it stands the demand for money is not at all dependent upon wealth. This means that if the personal sector holds only financial assets, then individuals will desire to hold all changes in wealth in the form of bonds (given no change in income or interest rates). Victoria Chick (1973) gives a good example of the kind of peculiar long-run behaviour implied by this simple model. It is essential, therefore, that the very short-run character of the model is recognised.

We have already referred to the static, equilibrium, nature of the *IS*/*LM* model, and this is its major weakness. It totally abstracts from the dynamics of adjustment and is incapable of analysing disequilibrium situations. The model can only be used to compare positions of equilibrium. But we should realise that in the real world the effect of, say, a change in tax rates takes a long time to reach equilibrium, and will almost certainly affect the wealth of the community. There is a conflict: within the model we can only compare equilibrium positions, but they take time to achieve, while on the other hand the model is only valid over the very short run.

Attempts have been made to introduce some form of dynamic reality into the model by showing that the *IS* and *LM* curves are not independent, e.g. because of wealth changes (Silber, 1970). Therefore both curves are moving together. However, even this is not sufficient in that it fails to recognise that the *IS* and *LM* curves are themselves drawn on the assumption of equilibrium. The *IS* curve requires equality between the *desires* to save and invest, not simply the statistical identity between *I* and *S* which is made true by definition. Similarly, the *LM* curve defines equilibrium in the money market. If there is a process of dynamic adjustment, during which the economy is not in equilibrium, we shall be at some point *off* the *IS*/*LM* schedules.

It should be clear by now that there are severe limitations to the use of the *IS*/*LM* model in describing the real world. We may be able to rescue it by emphasising its pedagogic use, as an *initial* simplification of a highly complex reality. The purpose of this chapter is to show the role that money plays within this familiar macroeconomic framework. In the final chapter we shall attempt to bring together some of the later arguments in order to develop an alternative model in which money plays a dominant role, and the disequilibrium nature of the adjustment process is emphasised. No model, however, can be justified in isolation, and can only be judged in comparison with some reasonable alternative. It is therefore important to understand the strengths and limitations of the *IS/LM* model, if only because this framework has dominated the teaching of macroeconomics for more than quarter of a century.

Expenditure Financing and Crowding-out

If we wish to employ this framework, while recognising its limitations, we should at least consider explicitly the financial aspects of economic activity. It is important to understand the implications of imposing financing constraints, derived from the logical necessity that all expenditures be financed. Although the model is only really applicable for comparing static-equilibrium positions, we can at least consider in outline the process through which adjustment will be achieved.

A typical starting-point is in considering the effect of a change in business expectations, i.e. what is normally classified as a rise in autonomous investment. If the process is described at all, the explanation generally seems to run as follows. In the first instance, as expectations improve so there is an increase in investment, and income rises. But as income rises so the (transactions) demand for money rises, and if the stock is fixed, supply and demand can only be equated if the rate of interest rises. This increase in the rate of interest tends to reduce the level of investment from what it would otherwise have been.

The major weakness of this explanation lies in its complete failure to consider how the new investment is financed in the first place. We should perhaps emphasise that we are now concerned with the final equilibrium position as much as the process through which this equilibrium is brought about. Of course, there would be no financial constraint if the velocity of circulation of money were infinitely variable, though in that case neither would there be any subsequent pressure for the interest rate to rise. It would, however, be most unrealistic to make such an assumption. That there is some short-run interest-elasticity is undoubtedly true – although times of tight money, when this should otherwise be most noticeable, are probably also associated with increased uncertainty. And it is also true that increases in efficiency and the innovation of new techniques by the financial intermediaries will increase velocity over time. What is equally true is that any short-run variability is strictly limited; otherwise there would never be such things as liquidity crises in the economy. Direct controls on the banking system would have no effect; there would be no need for interest rates to change; or for the government to print more money.

We need, therefore, to take account of the fact that finance is a scarce resource. When business expectations improve it is necessary to obtain the finance *before* any additional investments can be undertaken. This demand for funds pushes up the rate of interest, which results in the direction of funds to the industry concerned. In fact the process is somewhat more complicated than that. First, the rate of interest rises so that funds are obtained, thereby financing an increase in expenditure, but as expenditure rises so the demand for money to hold rises, pushing up the rate of interest and so cutting off some of the potential investment. What in fact we are saying is that in any adjustment from one equilibrium to another interest-rate changes *precede* quantity or price changes. The extent of the effect of an increase in expectations upon the total level of investment, and through this upon the level of income, real or nominal, will depend upon the degree to which *new* finance is generated. And with a fixed money supply this can only be at the expense of previous hoarding.

This way of viewing the adjustment process is, I would argue, entirely consistent with Keynes's own description. In 1937, the year following the publication of *The General Theory*, Keynes published two papers in the *Economic Journal* in which he argued that additional saving will not be available simply because some additional investment or consumption is *planned*. Additional saving will only occur when the extra *net* investment has actually been made. But for the net increase in expenditure to take place, extra finance must first be made available. This will not be permitted by increased saving but by an expansion of credit – and that depends crucially on the financial system in general, and liquidity preference (i.e. the demand for money) in particular. Therefore a *planned* increase in output should lead to a rise in the rate of interest. This Keynes (1937b) considered to be the 'coping-stone to the liquidity theory of the rate of interest'.

Because finance must be obtained before expenditures are made,

> the transition from a lower to a higher scale of activity involves an increased demand for liquid resources which cannot be met without a rise in the rate of interest, unless the banks are ready to lend more cash or the rest of the public to release more cash at the existing rate of interest. If there is no change in the liquidity position, the public can save ex-ante and ex-post or ex-anything-else until they are blue in the face, without alleviating the problem in the least – unless, indeed, the result of their efforts is to lower the scale of activity to what it was before (Keynes, 1937b).

It should be clear from what has been said above that with a fixed supply of money one individual, or sector, may only be able to obtain finance for expansion at the expense of another individual, or sector. This possibility has been called 'crowding-out'. This now popular phrase was coined by Culbertson (1968) to describe the process whereby an increase in the demand for finance withdrew funds from alternative uses. In particular the expression is employed with reference to the pre-empting of financial resources by the public sector at the expense of the private sector, though it need not necessarily be so restricted. Various degrees of crowding-out are possible depending on the interest-elasticity of expenditures, the demand for and supply of money, and the extent of administrative controls of finance.

When the phrase was first employed it quite clearly referred to the competition for finance. Since then, however, others have used the term to refer to the pre-empting of real resources by one sector, particularly the public sector at the expense of the private sector. Brunner and Meltzer (1976), for example, argue that crowding-out occurs as the result of changes in prices. This, however, is something completely different. We might argue that a fiscal stimulus at full employment can increase imports or prices, but it cannot, by definition, increase output or employment. However, neither imports nor prices could increase if there were complete *financial* crowding-out; in that case pressure would never have reached resource markets. It is therefore necessary to identify, at a minimum, two separate forms of crowding-out: financial crowding-out and resource crowding-out. We shall concentrate on the former of these since this is what the term originally referred to, and is what this section is all about.

In analysing this question it is useful to think of the *IS* and *LM* curves as representing the demand for, and supply of, finance. All expenditure has to be paid for (since it also represents income to someone else), whether out of current income, past saving or borrowing. An increase in business expectations, or the public-sector deficit, i.e. a rightward shift of the *IS* schedule, represents an increase in the demand for finance. The supply response to this increase in demand, in the absence of an increase in the supply of money, will be determined by the ability and willingness of wealth-holders to economise on existing money balances – as represented by the *LM* schedule.

An improvement in business expectations shifts the *IS* schedule to the right by the amount of the consequent investment, times the multiplier, that would result *if the finance were available*, while the actual increase in total income is only by the extent to which new funds are provided. If the industry within which business expectations have risen obtains all the finance it demands, this can only be, to a large extent, at the expense of some other industry. It should perhaps be emphasised that this is under the present assumption of a fixed money supply. If the money supply were perfectly elastic with respect to the rate of interest, then all groups in society could obtain the funds they desired at the fixed price. In the United Kingdom the apparent flexibility imparted to the financial system by the existence of unutilised overdraft facilities is only really significant to the extent that the authorities are prepared to provide the necessary reserves to validate the use of these facilities.

The same argument must apply equally to the government. If it sells bonds equal to $G - T$, but there is little generation of new finance, this can only be at the expense of the private sector. For example, consider Figure 2.5. As the result of an increase in government expenditure the *IS* schedule shifts to the right by $\Delta G(= ac$, for example), times the multiplier (total = *ae*). However, if the interest-elasticity of hoarding is such that only *ab* is covered by new finance (given by the intersection of the IS_1 and LM_0 schedules), while at the same time the total increase in government expenditure is realised – financed by the sale of bonds – then private-sector expenditure must have fallen by *bc*. This follows from the obvious requirement that all expenditure has to be financed. What is more, private-sector investment will have fallen by much more, since as income rises so consumption is assumed to rise. Therefore the increase in income of *ab* has been accompanied by a switch in private-sector expenditure in favour of consumption.

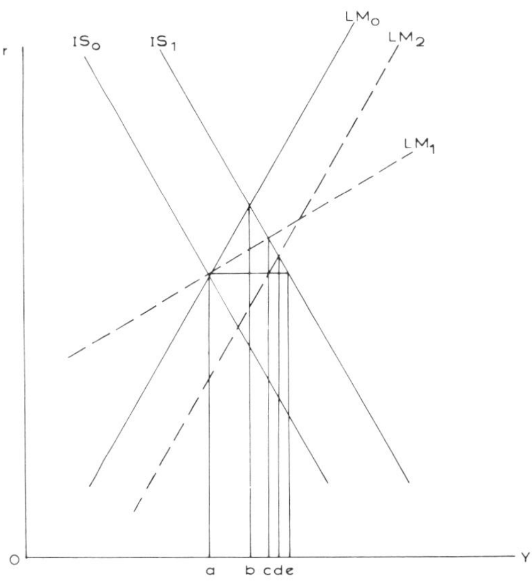

Figure 2.5 Demand for and Supply of Finance

Naturally if we make the supply of money interest-elastic, this will increase the elasticity of the *LM* schedule. Thus it would be possible to have a schedule such as LM_1 which just covered the increase in government expenditure. On the other hand, if we keep the elasticity of the first schedule *but* increase the supply of money so that, times the money multiplier $(1/e_1)$, it exactly equals the increase in government expenditure, this will give us LM_2, and permit income to rise by *ad*. The full expansion, *ae*, will only be possible if the supply of, or demand for, money are infinitely elastic to the rate of interest.

In the short run, with a fixed money supply, financial crowding-out depends crucially on the interest-elasticity of the demand for money relative to the interest-elasticity of expenditures. In addition there could also be crowding-out in resource markets. This could be the case even, or especially, if the money supply is increased. If the public sector can obtain finance more cheaply than the private sector, say by printing money or by not being required to earn a profit on the money spent, the former will have a competitive advantage over the latter in resource markets. In this case it is price changes that crowd out the private sector rather than interest-rate changes.

In the long run the extent of crowding-out depends to some extent on the self-stabilising properties of the economy. If an underemployed economy would continue to stagnate over the long run in the absence of increased public-sector expenditure, then such expenditure will not result in any significant crowding-out in the long run. How soon it is before some form of resource constraint is met will depend on how specific the incremental demands are. If the depressed state of the economy is only temporary, and if the economy would return to a 'natural' level of employment on its own, then all *maintained* fiscal expansion will crowd out potential private expenditure. The long-term policy mix should therefore be determined by some rational economic criteria. In the short term, however, it does not exclude the possibility of operating fiscal stabilisation policy.

This discussion can perhaps be clarified with the aid of Figure 2.6. This diagram illustrates the production possibilities that exist for all combinations of public- and private-sector output.[3] The line *PP′* represents the maximum combinations attainable. If the economy is at *c* it may be possible to move to a point such as *a* where both private- and public-sector produc-

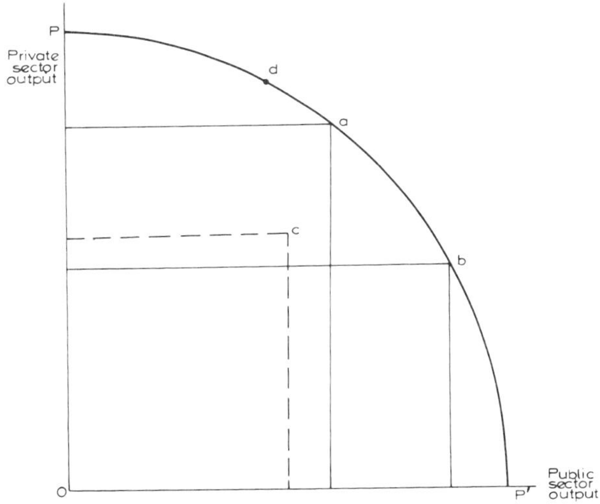

Figure 2.6 Production Possibilities for Private- and Public-sector Output

tion are increased. However, starting from a point on the frontier like *a*, an increase in public-sector expenditure can only be achieved at the expense of private-sector output. Even for the movement from *c* to *a* not to represent any crowding-out in the long run requires *c* to be a long-run equilibrium, and that a point like *d* would not eventually have been achieved.

Starting from a position of full employment, an expansion of public-sector expenditure will crowd out an equivalent amount of private-sector expenditure. This will happen however the crowding out occurs. With complete financial crowding-out there need be no increase in the competition for resources, and therefore no change in the level of prices.[4] If there is no financial crowding-out, i.e. the money supply is increased, then prices must be allowed to rise and the crowding-out of private sector is the counterpart of the tax-collecting effect of inflation (see Bailey, 1956). At a position of full employment the financing of the deficit is therefore important for inflation (and the balance of payments) but irrelevant from the point of view of crowding-out broadly defined.

We should also note that evidence of crowding-out in

financial markets should not be restricted to relatively high interest rates offered on public-sector debt. It is also necessary to take account of non-market controls on lending to the private sector. Limitations on the operations of markets can be very important but are too often neglected.

Finally, we should note that Friedman's (1968) now famous description of the operation of monetary policy can be interpreted as an argument in favour of complete resource crowding-out. It is of course the same conclusion arrived at by the early quantity theorists (see above). He suggested that a change in the supply of money will be distributed between output, prices and velocity changes as follows:

(i) The impact effect will be almost entirely reflected in changes in real output, and possibly velocity, but hardly at all in changes in the price level, i.e. little crowding-out in the short term.

(ii) Over time the effect on real output will be reversed, probably as part of a 'cyclical adjustment process', and the effect on the price level will build up. The change in velocity to be expected is unclear.

(iii) In the long run, after long and variable lags, the effect of a change in the supply of money will have been transmitted almost entirely to the price level, the effect on real output being reduced to minor proportions, and with velocity changes reflecting the long-run demand for money, i.e. practically complete crowding-out in long run.

Including an External Sector

The *IS*/*LM* model we have been looking at so far has been restricted to a closed economy. We noted above that the existence of overseas trade could apparently affect the extent of crowding-out by attracting extra resources from abroad. There are, however, constraints on the extent of this process, and it is anyway necessary to consider the transmission mechanisms through which such adjustments can take place. The discussion included here is only very brief, but it does show how the simple model developed so far can be amended to take account of external flows in commodities and finance. The inter-relationships between the domestic and external economies will be developed further in later chapters.

The current account of the balance of payments (CUR) is equal to exports (X) minus imports (Z), measured in real terms:

$$CUR \equiv X - Z \tag{2.16}$$

It is normally assumed in simple macroeconomic models that exports are exogenously determined and that imports are endogenous. However, exports are obviously not given exogenously and it is more realistic to assume that both these variables are behaviourally determined. In reality attention should be given to the supply side of the relationships, particularly for exports. For present purposes it is sufficient to introduce the external side of the economy by following convention and concentrating only on the demand side.

The main influences to be considered are domestic and foreign demand, relative prices and the exchange rate.[5] An increase in domestic demand, as given by domestic income, should increase the demand for imports and reduce the demand for exports; an increase in foreign demand will have the opposite effect. An increase in domestic prices, P, relative to foreign prices in terms of domestic currency (i.e. the foreign currency price divided by the exchange rate), Pf, will tend to reduce exports and increase imports.

The current account can therefore be written as:

$$CUR = -f_1 e + f_2 FD - f_3 (P - Pf) - f_4 Y \tag{2.17}$$

The capital account of the balance of payments (CAP) is often assumed to depend solely on the level of domestic interest rates (r) relative to interest rates abroad (rf), as suggested by Mundell (1960):

$$CAP = f_5 (r - rf) \tag{2.18}$$

These two relationships can be added to the IS/LM model as shown in Figure 2.7.[6] This diagram shows how changes in real income and the domestic rate of interest can result in changes in the current and capital accounts of the balance of payments. The story is, however, incomplete. Equilibrium on the overall balance of payments (BOP) is only achieved when there is no money flowing in or out of the country, i.e. when the capital account is equal and opposite to the current account; for the

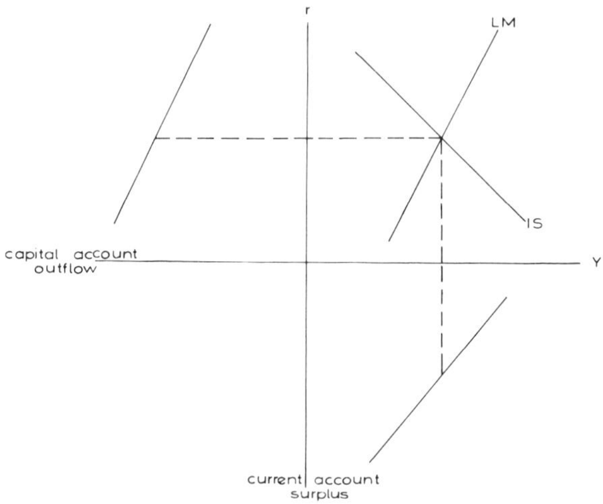

Figure 2.7 Adding the Current and Capital Accounts to the *IS*/*LM* Model

moment assuming no limit to the capital-account deficits that it is possible to finance. If

$$BOP \equiv CUR + CAP = 0$$

then

$$CAP = -CUR$$

Substituting from (2.17) and (2.18) gives

$$f_5(r - rf) = f_1 e - f_2 FD + f_3(P - Pf) - f_4 Y$$

and

$$r = \frac{1}{f_5}[f_1 e - f_2 FD + f_3 (P - Pf) - f_4 Y] + rf \quad (2.19)$$

The equilibrium requirement could be illustrated by including a 45° line in the fourth quadrant of Figure 2.7. An alternative procedure, and one which is more in keeping with the *IS*/*LM* framework, would be to include the equilibrium requirement for the balance of payments directly in the two-dimensional *IS*/*LM* diagram (see Figure 2.8). This can be done because equation (2.19) above has exactly the same charac-

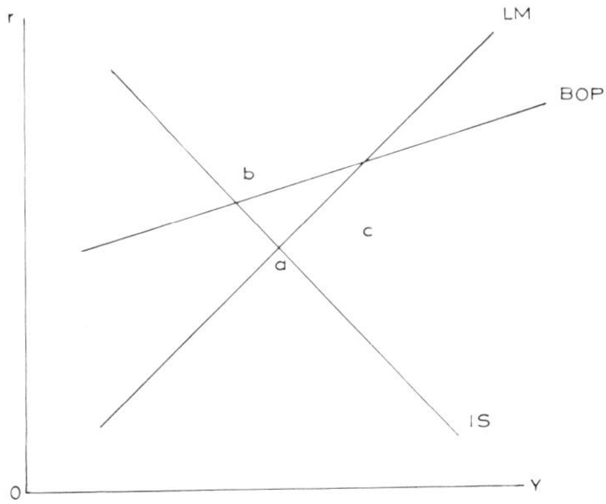

Figure 2.8 *IS/LM* as applied to an Open Economy

teristics as the *IS* and *LM* curves (equations (2.9) and (2.10)), i.e. the rate of interest is defined in terms of real income and a number of exogenous variables, including relative prices. Because r is positively related to Y we draw the balance-of-payments line, along which the balance of payments is in equilibrium, as upward-sloping (see Mundell, 1960).

If international capital flows were infinitely interest-elastic (i.e. $f_5 \simeq \infty$), the *BOP* line would be a horizontal line at an interest rate equal to the world rate. Therefore any marginal increase in domestic interest rates relative to the rest of the world would result in infinite capital flows. This would imply that any current-account deficit would be compatible with equilibrium on the balance of payments, since capital flows would simply adjust to offset the deficit (or surplus). Such flexibility might be thought to be rather unrealistic, and we shall consider this further below. If, on the other hand, international capital flows were not at all interest-elastic (i.e. $f_5 \simeq 0$), the *BOP* line would be vertical at whatever income resulted in zero balance on the current account. In this case it is impossible to offset any current-account deficit through flows on the capital account. A more realistic assumption would be to assume some interest-elasticity between zero and infinity, resulting in an upward-sloping *BOP* line, as in Figure 2.8.

In the diagram we can see that the economy is not in

equilibrium, since all the curves do not intersect at the same point. We therefore need to consider what sort of mechanisms exist to bring about equilibrium. Before doing that we need to redefine the money-supply process. If the exchange rate is floating, so that any disequilibrium on the balance of payments changes the exchange rate to restore equilibrium, the previous assumption can be retained, i.e. that the money supply is exogenously determined by the monetary authorities (see p. 18).[7] However, as soon as a fixed exchange rate is assumed it becomes necessary to change the money-supply assumption. In highly simplified terms the money supply will depend upon domestic credit (DC) and foreign credit, i.e. lending from overseas to the non-bank private sector, equal to the stock of foreign reserves (R). The change in foreign reserves (ΔR) we shall assume is the same as any net flows on the balance of payments (i.e. $\Delta R = BOP$). This is the normal assumption (but see Chapter 10 for a more exact definition).

$$M^s \equiv DC + R \tag{2.20}$$

DC is generally assumed to be determined by the monetary authorities, but with a fixed exchange rate e, R (and therefore M^s) is endogenous, and determined by the balance of payments.

Let us now return to Figure 2.8 and see how adjustment will take place. It will be convenient to assume that the economy is at less than full employment, and that all income movements represent changes in quantity rather than prices.

Starting from point a, in which real and money markets are in equilibrium but there is a deficit on the balance of payments (i.e. income is too high relative to the rate of interest), if the exchange rate is floating, it will depreciate. The fall in the exchange rate will lower the BOP line (see equation (2.19)), and also cause the IS line to move up and to the right in response to the increased demand for exports. Equilibrium will therefore be achieved along LM some point to the right of a. At this point the balance-of-payments deficit will have been corrected and unemployment will have been reduced.

The next example is to consider what will happen if, starting from the same position, the exchange rate is held fixed by the authorities intervening in the foreign exchange market. In this case the stock of foreign reserves will decline, and with it the money supply. The money supply will continue to decline, with the *LM* curve shifting to the left, until equilibrium is restored at point *b*. This will increase the level of unemployment, and the authorities may try to prevent this from happening by changing domestic credit to offset the decline in reserves. It is, however, questionable to what extent this is a realistic long-run policy alternative, and this is discussed further below.

The international monetarists lay stress on the long-run equilibrium properties of this model (see Frenkel and Johnson, 1976; Coghlan, 1978). They view the domestic economy as being a 'small country', i.e. so small that prices and interest rates can be thought of as being determined in world markets independently of the individual country. Each country is therefore treated as the individual unit making up a perfectly competitive market, and satisfying all necessary conditions for such a market organisation: 'The small country is a price taker facing perfectly elastic demand and supply of assets and goods' (Dornbusch, 1971).

However, while it may be a reasonable approximation to view an individual country as a price-taker, we need to be careful how we define the relevant prices. The expected return to a foreign investor holding U.K. financial assets depends not only on the rate of interest payable but also on expected exchange-rate movements. Quite apart from anything else these expectations are likely to be influenced by the size and duration of any current-account deficit. A large, and long-lasting, current-account deficit is likely to create the expectation that the exchange rate will depreciate. Therefore the greater the need for capital flows to offset a current-account deficit, the higher will interest rates have to be. In order to finance a continuing current-account deficit it will probably be necessary to pay ever higher rates of return as expectations of an exchange-rate depreciation grow ever stronger.

The analysis outlined only really makes any sense as a description of the short run since it assumes that a continuing balance-of-payments deficit can be counterbalanced by a continuing inflow on the capital account. This is also true of the possibility suggested above, i.e. of trying to maintain demand in the face of a sustained balance-of-payments deficit. Such sterilisation policies will be limited by the finite stock of foreign reserves – which cannot be depleted continuously. It is misleading to discuss the long run in terms of the *IS/LM* model; it is only applicable to the very short run. This is particularly noticeable in discussing the arguments of the international monetarists, but it is also true of any form of *equilibrium* adjustment. In using this model we are following convention, but it does give us some valuable insights into the working of the economy, as long as we are aware of its limitations. As we progress a more dynamic model will evolve which does not lay stress on equilibrium relationships. This will be presented in Chapter 10, but even then it is necessary to remember that all economic models must abstract to some extent from complex reality.

A further argument often employed against the assumption of infinite capital flows is that the portfolio theory which underlies capital flows is based upon the assumption of stock adjustment. It might therefore be suggested that capital flows only arise from *changes* in interest rates, i.e.

$$CAP = f_6 \Delta(r - rf) \qquad (2.21)$$

However, stock-adjustment behaviour based on the assumption that the *proportion* of world wealth, W, held in the form of domestic assets, A, depends on relative interest rates, i.e.

$$\frac{A}{W} = f_7 (r - rf) \qquad (2.22)$$

still results in persistently higher capital flows as long as world wealth is increasing. Equation (2.22) can be rewritten as

$$A = f_7 (r - rf) W$$

and the first difference, which represents the capital inflow from abroad to purchase domestic assets, is

$$\Delta A = f_7 \Delta(r - rf) W_{-1} + f_7 (r - rf) \Delta W \qquad (2.23)$$

Therefore, although there will be an inflow associated with the *change* in interest differentials, the higher *level* of the differential will also result in a greater proportion of the *increase* in world wealth being allocated to domestic assets. Moreover, interest-elasticities can still be very high if domestic and foreign assets really are highly substitutable.

The major deficiency of this last argument is that it has been in terms of the rate of interest, whereas it was argued above that the rate of return expected should take account of any exchange-rate expectations. These exchange-rate expectations are probably more important than the question of whether interest rates are determined in stock or flow markets. What is more, expectations are likely to depend on a great variety of factors, and it may well be that the authorities will find it impossible to control capital flows in the way desired.

If we ignore these problems for the moment, and assume that the authorities are in complete control of all instruments of policy, it may be of interest to consider how the authorities might achieve a position of equilibrium at a point like *c* in Figure 2.8. First, the exchange rate will need to be devalued in order to lower the *BOP* line. This, as we have seen, will also have the effect of shifting *IS* to the right. It would, however, be strange if this were exactly sufficient to achieve an intersection at *c*; so we must also operate on fiscal policy to get *IS* in the right place. Finally, the money supply will have to be increased, shifting *LM* to the right.

This example illustrates an important point: that the authorities will generally require as many policy instruments as the number of ultimate objectives they wish to achieve. This is an example of the policy trade-offs first analysed by Tinbergen (1952). Mundell (1962) has since added his own 'principle of effective market classification', which states (as might seem obvious) that instruments should be paired with those objectives on which they have the most influence. Given two objectives and two instruments, an instrument is employed for a particular purpose when the ratio of its effect on that objective to its effect on the other target is greater than the ratio of the effect of the alternative instrument on these two targets. So if aM is the effect of M on A, and bF is the effect of F on B, etc., then M is chosen for A when $aM/bM > aF/bF$.

In this case the objectives were balance-of-payments equilibrium and particular levels of income and interest rates; the instruments were exchange-rate policy (devaluation) and fiscal and monetary policy. It is usually very simple to see how a single objective can be achieved; what is difficult is the simultaneous reconciliation of a number of different objectives. In the real world it may not always be possible to achieve simultaneously all of one's objectives, and it is important that rational criteria are applied when choices have to be made. To this end the model developed here will be too simple, but it is a start, and at least it does include monetary influences. A clear understanding of the financial aspects of the economy is essential to the formalisation, and understanding, of economic policy.

Appendix Diagrammatic Derivation of the *IS/LM* Model

Goods market

$$Y \equiv C + I + G \qquad \text{Income identity} \tag{2.4}$$

$$C = c_0 + c_1(Y - T) \qquad \text{Consumption function} \tag{2.5}$$

$$I = A - ar \qquad \text{Investment function} \tag{2.6}$$

with the variables as defined in the main text (see Figures 2A1 and 2A2).

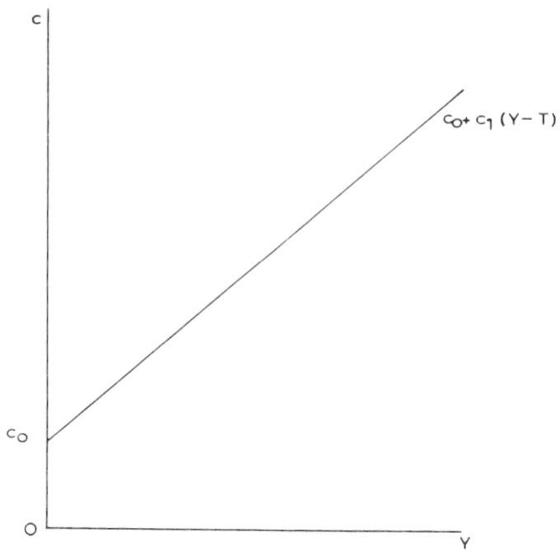

Figure 2A1 Consumption Function

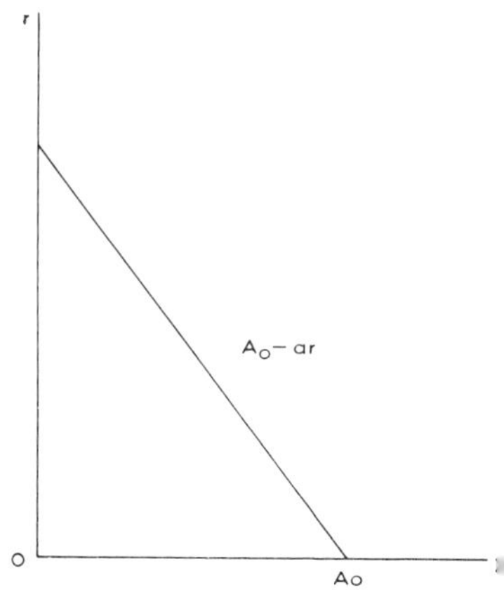

Figure 2A2 Investment Function

Saving by the personal sector will equal its disposable income minus consumption expenditure (see Figure 2A3):

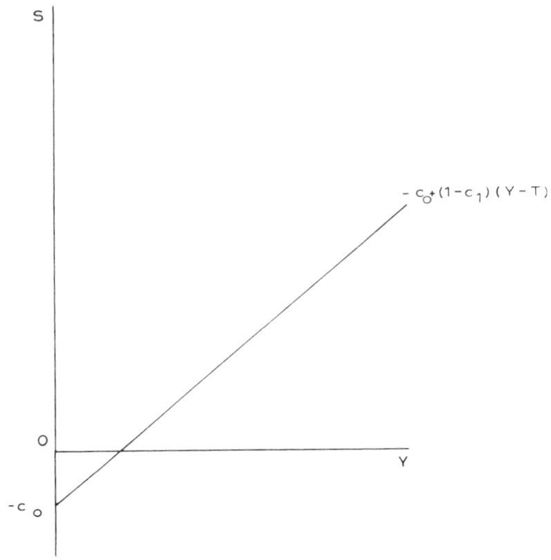

Figure 2A3 Saving Function

$$S = (Y - T) - C = (Y - T) - c_0 - c_1(Y - T)$$
$$= -c_0 + (1 - c_1)(Y - T)$$

In equilibrium desired saving must be equal to desired investment plus government expenditure:

$$(A + G) - ar = -c_0 + (1 - c_1)(Y - T)$$

This is illustrated in Figure 2A4.

Money market

$$\frac{M^d}{P} = e_1 Y - e_2 r \quad \text{Money demand (real)} \qquad (2.7)$$

$$M^s = M \quad \text{Money supply (nominal)}$$

$$\frac{M^d}{P} = \frac{M^s}{P} \quad \text{Equilibrium condition} \qquad (2.8)$$

(See Figures 2A5 and 2A6.)

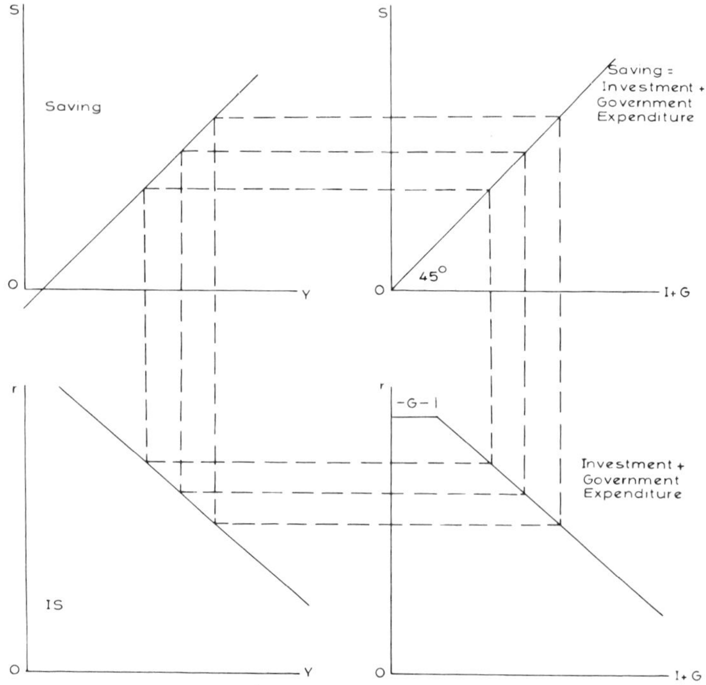

Figure 2A4 Deriving the *IS* Schedule

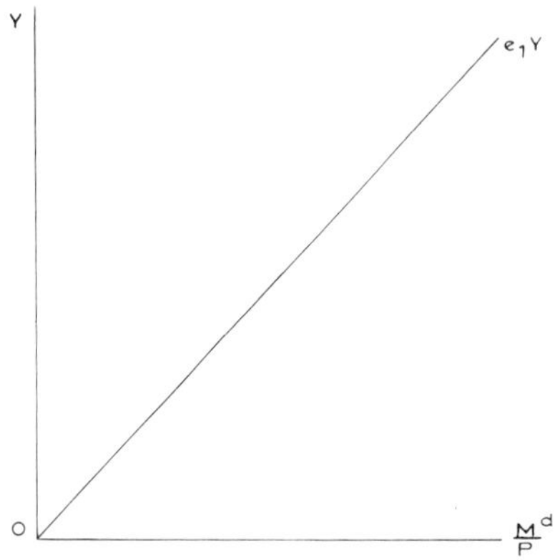

Figure 2A5 Relationship between the Demand for Money and Income

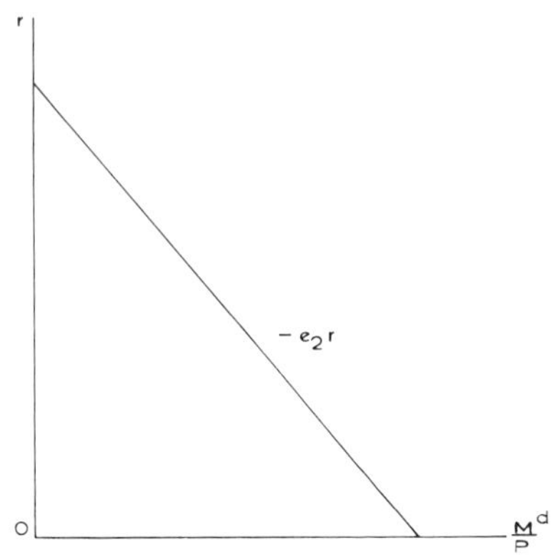

Figure 2A6 Relationship between the Demand for Money and the Rate of Interest

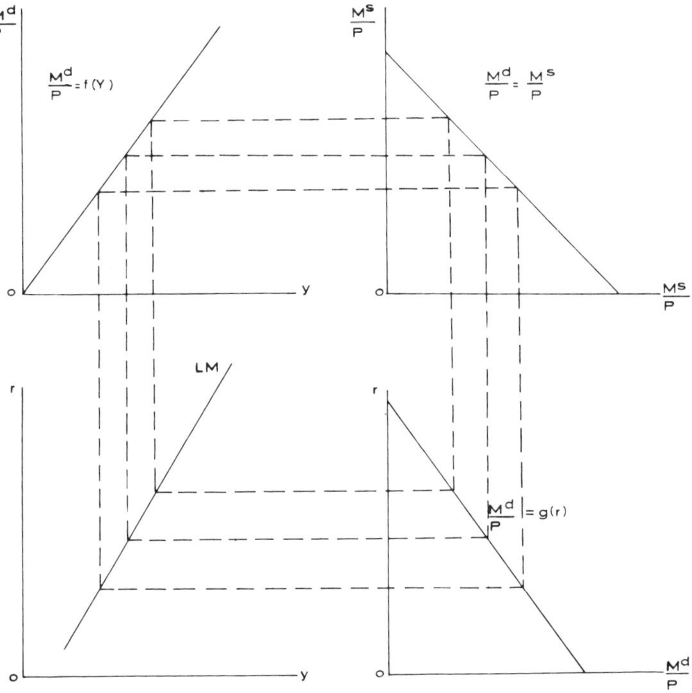

Figure 2A7 Deriving the *LM* Schedule

In equilibrium the demand for money will be equal to supply, as illustrated in Figure 2A7.

3. THE CAUSALITY DEBATE

In recent years the monetarist approach to macroeconomic analysis has gained increasing acceptance as a framework for interpreting economic behaviour, and has consequently become more important in discussing the policy options facing the authorities. Monetary variables have come to play an increasing role in the large scale macroeconomic models, particularly in the United States; for a comprehensive survey, see Fisher and Sheppard (1972). The monetarists have, however, tended to concentrate on simpler, highly aggregative, reduced-form models in their attempt to demonstrate the overwhelming influence of money on the economy, in particular on prices and the rate of inflation. Strangely, this work has received scant attention in macro and monetary textbooks, and yet it would seem essential to a proper understanding of the monetarist position. This chapter therefore briefly summarises the debate, and the evidence that has been presented.

Outline of Debate

The greatest problem is to decide the limits of the exercise. The arguments have ranged across the whole broad frontier of macroeconomics, incorporating such issues as the fundamental characteristics of a modern developed economy and the research methodology employed in its study. There are really two related questions that the monetarists have attempted to answer in this work:

(i) Does the simple Keynesian expenditure multiplier model or the monetarist's quantity theory provide the most illuminating characterisation of the actual economic structure?

(ii) Less fundamental from a theoretical point of view, though probably of more practical importance, does monetary policy or fiscal policy exert the greater influence over the economy?

The first of these questions was asked by Friedman and Meiselman (1964), who tested the hypothesis econometrically, employing single equations, supposedly representing reduced forms of the complete macro economy. This approach accorded with the 'positivist' research methodology espoused by the monetarists according to which models should be judged only on their predictions, not on their underlying assumptions, and are ranked inversely according to their size, i.e. the ability to predict something large from something small was interpreted as a virtue.[1]

In outline, Friedman and Meiselman regressed the level of consumption (representing endogenous income) on the stock of money and the level of autonomous expenditure over a long span of history, interpreting the coefficients as money and expenditure multipliers. What they claimed as a result of this exercise was that the money multiplier was much larger and more stable than the expenditure multiplier, from which it followed that the quantity theory provided a better characterisation of the world than simple Keynesian economics.

This conclusion was based upon a comparison of simple and partial correlation coefficients[2] from equations (3.1) to (3.6) below, estimated for annual (1897–1958) and quarterly (1945–58) data for the United States:

$$C = a_1 + b_1 A \qquad (3.1)$$

$$C = a_2 + c_2 M \qquad (3.2)$$

I

$$C = a_3 + b_3 A + d_3 P \qquad (3.3)$$

$$C = a_4 + c_4 M + d_4 P \qquad (3.4)$$

II

$$C = a_5 + b_5 A + c_5 M \qquad (3.5)$$

$$C = a_6 + b_6 A + c_6 M + d_6 P \qquad (3.6)$$

III

where

C = consumption (durables, non-durables and services) measured in current dollars.

A = autonomous expenditures (net private domestic investment, the government deficit on income and product account, and the net foreign balance) measured in current dollars.

M = money supply (currency in circulation with the public, adjusted demand deposits and commercial bank time deposits).

P = consumer price index.

Most of these equations cannot be derived from any formal model, but are rather *ad hoc* extensions of a very simple, dichotomous, view of alternative theories (see Edge, 1967). The alternatives are extreme characterisations of the Keynesian and monetarist approaches[3] whereby

$$Y = \alpha + k'A \tag{3.7}$$

and

$$Y = a + V'M \tag{3.8}$$

Because, by definition,

$$Y \equiv C + A$$

any correlation of Y with A involves correlation of Y with part of itself, and does not therefore represent the true ability to explain the endogenous component of Y. For this reason Friedman and Meiselman replace Y by C, so that now

$$C = \alpha + kA \tag{3.7a}$$

where $k = k' - 1$,[4] and

$$C = a + VM \tag{3.8a}$$

'where V has no such simple arithmetic connection with V' as k with k''.[5] They also combine the equations in arbitrary fashion, writing[6]

$$C = \alpha + VM + kA \tag{3.9}$$

in order to obtain the partial correlations between C and M, and C and A, taking explicit account of the correlation existing between M and A. Finally, prices are added, in an equally *ad hoc* fashion, in order to attempt to identify any separate price effect.

Friedman and Meiselman obtain correlation coefficients for each of these equations for the whole period and for a variety of sub-periods. The results consistently reveal that the correlation between *C* and *M* is greater than that between *C* and *A*, with the single exception of the period 1929–36: 'Except for the early years of the Great Depression, money is more closely related to consumption than autonomous expenditures . . . the results are strikingly one sided'; and 'the stock of money is unquestionably far more critical in interpreting movements in income than is autonomous expenditures'. Furthermore, Friedman and Meiselman claim that the relation found between autonomous expenditure and consumption was primarily a disguised reflection of the effect of money on consumption, *M* and *A* being positively correlated. Their conclusion from all this was that 'the income velocity of circulation of money is consistently and decidedly stabler than the investment multiplier except during the early years of the Great Depression after 1929'.

The publication of this research was greeted with an immediate response from Keynesian economists Ando and Modigliani (1965) claimed that 'the strikingly "one-sided" results of Friedman and Meiselman are largely accounted for by their strikingly one-sided procedure'. Certainly, on points of detail this counter-attack demonstrated that alternative definitions of the variables employed could in fact reverse the conclusion. Perhaps more fundamentally it questioned the whole research methodology, both in principle and in its particular application. These questions will be discussed below. As a result of this controversy, it cannot be claimed that Friedman and Meiselman achieved their objective of showing that money was all that mattered, but they did demonstrate that money was important and could not easily be dismissed. At the time even this was a major achievement, though, as became clear from the discussion, many self-professed Keynesians did not belong to the '45° line school' of Keynesianism caricatured by Friedman and Meiselman, but did accept that money had an important role to play.

The second approach put the question in a slightly different form. It was developed by Andersen and Jordan (1968), at the Federal Reserve Bank of St Louis, who asked whether fiscal policy or monetary policy had the larger, more predictable and faster-acting influence on economic activity. The conclusion was overwhelmingly in favour of monetary policy.

The approach was again to estimate reduced-form-type equations, this time with changes in nominal G.N.P. being explained by changes in measures of fiscal (FP) and monetary policy (MP), and a constant (k). Fiscal policy was measured by full-employment expenditures, receipts or surpluses, and monetary policy by the monetary base or the stock of money narrowly defined. The equations were estimated employing quarterly data and incorporating lags of approximately four quarters, e.g.

$$\text{G.N.P.} = k + \sum_{i=0}^{3} fi\, \Delta FP_{-i} + \sum_{j=0}^{3} mj\, \Delta MP_{-j} + u \tag{3.10}$$

where u is a randomly distributed error term with zero mean and constant variance.

Attention was concentrated on full-employment measures of fiscal policy in order to obtain a better measure of autonomous policy actions by abstracting from any automatic, income-related changes.

To explain this concept we start by assuming that public-sector expenditure on goods and services (G) is given, and that taxes (less subsidies) are related to income, i.e.

$$G = \overline{G} \tag{3.11}$$

$$T = t_0 + tY \tag{3.12}$$

The total budget position is shown diagrammatically in Figure 3.1.

As an example, consider the case where fiscal policy is measured by the public-sector deficit. If we start at income Y_1 the unnormalised deficit will be zero. By increasing the marginal tax rate, and assuming no change in income, the deficit would be reduced from zero to D_1, i.e. the public sector would run a surplus. However, an identical surplus could emerge if tax rates remained unchanged but income rose from Y_1 to Y_2. Therefore the deficit does not give an unambiguous measure of *discretionary* fiscal policy. Such a measure can be obtained by normalising the deficit on a particular level of income, conveniently at full employment. If that is done, automatic changes in the deficit resulting from changes in income will be

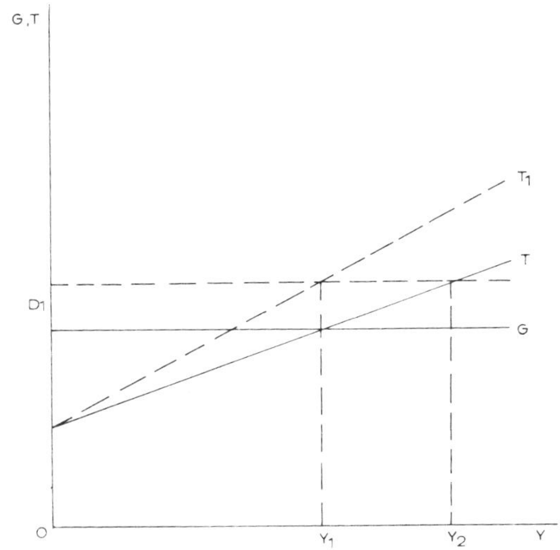

Figure 3.1 Measuring Fiscal Policy

eliminated, and only discretionary policy changes, e.g. adjustments in tax rates, will be included.

There is an intuitive appeal to this approach, though, as we shall see below, it still does not ensure the exogeneity of the variable so obtained. In addition there are considerable difficulties associated with the attempt to estimate the values of the particular fiscal variables at any particular level of income. This has been clearly illustrated by the almost total inability of the U.K. authorities to predict the budget deficit over the 1970s, even when income was forecast fairly accurately. Even if this problem can be satisfactorily resolved, the question remains of how such variables are supposed to affect the economy. For example, it is possible to derive a theoretical multiplier which relates a change in actual public-sector expenditure to a change in income; but it tells us nothing about the effect of a change in some abstract, full-employment measure of expenditure.[7]

There are anyway many difficult questions of detail. For example, how are we to define full employment? Is the percentage unemployment which can be considered 'normal' or 'natural' a constant, or is it rising with improved social benefits, and so on? This is a crucial prior question about which there is little consensus. Or, to take another example, should full-employment public-sector expenditure on goods and services be taken as given, so that the only changes are interpreted as the direct result of discretionary policies. Over the past twenty-five to thirty years public-sector expenditure in most developed countries has been growing at, or above, the rate of growth of the economy. The question therefore arises whether or not some part of this growth has become embedded in the system and would be better thought of as endogenous. This ingenious way of measuring (discretionary) fiscal policy is now very often used, but we should be aware that in fact it is likely to create as many problems as it solves.

Monetary policy is also thought to be more accurately explained in terms of either narrow money or the monetary base, i.e. those assets held by the banks as reserves, since these are more likely to be under the control of the monetary authorities. There is, however, a big jump from recognising the potential ability to control and the actual assumption that this control is effective. As we shall see below, the ability to control a variable does not ensure its exogeneity, and it is this last quality that is desired if the reduced-form equations are to be interpreted as causal relationships.

Lags on the explanatory variables were estimated with quarterly data, employing the Almon technique,[8] for the period 1952 (1) to 1968 (2). A typical example of the lags found is given in Table 3.1. The dependent variable is the change in nominal

Table 3.1 Andersen and Jordan's Reduced-form Results

$$\Delta \text{G.N.P.} = \underset{(2.76)}{2.28} + \sum_{i=0}^{3} e_i \, \Delta E_{-i} + \sum_{i=0}^{3} m_i \Delta M_{-i}$$

$\bar{R}^2 = 0.60$

S.E. $= 4.01$

D–W $= 1.78$

$e_0 =$	0.40	(1.48)	$M_0 =$	1.54	(2.47)
$e_1 =$	0.54	(2.68)	$M_1 =$	1.56	(3.43)
$e_2 =$	−0.03	(0.13)	$M_2 =$	1.44	(3.18)
$e_3 =$	−0.74	(2.85)	$M_3 =$	1.29	(2.00)
$\Sigma e_i =$	0.17	(0.54)	$\Sigma M_i =$	5.83	(7.25)

Notes: $\bar{R}^2$ is the coefficient of determination corrected for degrees of freedom; S.E. is the standard error of the estimated equation; D–W is the Durbin–Watson statistic to measure the degree of first-order autocorrelation; t statistics are given in parenthesis with each regression coefficient.

G.N.P. and this is explained by the changes in nominal high-employment expenditures of the Federal Government and the narrowly defined money stock.

The results given in Table 3.1 show that fiscal policy does seem to have an immediate effect on nominal income, but that by the end of a year this has become very small. This implies that the public-sector expenditures 'crowd out' an almost equivalent amount of private-sector expenditures. For example, the long-run effect of an increase in public-sector spending of $1 billion is to raise G.N.P. by only $170 million. Monetary policy, on the other hand, seems to have a substantial long-run effect, with an equivalent increase in the money supply raising G.N.P. by $5.8 billion after a year.

This work resulted in similar reaction to that of Friedman and Meiselman – somewhat more subdued but seemingly longer lasting. Again it was shown that by changing the definitions of fiscal policy (and the estimation period), it became more important in explaining changes in income. Monetary policy, however, continued to have a major impact on nominal income. The more fundamental questions associated with this debate are dealt with below.

The Federal Reserve Bank of St Louis has retained substantial interest in this area and has continued to publish regular articles supporting the monetarist position. In 1970 it published a more complete model, by Andersen and Carlson, which included separate price, demand pressure, unemployment and interest-rate equations. Income was determined as before, but now it could be broken down into its separate output and price components. An outline of the model is given in Table 3.2, together with a flow diagram (Figure 3.2) which emphasises the direction of causality assumed in this model.

An advantage of this model over the previous single-equation studies was seen to be that it was now possible to distinguish between *real* effects, e.g. on output and employment, and price effects. This was a considerable advance since, as we saw in Chapter 2, the monetarists expect an increase in the money supply to have its major long-run impact on the price level, with hardly any long-run effect on real income, though in the short run they expect the impact effects to be the exact opposite of this.

Table 3.2 Model in Algebraic Form

(1) Total spending equation $\Delta Y_t = f_1(\Delta M_t \ldots \Delta M_{t-n}, \Delta E_t \ldots \Delta E_{t-n})$

(2) Price equation $\Delta P_t = f_2(D_t \ldots D_{t-n}, \Delta P^A{}_t)$

(3) Demand pressure identity $D_t = \Delta Y_t - (X^F{}_t - X_{t-1})$

(4) Total spending identity $\Delta Y_t = \Delta P_t + \Delta X_t$

(5) Interest-rate equation $R_t = f_3(\Delta M_t, \Delta X_t \ldots \Delta X_{t-n}, \Delta P_t, \Delta P^A{}_t)$

(6) Anticipated price equation $\Delta P^A{}_t = f_4(\Delta P_{t-1} \ldots \Delta P_{t-n})$

(7) Unemployment-rate equation $U_t = f_5(G_t, G_{t-1})$

(8) G.N.P. gap identity $G_t = \dfrac{X^F{}_t - X_t}{X^F{}_t}$

Endogenous variables	*Exogenous variables**
ΔY_t = change in total spending (nominal G.N.P.)	ΔM_t = change in money stock
ΔP_t = change in price level (G.N.P price deflator)	ΔE_t = change in high-employment Federal expenditures
D_t = demand pressure	$X^F{}_t$ = potential (full-employment) output
ΔX_t = change in output (real G.N.P.)	
R_t = market interest rate	
$\Delta P^A{}_t$ = anticipated change in price level	
U_t = unemployment rate	
G_t = G.N.P. gap	

*Other than lagged variables.

The model was estimated incorporating reasonably long lags in the explanation of behaviour, again mostly on the basis of the Almon technique. Long-run simulations with the model provided strong support for the monetarist thesis, resulting in the conclusion that 'monetary actions have no effect on real magnitudes; the rate of growth of output, the unemployment rate, and the real rate of interest all tend to move toward some equilibrium rate, regardless of which rate of money growth is maintained. The effects of alternative rates of monetary expansion are on nominal magnitudes, namely total spending,

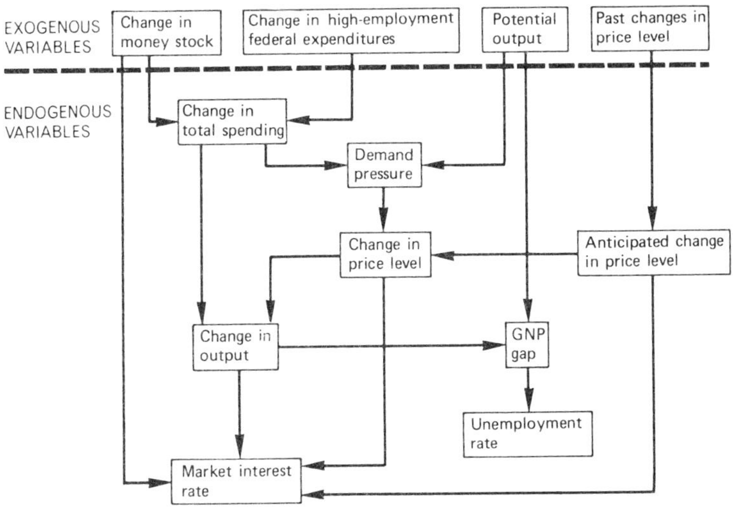

Figure 3.2 Flow Diagram of model

prices, and market interest rates' (Anderson and Carlson, 1970).

Many more models are now being constructed that incorporate direct effects of money on income and prices. This work is likely to continue for some time to come, and is almost certain to prove as controversial as previous studies.[9] It is also clear that economists, politicians, workers and businessmen are becoming increasingly aware of the role played by money in the economy, and attempts have got to be made to try to quantify this effect. It is, however, also important to recognise the limitations of these studies. Before going on to discuss some of these problems, we shall briefly consider the application of this approach to the United Kingdom.

Evidence for the United Kingdom

In fact very little work has been done in the United Kingdom on examining the role of money as a causal factor in determining output and prices. The more general view has been that the supply of money has responded to developments in 'real' markets, and it is for that reason only that velocity has been stable (see, for example, Kaldor, 1970). However, the two major American studies by Friedman and Meiselman and Andersen and Jordan, referred to above, have been replicated for the United Kingdom by Barrett and Walters (1966) and Artis and Nobay (1969).

Barrett and Walters took rather more care in deriving the reduced-form equations they were to estimate, though they do not explain why they defined the variables in logarithmic form. The reduced forms were estimated for annual data over the period 1878 to 1963, excluding the war years, and attention was concentrated on three particular sub-periods: 1878–1914, 1921–38 and 1948–63. Table 3.3 gives an example of the type of results obtained.

Table 3.3 Barrett and Walters's Multiplier/Velocity Results

	M	A	R^2	$r_{CM.A}$	$r_{CA.M}$
1878–1914 levels	0.6*	0.2*	0.98	0.76	0.37
First differences	0.6*	0.09*	0.58	0.56	0.20
1921–38 levels	0.16*	0.23*	0.90	0.31	0.80
First differences	0.25	0.19*	0.68	0.20	0.65
1948–63 levels	0.76*	0.52*	0.99	0.70	0.93
First differences			Not significant		

* Statistically significant at the 5 per cent level.
$r_{CM.A}, r_{CA.M}$ = the partial correlation coefficient of C on M holding A constant, or of C on A holding M constant.

These results illustrate the conclusion drawn by Barrett and Walters: 'Money seems to have had special importance in the relatively full-employment conditions up to the First World War. With high unemployment between the wars, and prices falling for most of the period, autonomous expenditure accounted for most of the variability in consumption. The explanatory power of both variables declines for the postwar economy.' There is therefore no strong support for Friedman and Meiselman, though money does seem to have a role to play, which, given the contrary views of many economists at that time, might have been thought victory enough.

The attempt to replicate the Andersen and Jordan study for

the United Kingdom turned out to be even less successful. Artis and Nobay do derive full-employment measures of government expenditure and income, but they are not particularly confident about the estimates obtained. They therefore consider an alternative measure of fiscal policy – the government fiscal measure (G.E.M.), which measures the (cumulated) impact of the 'first-round' effects on G.D.P. of defined taxation changes (and hire-purchase terms) – always assuming, of course, that these 'impact' effects have been identified accurately. This last measure of fiscal policy provides the most significant fit, and the broad definition of money is the 'best' monetary variable.

The Almon-lag results are invariably very poor, and Artis and Nobay are sceptical of the method: 'the assumptions which have to be made in deploying this technique appear to be very restrictive, and the results rather arbitrary'. The results, for what they are worth, and Artis and Nobay stress their doubts about the whole procedure, are exactly the reverse of those obtained by Andersen and Jordan, i.e. 'fiscal policy works faster and performs better in explaining changes in G.D.P. than measures of monetary policy'.

In 1970 the Bank of England published a review of the importance of money (Goodhart and Crockett, 1970) which contained estimates of the effect of money on output, derived from a quarterly equation of the following form:[10]

$$Y = (a_0) + \sum_{i=0}^{7} a_i M_i + u \tag{3.13}$$

where $Y =$ G.D.P. at factor cost, or industrial output, both measured at current prices, $M =$ QM1, QM2 or M3 (the Q suffix is included to indicate that the narrower definitions are quasi-definitions including data on deposits only with the London clearing banks), QM1 = currency and net current-account deposits of the London clearing banks, QM2 = currency and net deposits of the London clearing banks, and M3 = currency and net deposits of U.K. residents with the U.K. banking sector. The results obtained are given in Table 3.4.

The evidence suggests that money can to some extent 'explain' output even in the United Kingdom, though the authors are careful to point out that 'the apparent connection

Table 3.4 Goodhart and Crockett's money multiplier results

Money series	*Constant*	ΔM_0	ΔM_{-1}	ΔM_{-2}	ΔM_{-3}	ΔM_{-4}	ΔM_{-5}	ΔM_{-6}	ΔM_{-7}	*Estimated money Multiplier**	*Coeffi-cient of deter-mination*	*Standard error of estimate*	*Durbin–Watson statistic*
					Dependent variable–G.D.P.								
M_1	77.1		0.42 (0.15)	−0.38 (0.16)	0.40 (0.15)		0.33 (0.15)	−0.27 (0.15)		0.50	0.216	70.6	2.69
(1957:2–1969:3)	Suppressed	0.35 (0.17)	0.28 (0.18)		0.49 (0.15)		0.63 (0.17)	−0.39 (0.20)	0.45 (0.18)	1.81	0.565	83.7	2.17
M_2	64.6	0.25 (0.14)					0.37 (0.17)	−0.29 (0.16)		0.33	0.086	76.1	2.72
(1957:2–1969:3)	Suppressed	0.34 (0.12)			0.27 (0.15)		0.49 (0.16)	−0.45 (0.19)	0.27 (0.16)	0.92	0.629	77.3	2.47
M_3	91.7			0.19 (0.13)	−0.36 (0.13)	0.27 (0.13)		†	†	0.10	0.343	73.9	2.79
(1964:3–1969:3)	Suppressed			0.28 (0.11)	−0.31 (0.12)	0.32 (0.12)	0.20 (0.11)	†	†	0.49	0.742	74.4	2.54
					Dependent variable – industrial output								
M_1	21.9	0.11 (0.05)	0.17 (0.05)	0.15 (0.06)		0.12 (0.06)				0.55	0.276	37.0	1.82
(1953:2–1969:3)	Suppressed	0.14 (0.06)	0.22 (0.06)	0.18 (0.06)	0.12 (0.06)	0.15 (0.06)	0.09 (0.06)			0.90	0.588	39.0	1.64
M_2	14.9		0.22 (0.06)		0.10 (0.07)					0.32	0.212	38.6	1.53
1953:2–1969:3)	Suppressed	0.09 (0.07)	0.22 (0.07)		0.14 (0.06)					0.45	0.585	39.1	1.49

M_3	−57.0	0.08	0.09	0.23	0.12	†	†	0.53	0.516	34.2	1.46
		(0.06)	(0.05)	(0.06)	(0.06)						
(1964:3–	Suppressed		0.07	0.20		†	†	0.27	0.772	36.3	1.51
1969:3)			(0.05)	(0.05)							

Note: Standard errors of the estimated coefficients are shown in parentheses
* The sum of the estimated coefficients of ΔM_0 to ΔM_{-7}, measuring the expected effect of a change in the money stock during the first eight quarters from its occurrence.
† These variables were not included in the estimation.

Source: Goodhart and Crockett (1970).

between changes in money and changes in output is merely a reflection of cyclical influences acting on both variables, with no direct causal connection'. It is interesting to note that 'M3 appears to give the best explanation of changes in output whichever output measure is used', even though 'M3 performed no better than M1 and M2 in the estimates of the demand-for-money functions'. As will be made clear below, these findings are quite consistent with the view that broad money, M3, is determined by factors affecting its supply, and that the determinants of demand then adjust in order to bring about equality.

Economists at the London Business School (1977) have also experimented with simple money–income relationships. For example, they have related changes in real final expenditure to the current and lagged changes in real money supply (i.e. the nominal money supply deflated by the expenditure deflator). As the equation in Table 3.5 illustrates, the simple relationship employing quarterly data for the period did prove reasonably successful.

Table 3.5 London Business School's Money Multiplier: 1969(1)–1976(2)

$$\Delta_4 \ln E = \underset{(3.61)}{0.938} + \underset{(7.78)}{0.622}\,\Delta_4 \ln \left\{\frac{M}{P}\right\} - \underset{(3.76)}{0.301}\,\Delta_4 \ln \left\{\frac{M}{P}\right\}_{-1} + \text{dummies}$$

$\bar{R}^2 = 0.85$
$D\text{–}W = 2.1$
$S.E. = 1.37$

where E = total domestic expenditure at constant (1970) prices
M = M3 definition of money
P = price deflator of total domestic expenditure
Δ_4 = four-quarter change

Notes: Dummies were included to capture the effects of the strike in 1973(1) and the three-day week in 1974(1); t statistics are given in parentheses.
Source: London Business School (1977).

The other side of the money multiplier relationship has also been under scrutiny at a less formal level. In 1976 the editor of *The Times* (Rees-Mogg, 1976) attempted to demonstrate the broad relationship between inflation and changes in the stock of money which occurred two years previously. This proposed relationship was in turn completely rejected by Tarling and

Wilkinson (1977). It should be noted, however, that a more objective interpretation of the reported results, regressing inflation on the growth of the lagged money supply, hardly supports such a conclusive dismissal.

Tarling and Wilkinson presented the monetarist case in its 'popular' form, with emphasis placed on the long-run equilibrium conditions. The starting-point is the perennial quantity equation (identity) (see above):

$$MV \equiv PT \tag{3.14}$$

Taking logs and first differencing gives:

$$\Delta \ln M + \Delta \ln V \equiv \Delta \ln P + \Delta \ln T$$

If V is constant, so that $\Delta \ln V = 0$, and transactions follow a steady growth path, i.e. $\Delta \ln T = k$, then (3.14) can be written as

$$\Delta \ln P = -k + \Delta \ln M \tag{3.15}$$

Allowing for lags in the effect of money on prices we can write:

$$\Delta \ln P = -k + \sum_{i=0}^{n} W_i \Delta \ln M \tag{3.16}$$

This is the equation estimated by Tarling and Wilkinson, with the expectation that $\sum_{i=0}^{n} W_i$ should be approximately unity.

Tarling and Wilkinson present a table of results from which they conclude that the hypothesis is not supported by the data. The results, however, are not conclusive, particularly given the limited degrees of freedom available. Although the hypothesis being tested is of the very simplest variety and might not be expected to 'work' even by a convinced monetarist, it did seem worth re-estimating the longest lagged of these equations. The data employed are M3 and the market price deflator of total final expenditure (T.F.E.). Table 3.6 reports the results of reestimating the equations from 1960 (with lags calculated back to 1956). These show that as the data period is extended into the 1970s, so the results conform more closely to the monetarist hypothesis. There is, however, also an all-round improvement in the quality of the equation.

It should be noted that the growth of the money supply

Table 3.6 The Determination of the Inflation by growth in the Money Stock (Regressions from 1960)

	k	$\Delta\ln M$	$\Delta\ln M_{-1}$	$\Delta\ln M_{-2}$	$\Delta\ln M_{-3}$	$\Delta\ln M_{-4}$	$\overline{R}^2$	S.E.	D–W	$\sum_{i=0}^{4} M_i$
1960–70	−0.003	0.115	0.147	0.250	0.351	−0.105	0.416	0.013	1.140	0.758
	(0.20)	(0.71)	(0.99)	(1.55)	(2.34)	(0.50)				
1960–71	−0.010	0.168	0.217	0.151	0.364	0.042	0.491	0.014	1.068	0.942
	(0.66)	(0.96)	(1.39)	(0.93)	(2.20)	(0.20)				
1960–72	−0.006	0.086	0.186	0.122	0.400	0.106	0.561	0.013	1.310	0.898
	(0.50)	(0.97)	(1.35)	(0.83)	(2.74)	(0.64)				
1960–73	−0.003	0.082	0.134	0.097	0.377	0.144	0.726	0.013	1.319	0.834
	(0.24)	(0.97)	(1.33)	(0.72)	(2.80)	(0.99)				
1960–74	−0.015	−0.012	0.201	0.269	0.411	0.243	0.884	0.014	1.439	1.111
	(1.63)	(0.16)	(1.88)	(2.46)	(2.74)	(1.60)				
1960–75	−0.017	−0.010	0.181	0.281	0.456	0.247	0.943	0.014	1.368	1.155
	(2.24)	(0.14)	(1.97)	(2.79)	(4.54)	(1.70)				
1960–76	−0.011	0.003	0.159	0.365	0.408	0.074	0.938	0.015	1.561	1.009
	(1.54)	(0.03)	(1.63)	(3.84)	(3.92)	(0.67)				

Note: The figures in parentheses are t statistics.

lagged three years and is consistently significant. This would seem to suggest that the time lag of the effect of money on prices is somewhat longer than the two years sometimes suggested. The alternative view, that money simply accommodates price changes, gets little support, with the current rate of change in the money supply not even approaching significance.

It is not possible to argue that such a simple test 'proves' the monetarists' position; alternatively, neither does it permit the unqualified rejection of their argument, as Tarling and Wilkinson have suggested.

A more stringent test of any econometric result is the accuracy with which the estimated relationship is able to forecast outside the estimation period. This equation has therefore been used to forecast the rate of inflation (as measured by the T.F.E. deflator) for 1977 and 1978 under the assumption of a 13 per cent increase in M3 over each of those two years (see Table 3.7). These forecasts can only be as good as the model that generated them, and this, as we have seen, is extremely naïve. However, that is not an argument for rejecting the theory but rather for formulating improved tests.

Table 3.7 Forecasting Inflation

	Assumed rate of change in M (%)	*Forecast inflation (%)*
1977	13	10.45
1978	13	9.04

Criticisms and Comments

This debate seems to have raised as many questions as it has answered. The main points of discussion can be summarised under the following three broad headings:

(i) Reduced-form models versus behavioural system
(ii) Discretionary policy versus rules
(iii) Endogeneity versus exogeneity

A number of questions can be asked under each of these headings:

Reduced-form models versus behavioural system

(1) In the course of this debate it became clear that most of the equations estimated did not even represent a true reduced form of any structural model. The quasi-reduced forms actually employed are therefore open to alternative interpretation; and, as we saw above, even the sign to be expected cannot be taken for granted.

Consider, for example, the reduced-form equation (2.15) on page 25 above. It can be seen that the same parameters enter into both multipliers. Thus, while it is possible to compare the relative sizes of the two multipliers, it is not really valid to compare their stability; they should both be stable, or both unstable.

(2) What is the transmission mechanism underlying monetary models that relates changes in money supply/policy to income and expenditure? Friedman has at times argued that it is possible to think in terms of a single interest rate; this is particularly true of his 'reformulation' of the quantity theory into a demand theory (see Chapter 4). He has, however, proposed a radical alternative, the best exposition of which is contained in the paper by Friedman and Meiselman referred to above. The argument centres on money serving as a generalised substitute for all assets, financial and real, and being no more substitutable for short-term financial assets than for equities or durable goods. For example:

> The crucial issue that corresponds to the distinction between the 'credit' and 'monetary' effects of monetary policy is not whether changes in the stock of money operate through interest rates but rather the range of interest rates considered. On the 'credit' view, monetary policy impinges on a narrow and well defined range of capital assets and a correspondingly narrow range of associated expenditures. To these assets and these expenditures, there corresponds a set of market yields that can conveniently be summarised by 'a' rate of interest. Hence, it is useful to make this rate of

> interest the pivot of the analysis. On the 'monetary' view, monetary policy impinges on a much broader range of capital assets and correspondingly broader range of associated expenditures. In principle, yields or rates of interest can be defined to correspond with each item in the range but many of these will be implicit and unobservable, and an interest rate may not be a satisfactory way to summarise the terms and conditions on which some assets can be acquired. Hence, while it is always possible to describe the effect of changes in the stock of money on income as operating through interest rates, it may not be very useful or illuminating to do so. . . .
>
> On this alternative view, the conception of assets is as broad as the conception of expenditures: to each there corresponds a stream of expenditures and to each stream of expenditures an asset. That is why there is such a close link between the 'monetary' view and the quantity-theory approach. If monetary policy impinges on the whole balance sheet, its effects can be manifested in the whole range of expenditures. Conversely, if changes in the stock of money working themselves out through a stable velocity dominate changes in money income, then we must look for the effects of monetary policy on the assets corresponding to all parts of the stream of income (Friedman and Meiselman, 1963, pp. 217–18).

Because of the sheer inability to measure the great majority of the relevant interest rates (one for each asset yielding future services), complicated by changing market conditions for individual items and inflationary expectations, it is entirely misleading to measure the effect of a change in the money supply operating through a narrow sub-set (generally consisting of one) of measured nominal interest rates. Support for this view can be found in an excellent paper by Hicks, published as long ago as 1935, in which he attempted to establish a framework for integrating monetary and value theory.

Although this alternative transmission mechanism may eventually be proved to be substantially incorrect, it does at present represent a serious challenge to the Keynesian mechanism which ranks substitutes in terms of liquidity, with the main effect of changes in money supply being concentrated in financial markets. The monetarist transmission mechanism tells us what is inside the 'black box' but does not allow us to measure it. That does not, however, give grounds for rejecting it; even in the physical sciences there is much that is 'understood' but not observed directly.

It has been argued by Keynesian model-builders that they are not only interested in predicting the economy but also in understanding how it operates. For this reason disaggregation is essential. However, that argument can be turned around to claim that the actual transmission mechanisms specified, incorporating a narrowly defined range of interest rates, fail to measure the true impact of money on expenditures. Therefore the reduced form is an attempt to understand how the economy really responds to monetary changes, while the Keynesian approach is dominated by disaggregated responses to tax and 'exogenous' expenditure changes, but is importantly mis-specified by its neglect of monetary factors.

(3) If we accept that this transmission mechanism deserves serious consideration, we are then faced with the question of how to model the economy in such a way as to provide an adequate test. It may be that the direct correlation between money (lagged) and income is to some extent the result of such a mechanism. There is, however, a problem in estimating reduced forms in that this procedure is unable to distinguish the separate influences between variables. If the change in money and the fiscal policy variable are themselves a function of G.N.P., this is incorporated in the coefficient estimate. This will be further discussed later (pp. 70–1). It does not imply that there is no direct effect of money on income, only that the test is invalid. What is required, therefore, is a simultaneous model with income determined by the money supply and fiscal policy but including separate *reaction functions*[11] for the policy variables.

(4) It is not only the monetarists who have expressed concern at the apparent shortcomings of short-term stabilisation policies and the large-scale quarterly models that have been developed. A medium-term Keynesian alternative has also been put forward, for example by the Cambridge Economic Policy Group (Godley and Cripps, 1974, and Cripps, Godley

and Fetherston, 1974). This approach considers the short-term models to be so complicated that they have lost sight of the real issues, and that consequently they fail to take adequate account of the longer-run implications of policy changes (or any other exogenous shift). The approach is still in the process of development, but it does share with the monetarists the view that policy actions ought not to be dictated by short-run expediency but rather determined in the light of their longer-run effects. This argument is included to demonstrate that criticism of short-term quarterly models does not necessarily imply the adoption of monetarism.

Discretionary policy versus rules

Both the medium-term model-builders and the monetarists would argue that there should be less demand management. There are two main reasons:

(i) even in perfect conditions economic relationships are not understood well enough to enable fine-tuning of the economy – lags in the availability of information, reaction and operation are likely to result in perverse timing; and
(ii) the political importance of certain economic variables means that economic policy is often employed to register short-term political gains.

As far as the monetarists are concerned, an essential safeguard is the existence of an independent monetary authority imposing strict limits on the growth of the money supply. For the medium-term model-builders, including many other eclectic Keynesians, it is more a question of degree. There does seem to be increasing support for the view that the economy is *relatively* stable, and in this context it is perhaps instructive to refer to a recent paper by one of America's leading Keynesian economists. Modigliani (1977) in his presidential address to the American Economic Association went so far as to say: 'Milton Friedman was once quoted as saying, "we are all Keynesian now", and I am prepared to reciprocate that "we are all monetarists" – if by monetarism is meant assigning to the stock of money a major role in determining output and prices.'

He then proceeded to refute the claims that have been made against fiscal stabilisation, but accepted that 'the monetarists have made a valid and most valuable contribution in establishing that our economy is far less unstable than the early Keynesians pictured it and in rehabilitating the role of money as a determinant of aggregate demand', and 'have made an important contribution in pointing out that [stabilisation] policies might in fact prove destabilising'. According to this view there still remains an important role for stabilisation policies, though it is not clear whether these should be fiscal, or monetary, or both.

Endogeneity versus exogeneity

(1) A number of arguments have been put forward to suggest that the money supply is endogenous. The most important of these are based on the authorities' concern with stabilising interest rates and the exchange rate. Without going into possibilities of the joint operation of both policies, it is only necessary to note that strong arguments can be put forward to the effect that the adoption of either policy will cause the money supply to be endogenous. Of rather more academic interest is the argument that the banking system can, within significant limits, obtain or 'manufacture' reserves as and when required.

These arguments can be used to support the view that the money supply has simply responded to demand pressures and has therefore been endogenous. It should, however, be clear that they do not necessarily imply that changes in the money supply will have no independent effect on the rest of the economy, only that the simple reduced forms will not be able to identify the true causal relationships. An argument in support of an independent money-supply variable is contained below.

(2) It can be, and often has been, claimed that since the monetary base is under the control of the authorities this is the relevant exogenous variable. The same argument has been used with respect to the fiscal measure. Researchers have gone to great lengths to eliminate any endogeneity by employing full-employment measures of fiscal policy in order to obtain a variable which is supposed to be under the control of the

government. (It was noted above that the value of such variables to achieve even this objective is now being questioned.)

In discussing this question it will be helpful to distinguish between what might be called 'autonomous' and 'exogenous' variables: which are defined respectively as 'under the control of the authorities' and 'determined outside the model system'. As we have seen above, it has often been argued that evidence of autonomy could be interpreted to mean exogeneity. However, once we recognise that a policy variable is by its very nature 'varied' in order to achieve some economic objective, it can no longer be thought of as exogenous to the system. This is very important since, as was argued above, the reduced form tells us nothing about the separate influences involved. Even the sign of any correlation ceases to be meaningful.

To take an example, if fiscal policy were operated *successfully* to stabilise an economy which would otherwise be subject to cyclical disturbances, there would be no correlation between the cyclical variation of fiscal policy and the constant level of income. So the very low correlation for fiscal policy with income is open to the interpretation that it implies the greater significance of fiscal policy as a stabilisation instrument. One possible solution is to allow for such interrelationships by simultaneously estimating the policy reactions of the authorities.

Before leaving this important question it should perhaps be added that most large-scale Keynesian models also abstract from this problem by assuming exogenous policy actions. Because of the degree of disaggregation adopted, this may not be particularly important for the estimation of individual parameters. However, the errors are likely to accumulate so that the total policy multipliers estimated may be very unreliable. Goldfeld and Blinder (1972) believe that 'the differences between ignoring and taking account of correctly estimated reaction functions seem far more important than any structural estimation problems'.

Conclusion

What are the main conclusions to come out of this brief survey of simple, monetary models of the macro economy? The main point to note is that the monetarists have had reasonable success in obtaining results that broadly conform to their *a priori* expectations. These results have, however, not gone unchallenged, though more in terms of detail than principle, and there does seem to be a broad measure of agreement that money is likely to be an important determinant of economic activity. Disagreement is more concerned with the channels through which money has its effect than with the existence or otherwise of such an effect.

Much of the debate surrounding this question has concerned the technical aspects of analysis: how tests should be formulated, and conducted, and what the actual tests carried out have succeeded in showing. This debate is likely to continue for some time yet, and all the while attempts will be made to improve the tests employed. In addition, theoretical developments are required to improve our understanding of the basic relationships under study. This is just one aspect of the evolution of macroeconomics which contributes to the present interesting state of the subject. The one conclusion we should perhaps emphasise is that the evidence at least does not suggest that money is unimportant.

Appendix Statistical Evidence of Monetary Causality

An example of the search for some purely statistical evidence on the question of monetary causality in the United Kingdom is provided by Crockett (1970). This study did not pretend to be explaining any form of economic behaviour, simply it was intended to identify the statistical correlations between the leads and lags of pairs of economic time series. The approach adopted was that of the *cross-correlogram*: 'a series of coefficients of correlation which can range between +1.0 and −1.0 and which measure the closeness of linear association (positive or negative) between two series with a given lead or lag'. For example:

ΔG.D.P. and	ΔM_{-2}	r_{+2}
" "	ΔM_{-1}	r_{+1}
" "	ΔM	r_0

ΔM	and ΔG.D.P.	r_0
"	" ΔG.D.P.$_{-1}$	r_{-1}
"	" ΔG.D.P.$_{-2}$	r_{-2}

These correlations can then be plotted on a chart (as shown in Figure 3A1).

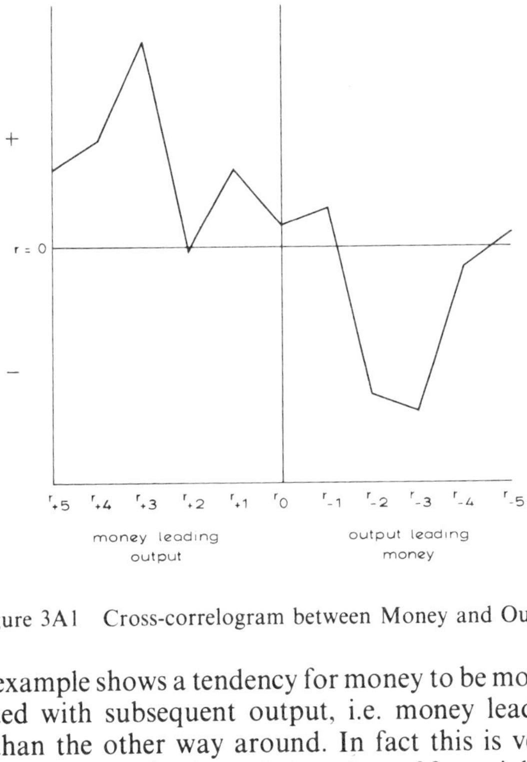

Figure 3A1 Cross-correlogram between Money and Output

This example shows a tendency for money to be more closely correlated with subsequent output, i.e. money leads output rather than the other way around. In fact this is very much what Crockett's results showed. A variety of financial variables (but not M3) and measures of economic activity were tried, and in all cases the financial variables seemed to lead activity. The most clear-cut results were in favour of narrow money (quasi-M1, as defined in the main text).

A further refinement of this type of statistical approach was made by Granger (1969), who provided a particular statistical definition of causality and suggested various methods for measuring it. This endeavoured to introduce more rigorous and scientific criteria to answer such questions of causality. It should, however, be emphasised that any purely statistical test can, at best, only be suggestive of a particular causal relationship, and it should not be interpreted as 'proof' of causality. The first application of this approach was by Sims (1972), who examined the causal relationship between money and income in the United States. This involved prefiltering the series in order to eliminate any trend or systematic component. These filtered series were then regressed on each other. Income was regressed on lagged, present and future values of the money stock, narrowly defined (or money base), and also money was regressed on lagged, present and future values of income. If money causes income in this sense, and income does not influence the money stock, then future values of money will be insignificant in explaining income, but future values of money will be insignificant determinants of money. And this, in fact, is the result that Sims found.

In 1976 Williams, Goodhart and Gowland published the results of applying a modified Sims approach to the United Kingdom. As before, the money series were the quasi-M1 and quasi-M2 series based only on London clearing banks figures. The results were very poor and, if anything, reversed Sims's conclusion, i.e. it seemed that income influenced the money stock, not the other way round. However, the poor quality of the results means that any conclusion would need to be treated with great caution. Moreover, one of the authors (Goodhart, 1975) has since questioned the whole approach on the grounds that the results are highly sensitive to the actual prefiltering procedure employed, and that the procedure has only considered the relationship between two variables, ignoring any further correlation with other, omitted, variables.

While these may seem to be admirable attempts to achieve scientific neutrality, they still depend crucially on the initial assumptions and the actual application of the approach. It is a relatively new methodology, and the results need to be treated with great caution. It could be that by giving prime importance to purely statistical causality, theoretical causality has actually been obscured.

4. THE THEORY OF THE DEMAND FOR MONEY

In Chapter 1 it was argued that the theoretical justification for the existence of money lay in the role money plays in reducing transactions costs. We also found that the temporal aspects of production and exchange necessarily imply that money must also serve as a store of value. Money therefore serves as a means of holding/storing wealth.

The objective of this chapter is to provide an introduction to the main theoretical justifications for the existence of a stable demand for money. The approach adopted is to begin with the three motives for holding money identified by Keynes in *The General Theory*: these are the transactions, precautionary and speculative motives. Since *The General Theory* each of these motives has been further refined, and the main developments are considered in turn. The final section is devoted to Friedman's reformulation of the quantity theory in terms of a theory of the demand for money.

Keynes – *The General Theory of Employment, Interest and Money*

Keynes systematically analysed the motives for holding money and gave original expression to the forces underlying the Cambridge quantity theory version of the demand for money (see Chapter 2). Keynes began by identifying three motives for holding money:

(i) the transactions motive;
(ii) the precautionary motive; and
(iii) the speculative motive.

Transactions demand (M_t^d)

This demand reflects 'the need of cash for the current transaction of personal and business exchanges' (Keynes, 1936, p. 170), and is derived directly from the means of payment function of money. This Keynes considered to be predominantly related to the anticipated level of income or transactions:

$$M_t^d = f(Y), \qquad f_Y > 0 \tag{4.1}$$

It has been argued that this transactions demand for money is not really *a demand* for money but merely a reflection of the 'pattern of transactions' (Hicks, 1967, p. 14). In a sense this is true, though it is also too simple a view, leaving open no possibility for the independent choice of the quantity of transactions balances held. The confusion arises because in the model from which this conclusion is derived money only comes into existence at the point of trade and is quickly cancelled out again. This, however, ignores the temporal aspect of exchange, the lags in the system between receipts and payments. Once these are taken into account it is only sensible to consider a *demand* for transactions balances.

Precautionary demand (M_p^d)

The precautionary motive is similarly related to the expected level of income or transactions, and stems from uncertainty about the future, and the possibility of being faced with unforeseen contingency payments, or unexpected changes in the pattern of receipts:

$$M_p^d = g(Y), \qquad g_Y > 0 \tag{4.2}$$

Keynes aggregated the precautionary and transactions demands together, and did in fact allow for these two demands to be a function of the rate of interest, though it was very much of secondary importance. The rate of interest enters as a determinant of the demand for money primarily through the third motive identified by Keynes.

Speculative demand (M_s^d)

The demand for speculative balances, what Keynes calls 'liquidity preference', only exists because of 'the existence of uncertainty as to the future of the rate of interest' (*The General*

Theory, p. 168), and the rate of interest is the reward for parting with liquidity (*The General Theory*, pp. 167, 174):

$$M_s^d = h(r), \qquad h_r < 0 \tag{4.3}$$

It is interesting to note that from whatever direction we approach the demand for money, *uncertainty* (of one form or another) is the dominant factor. If there were no uncertainty, there would be little demand for money.

Keynes assumed that each individual had a firmly held view of the *normal* rate of interest, and that if the actual rate diverged from this he would expect it to move back towards this normal rate. This then determined his expected capital gain or loss from holding bonds.

The analysis is reduced to a choice between money (M) and bonds (B) with a single expected rate of interest (r^e). The capital value (A) of a non-redeemable bond (i.e. the price you would have to pay for this bond) is equal to the coupon (R) (measured in monetary units) divided by the ruling rate of interest (r):

$$A = \frac{R}{r} = Rr^{-1} \tag{4.4}$$

The anticipated yield, in terms of money (Z), is equal to the coupon (R) plus any capital gain or minus any capital loss (g) due to an expected change in the price of the bond over the holding period. And any change in the price of the bond that is expected (with certainty) will depend on the current rate of interest relative to that considered to be 'normal'.

If we assume that $R = 1$, then

$$Z = R + g = R + \frac{dA}{dt} = 1 + \frac{dA}{dt} \tag{4.5}$$

Where $g = dA/dt$, i.e. the capital gain/loss is equal to the change in the asset price over the holding period dt.

Because we have assumed $R = 1$,

$$A = r^{-1}$$

Taking the total differential

$$dA = \frac{\partial A}{\partial r}\, dr = -r^{-2}\, dr$$

with respect to time gives:

$$\frac{dA}{dt} = -r^{-2}\frac{dr}{dt} = \frac{-1}{r^2}\frac{dr}{dt} \tag{4.6}$$

Substituting (4.6) into (4.5) gives:

$$Z = 1 - \frac{1}{r^2}\frac{dr}{dt} \tag{4.7}$$

The percentage yield (Z per cent), i.e. the monetary return as a proportion of the initial outlay, is

$$\frac{Z}{A} = Z\% = \left[1 + \frac{dA}{dt}\right]\frac{1}{A} \tag{4.8}$$

which gives

$$Z\% = r - \frac{1}{r}\frac{dr}{dt} \tag{4.9}$$

The next question to ask is at what point does an expected capital loss exactly offset the coupon return, i.e. where

$$Z = Z\% = 0$$

From (4.7)

$$0 = 1 - \frac{1}{r^2}\frac{dr}{dt}$$

gives

$$r^2 = \frac{dr}{dt} = r_c^2 \tag{4.10}$$

where r_c is the *critical* rate of interest, the point at which the expected capital loss is exactly equal to the rate of interest. And from (4.9)

$$0 = r - \frac{1}{r}\frac{dr}{dt}$$

$$r_c = \frac{1}{r}\frac{dr}{dt} \tag{4.11}$$

This tells us that in the absence of risk (and it is perhaps worth emphasising that all expectations are assumed to be held with complete certainty) an individual will be indifferent between holding money or bonds if the expected absolute rise in the rate of interest is equal to the square of itself (4.10). An alternative definition of this point of indifference is where the actual rate of interest is equal to its expected percentage change. For such analysis the planned holding period, dt, is obviously of considerable importance. Most theoretical and applied work assumes that it may be approximated by a year. This does, however, assume away a major problem.

Any individual expecting $r > r_c$ is assumed to hold all of his financial wealth, apart from his transactions and precautionary needs, in the form of bonds. On the other hand, the expectation that $r < r_c$ will result in the individual holding all of his wealth as money. An individual's demand curve for speculative balances will therefore be a discontinuous function. No money will be held, for this reason, if the expected capital loss fails to offset the interest to be earned over the planned holding period; only money will be held if the expected capital loss exceeds the rate of interest; and at the point of equality the individual will be indifferent as between money and bonds. This is illustrated in Figure 4.1, where W_S is the individual's financial wealth not required for transactions or precautionary purposes.

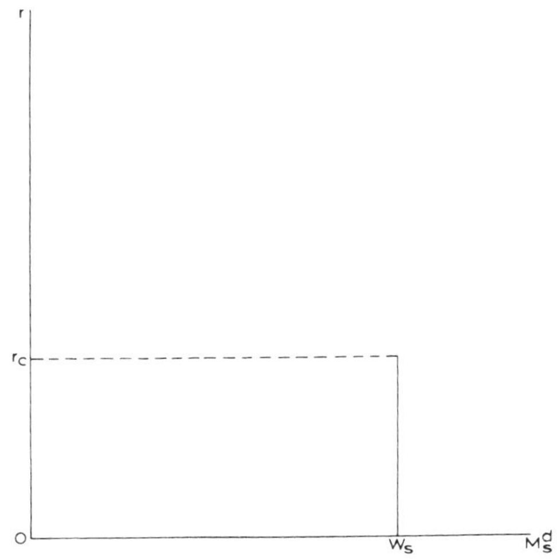

Figure 4.1 An Individual's Speculative Demand for Money

In order to obtain a smooth downward-sloping demand schedule Keynes assumed that while each individual held firm expectations of the normal rate, the rate considered normal was different between individuals. Furthermore, the frequency distribution of the 'true' rate over the whole economy was assumed to be approximately normal (see the top part of Figure 4.2).

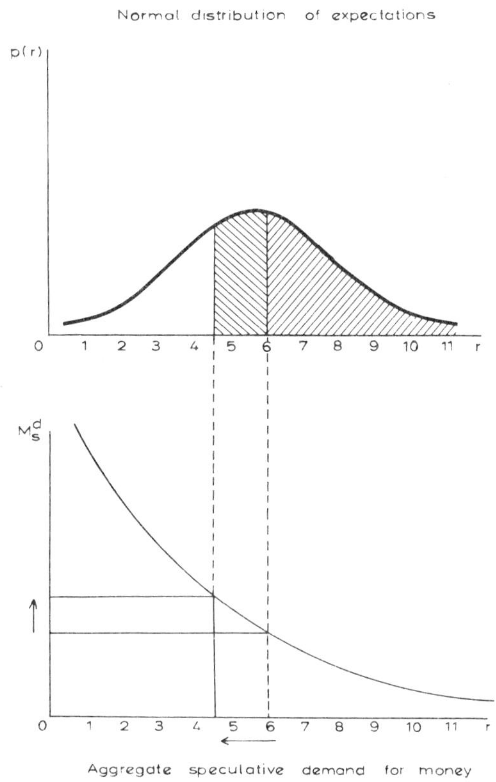

Figure 4.2

In this example, if the rate of interest falls below 6 per cent, *but does not change expectations of the normal rate*, more people will expect the interest rate to rise than to fall. Because the majority of the population now expect the price of bonds to fall, in order to return the rate of interest to its 'normal' level, there will be a reduction in the demand for bonds, or symmetrically, an increase in the speculative demand for money. A similar argument can be employed to show that an increase in the interest rate implies a reduction in the demand for money. In this way we can derive an *aggregate* demand for speculative balances schedule that slopes downwards as a function of the rate of interest (on bonds). Furthermore, this relationship is likely to be convex to the origin, since the further the interest rate moves away from what is considered normal (the mean of the distribution), the greater the percentage of people who will expect it to move back (see the bottom part of Figure 4.2).

We now have two separate demands for money: the speculative demand as a function of the rate of interest; and the transactions/precautionary demand determined by the level of income. These add up to the total demand for money, which in equilibrium must equal the supply of money. There may, in fact, be some overlap between these demands, but we can follow Keynes (1936, p. 199) in arguing that 'Whilst the amount of cash which an individual decides to hold to satisfy the transactions-motive and precautionary-motive is not entirely independent of what he is holding to satisfy the speculative-motive, it is a safe first approximation to regard the amounts of these two sets of cash-holdings as being largely independent of one another.' To see this the two demands are combined in Figure 4.3.

Looking at the total demand for money in this way reveals that the story is not yet complete. Before we know what the demand for money is, it is necessary to know the level of income. But the demand for money determines the rate of interest, which is in turn assumed to affect the level of income through its influence on investment. The full story of the determination of the demand for money requires us to take account of this interdependence. The model can be completed as shown in Figure 4.4 (which, incidentally, results in an alternative presentation of the complete *IS/LM* model developed previously).

Criticisms

Doubt has been cast on the speculative motive as an expla-

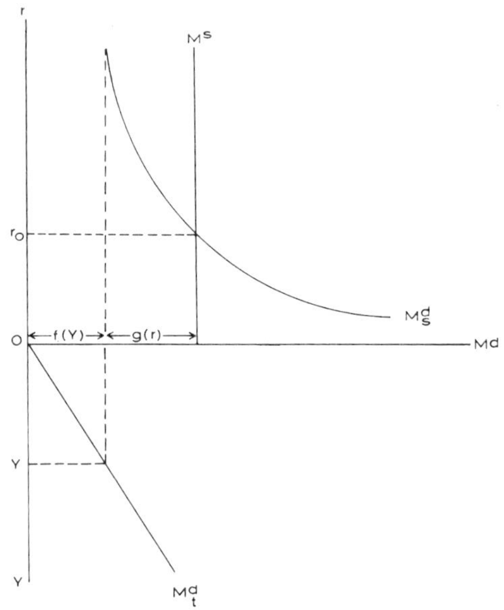

Figure 4.3 Speculative and Transactions/Precautionary Demands

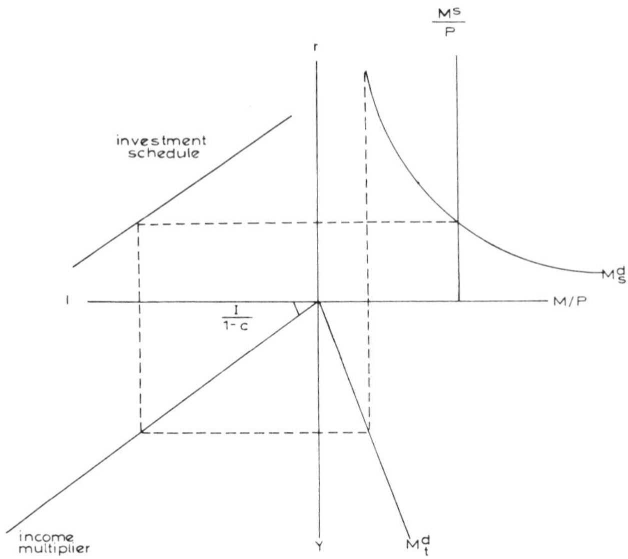

Figure 4.4 Determination of the Demand for Money (= Complete Model of the Economy)

nation of money holdings. It has been suggested that this motive is more likely to explain the choice between capital-safe assets yielding a rate of return and longer-term, capital-uncertain assets. If money is defined to exclude any interest-bearing assets, then why should anyone hold money as an asset when there are equally capital-safe assets yielding a positive monetary return (e.g. bank and building society deposits)? As long as money is defined narrowly to exclude interest-bearing deposits, this argument certainly seems valid. However, to apply the argument to money in general regardless of the definition of money ignores the fact that there are alternative, broad, definitions of money which include interest-bearing deposits, and are therefore reasonable capital-safe alternatives to 'bonds'. The failure to pay adequate attention to the actual definition of money is a source of constant confusion when discussing the demand for money, and is particularly noticeable in the specification of empirical equations (see Chapter 5).

Since 1945 there have been two major developments within the Keynesian tradition which have tried to base the demand for money on microeconomic behaviour at the individual level:

(1) The separation of the two demands for money into income-related and interest-related components has been challenged. It has been suggested that the transactions and precautionary demands for money are likely to be functions of the rate of interest. This possibility is examined in the two sections that follow.

(2) There have been two major queries raised against Keynes's analysis of the speculative motive – regardless of whether the demand under consideration is for money alone or some generalised set of financial assets. These may be summarised in the criticism that it is a 'boot-strap theory' of the rate of interest. This stresses the illogicality of assuming that the rate of interest is what it is only because it is expected to be something else: in other words it is held up by its own boot straps.

First, it seems illogical to assume firmly held expectations of what the interest rate will be, particularly when the majority must turn out to be wrong. It certainly does not fit easily alongside the importance placed on uncertainty.

Second, the assumption of *regressive* expectations (i.e. if the actual rate of interest moves away from what is considered normal, then it is expected to move back) is somewhat hard to justify in the short term and is counter to Keynes's more usual assumption of the formation of expectations in other contexts, e.g. business confidence. It is probably true to say that the more usual assumption is that, at least in the short term, expectations are formed extrapolatively: if interest rates change, then the rate considered normal also changes in the same direction.

The second important development in Keynesian theory has therefore been the introduction of risk into the individual decision-making process. This is considered below (pp. 93–105). The final section of the chapter concerns the attack on Keynesian theory by Milton Friedman.

Why the Transactions Demand for Money should be interest-elastic

Modern theories of a transactions demand for money originated in the work of Baumol (1952) and Tobin (1956), who adopted an inventory-theoretic approach. It is based on the existence of a time lag between payments and receipts, and the presence of short-term financial assets (which we shall call bills[1] to distinguish them from long-term bonds) other than money which yield an improved store of value since they are earning a rate of interest. The time lags are implicit in specialisation and the division of labour; the availability of a range of alternative assets depends upon the sophistication of the financial system. In addition there is also a cost involved in switching in and out of bills. However, if the yield is high enough, transactions costs low enough and the transactions period long enough, it will be worth while placing some of the money designated for spending during the period into bills.

According to this approach the demand for money can be shown to be a function of the rate of interest even in the absence of asset price uncertainty. The relevant behavioural determinants are:

(i) relative interest rates between money and bills;
(ii) the transfer cost involved in switching between money and bills; and
(iii) the length of the payments period.

The difference between the two theories developed by Tobin and Baumol is that Baumol assumed only fixed transfer costs, whereas Tobin included a variable cost as well, related to the size of the transaction. Since the results of both approaches are practically identical we shall only develop the simplest model.

The basic assumptions are that:

(1) Over any given time period the individual knows his income, Y, with certainty.

(2) The time path of expenditures is known and distributed evenly over the period summing to T, with $T = Y$, and that they all have to be paid for with money. This means that over any two sub-periods of equal length the value of transactions will be identical.

(3) The rate of interest, r, on the capital-safe alternative is fixed and known.

(4) The cost of switching from bills to money is a fixed amount, b (what Baumol calls 'the brokerage fee'), reflecting both subjective and objective costs. It is important to recognise the influence of subjective costs like the time and trouble taken to make any exchange. When we consider likely alternative assets, such as interest-bearing bank deposits, subjective costs will predominate, and it makes a lot of sense to include only a fixed transactions cost.

(5) The individual always transfers the same quantity of money out of bills each time, k, running this holding down to zero before making his next withdrawal.

At the simplest level it is easiest to assume that the individual is paid in bills which he then runs down over the transactions period. The analysis is not substantially altered if we allow payment in money and introduce a constant cost of switching $T-k$ of income into bills at the start. This simply adds a constant to the total cost and will not affect the result. In particular, if this cost is approximately equal to the brokerage cost, b, the model will be identical to that assuming initial payment in bills.[2] In this case, however, instead of the first transfer being out of bills into money, it is out of money into bills.

There are two types of cost incurred by the market operator:

(i) the brokerage charge, which is $b\,(T/k)$, i.e. the brokerage fee times the number of transfers made; and

(ii) the income forgone by holding money – since expenditure is assumed to be a constant flow, so that actual money balances are run down evenly over the holding period, the average money balance must be $k/2$. The cost is therefore this average holding times the rate of interest forgone, $r(k/2)$.

Since transactions are directly proportional to time, the pattern of money holding over time can be directly related to the income–expenditure pattern. This is illustrated in Figure 4.5.

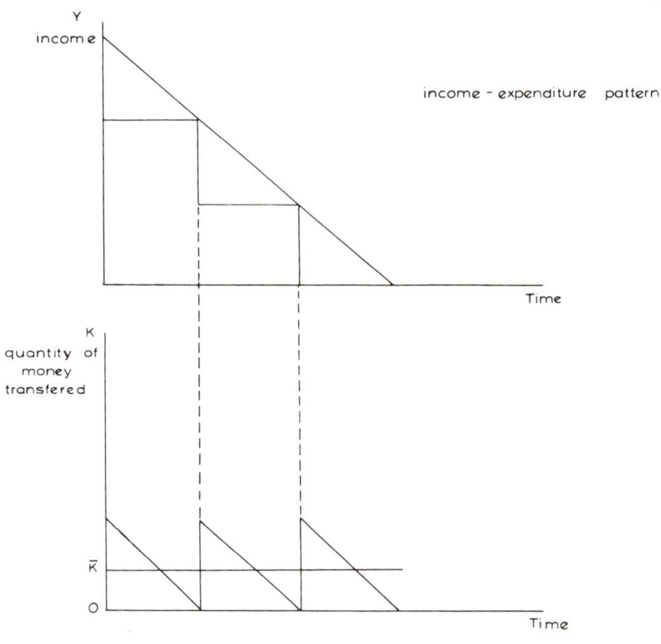

Figure 4.5 Pattern of Money Holding Over Time

The total cost, C, will be the sum of the two separate costs:

$$C = \frac{bT}{k} + r\frac{k}{2} \tag{4.12}$$

The value of k that minimises total costs is found by differentiating (4.12) with respect to k, and setting it equal to zero:

$$\frac{\partial C}{\partial k} = -\frac{bT}{k^2} + \frac{r}{2} = 0$$

Therefore

$$\frac{rk^2}{2} = bT$$

$$k = \sqrt{\frac{2bT}{r}} \tag{4.13}$$

For this to be a minimum a necessary condition is that the second derivative, $\partial^2 C/\partial k^2$, must be positive. In this case

$$\frac{\partial^2 C}{\partial k^2} = \frac{2bT}{k^3} > 0 \tag{4.14}$$

so that condition is satisfied.

The average transactions balance for the period was $k/2$, which since it reflects a demand for goods and services might be expected to represent a demand for real balances – in which case the demand for transactions balances in real terms can be derived as follows:

$$\frac{M^d}{P} = \frac{k}{2} = \frac{1}{2}\sqrt{\frac{2bT}{r}}$$

which can be rewritten as

$$M^d = \alpha T^{0.5} r^{-0.5} P \tag{4.15}$$

where $\alpha = \frac{1}{2}\sqrt{2b}$.

Before proceeding it may be helpful to give a diagrammatic representation of the above argument (see Figure 4.6). In this case the components of total cost will intersect, i.e. be equal, at

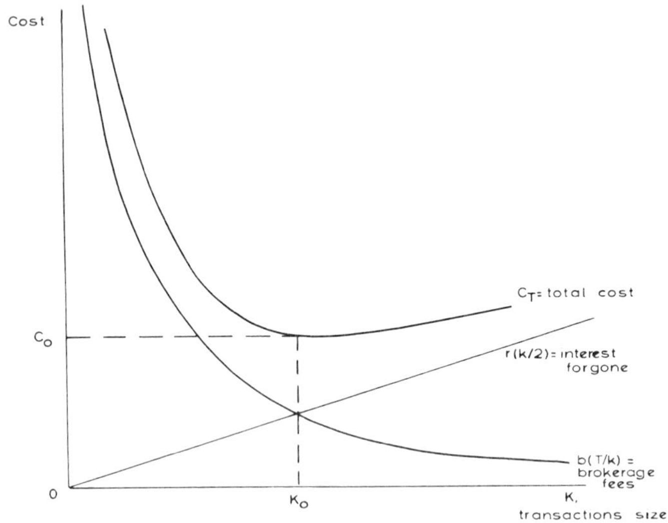

Figure 4.6 Minimising Transactions Costs

the value of K_0 for which total cost is at a minimum. This can be seen by setting the interest cost equal to the brokerage cost, i.e. $r(b/2) = b(T/k)$, which reduces to $k = \sqrt{2bT/r}$ and is equal to (4.13).

As the size of the transactions increases, the income forgone rises (with a fixed interest rate) but the cost of transactions is reduced. The objective is to choose the level of transactions to minimise total costs – the point where the two separate marginal costs are equal.

If we substitute $2M^d/P$ for k along the horizontal axis, we can see that the demand for money will be reduced as the result of an increase in the rate of interest, and increased if transactions costs rise.

Two implications of the so-called 'square-root formula' developed above which have attracted considerable attention are that:

(1) There are economies of scale in money holdings. The power of T, i.e. 0.5, can be interpreted as a constant elasticity. This means that the percentage change in M^d will only be half the percentage change in T.

(2) Because there are economies of scale in *individual* money holdings the aggregate demand for money will be a function of the distribution of incomes, i.e. the degree of concentration of income and expenditure.

We should, however, be cautious about accepting this square-root formula too literally. It is explicitly dependent on the assumptions that have been made, and it is possible to obtain other results by lifting some of the rigid assumptions that have been made.

At the individual level, transactions costs, subjective as well as objective, may be so high relative to the rate of interest and the level of income/transactions that this type of active cash management is impossible. Orr (1970, p. 136), for example, has claimed that with a brokerage fee of $2 and an interest rate of 6 per cent an individual would require a monthly salary of approximately $1600 before it would be economical for him to manage his funds in this way. In that case, there would be no interest-elasticity and the individual's demand for transactions balances would rise in line with his planned expenditure. An implication of this asymmetry is that aggregation from the individual to the total demand for transactions balances has the effect of increasing the income-elasticity and reducing the interest-elasticity (also see Brunner and Meltzer, 1967).

Optimal Precautionary Cash Balances

The second component of the demand for money which Keynes identified has a long history, going back at least to Edgeworth (1888). More recent developments have been by Patinkin (1965), Whalen (1966) and Orr (1970), among others. The approach adopted here principally follows Whalen.

The argument is very similar to that adopted for the transactions demand discussed above, but it allows for uncertainty regarding expected receipts and payments. It is, however, assumed that the individual can assign finite probabilities to the possible differences between receipts and payments – what we shall call net payments, N, over any specified period. Moreover, it is convenient to assume that the long-run objective is to spend all receipts so that the resultant probability distribution of net payments is centred on zero. As before, there are essentially two types of cost involved:

(1) The opportunity cost of holding money, i.e. the interest forgone. This is given by the stock of money held times the rate of interest to be earned on bills, r, i.e. Mr.[3]

(2) The cost of illiquidity. This is the cost of switching from bills to money if net payments exceed the money holding, i.e. if $N > M$. The probability of such an event is given by $p(N > M)$, while the cost, q, is assumed to be fixed independently of the size of the transfer, and therefore closely resembles the 'brokerage' fee associated with the transactions demand. The expected cost of illiquidity is therefore given by $p(N > M)q$.

Total cost is the sum of these two costs:

$$C = Mr + p(N > M)q \tag{4.16}$$

The next step is to relate the probability, $p(N > M)$, to an actual demand for precautionary balances. This analysis adopts Whalen's main case by assuming very conservative, risk-averse behaviour; to see the effect of alternative assumptions, see Whalen (1966).

The main conservative case is derived from Tchebycheff's inequality theorem (see Whalen, 1966), which states that the probability of a variable, in this case net payments, deviating from its mean by t times its standard deviation, s, is equal to or less than $1/t^2$. And with net payments having a mean of zero, this gives the probability of it deviating from zero. So the probability of net payments equalling M, which is $M/s(=t)$ standard deviations from zero, is

$$p(N > M) \leqslant \frac{1}{t^2} \tag{4.17}$$

Assuming the highest probability possible, thereby turning (4.17) into an equality, substituting M/s for t, and rearranging, gives

$$p(N > M) = \frac{s^2}{M^2} \tag{4.18}$$

where s^2 is simply the variance of the distribution of net payments.

Substituting (4.18) for $p(N > M)$ in (4.16) yields the following total cost function:

$$C = Mr + (s^2/M^2)q \tag{4.19}$$

As before, the value of M that minimises total costs is obtained by partially differentiating C with respect to M and setting the result equal to zero:

$$\frac{\partial C}{\partial M} = r - \frac{2s^2}{M^3}q = 0$$

Therefore

$$M^3 r = 2s^2 q$$

and

$$M = \sqrt[3]{\frac{2s^2 q}{r}} \tag{4.20}$$

Again, the second derivative is positive:

$$\frac{\partial^2 C}{\partial M^2} = \frac{6s^2}{M^4}q \tag{4.21}$$

confirming that we have in fact identified a minimum.

This model can also be illustrated with the aid of a diagram similar to that developed for the transactions demand, in this case starting with M on the horizontal axis (see Figure 4.7). The cost of illiquidity declines as M is increased, but the opportunity cost increases, given a fixed rate of interest. Total costs are minimised when money balances of M_0 are held.

It will be seen that precautionary balances will rise by the cube root of the variance, s^2, of the net payments distribution. Therefore, any increase in uncertainty regarding *expected* receipts and payments will be accompanied by an increase in the demand for money. Furthermore, it is through its effect on s^2 that an increase in income is translated into a demand for money. The actual relationship depends on the form of the net payments distribution, and the following example assumes a normal distribution.

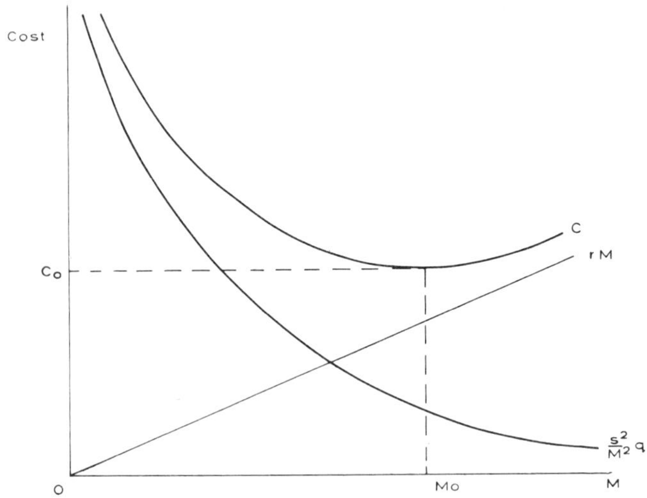

Figure 4.7 Optimising Precautionary Balances

If the value of individual receipts and payments stays the same but their number increases, the standard deviation will vary with the square root of the volume of receipts and payments, i.e. the variance will change proportionately. Since the demand for precautionary balances changes by the cube root of the variance, it will, in this example, change by the cube root of the average volume of receipts and payments, i.e. the elasticity will be $\frac{1}{3}$.

On the other hand, if the number of receipts and payments stays the same but their value increases, the variance will change with the square of the volume of receipts and payments, giving an elasticity of $\frac{2}{3}$. If the value of transactions increases because of an increase in the general level of all prices, *and* there is also an equivalent increase in the cost of illiquidity, the demand for money will have a price-elasticity of unity, an elasticity of $\frac{2}{3}$ associated with the change in the variance, and $\frac{1}{3}$ associated with the increase in the 'brokerage' fee. It is perhaps worth emphasising that it does require all prices to change by the same amount, not only commodity prices, but also the costs of financial transactions.

As with the transactions demand, the management of money balances in this way does require a fairly high minimum level of transactions. Because such money management will be uneconomic for many, if not most, individuals, we should perhaps expect the transactions-elasticity to be greater than $\frac{1}{3}$, and the interest-elasticity to be less than $\frac{1}{3}$.

Before leaving this discussion it is important to recognise that the precautionary demand is intimately related to the transactions demand for money. Precautionary balances are only required because of the uncertainty associated with the need to finance transactions over a particular period. It is, however, not possible to add together the transactions and precautionary demands since these demands will be closely related and the same money balances may partially satisfy both motives. The precautionary demand developed here is, however, not a complete replacement for the transactions demand since it only explains those money holdings required to finance net payments that diverge from the average, and not the money required to finance the expected average quantity of transactions.

Both these demands may be thought of as being concerned with the choice between capital-safe assets: in particular between money narrowly defined and a variety of deposit accounts with financial institutions (including banks), or short-term financial instruments. We might therefore expect these motives to explain the demand for narrow money but not broad money. The other area of development of the demand for money by the individual is with respect to the choice between capital-safe assets and capital-uncertain assets.[4]

Portfolio Analysis of the Demand for Money

This analysis is simply a special case of the standard theory of portfolio choice as developed by Markowitz (1952, 1959). In this case the choice is between an asset with a certain return, which we shall call money – with zero return – and a portfolio of uncertain assets, which we shall summarise in terms of a single asset called a bond – with an *expected* yield about which there is some uncertainty. The particular approach adopted here was developed by Tobin (1958), though the foundations were clearly outlined by Hicks as long ago as 1935.

It is normally assumed that a positive return enters positively into an investor's utility function, while risk enters negatively. In simple terms a positive return on money invested is good, the possibility of loss is bad. As we shall see below, there can be exceptions to this general rule, but it is assumed that the normal, risk-averse, investor chooses between money and bonds so that in equilibrium the additional interest earnings expected on any investment in bonds is just sufficient to offset the additional perceived risk incurred. There is therefore a trade-off between risk and return.

In this theory expected return and risk are measured by the mean and standard deviation of the subjective probability of the return of any investment. For this reason it is often referred to in the literature as 'the mean-variance approach' to portfolio choice. It is assumed that the individual knows the distribution of the possible outcomes of a particular investment. The expected capital gain $E(g)$ is the sum of all these possible finite outcomes (g_i) times their probability (p_i):

$$E(g) = p_1 g_1 + p_2 g_2 + \ldots + p_n g_n$$

$$= \sum_{i=1}^{n} p_i g_i \qquad (4.22)$$

where $\sum_{i=1}^{n} p_i = 1$.

For example, consider the following numerical example:

g_i (%)	p_i	$g_i p_i$ (%)
−15	0·05	−0·75
−10	0·10	−1.00
−5	0·20	−1.00
0	0.10	0.00
5	0.20	1.00
10	0.25	2.50
20	0.15	2.25
	$\Sigma p_i = 1$	$\Sigma p_i g_i = 3.00$

In this particular example it can be seen that the investors' expectations are strongly weighted in favour of a capital gain.

The standard deviation, $\sigma(g)$, of the probability distribution of anticipated outcomes is

$$\sigma(g) = \sqrt{\text{var}\,(g)} \tag{4.23}$$

and

$$\begin{aligned} \text{var}\,(g) &= p_1[g_1 - E(g)]^2 + \ldots + p_n[g_n - E(g)]^2 \\ &= \sum_{i=1}^{n} p_i[g_i - E(g)]^2 \end{aligned} \tag{4.24}$$

The variance of g, var (g), is simply the squared deviation of each g_i from the mean value weighted by its probability, p_i.

Assuming that all wealth, W, is held either in the form of money, M, or bonds, B, i.e.

$$W = M + B$$

it follows that

$$\alpha + \beta = 1 \tag{4.25}$$

where $\alpha = M/W$ and $\beta = B/W$.

The actual yield on the portfolio (R) is

$$R = \beta(r + g), \quad 0 \leqslant \beta \leqslant 1 \tag{4.26}$$

where r is the rate of return at the time the bond was purchased. This expression simply states that the return on the portfolio is equal to the return on bonds multiplied by the proportion of bonds held in the portfolio.

The analysis can be simplified by assuming $E(g) = 0$, unlike the example above, so that the *expected* yield on the portfolio reduces to

$$E(R) = \beta r \tag{4.27}$$

The standard deviation of the return expected on the portfolio is equal to the standard deviation of the possibility of capital gain or loss, $\sigma(g)$, times that proportion of the portfolio held in bonds:

$$\sigma(R) = \beta\sigma(g) \tag{4.28}$$

so that

$$\beta = \frac{\sigma(R)}{\sigma(g)} \tag{4.29}$$

Substituting (4.29) into (4.27) gives

$$E(R) = r\frac{\sigma(R)}{\sigma(g)} \tag{4.30}$$

with $0 \leqslant \sigma(R) \leqslant \sigma(g)$, i.e. the standard deviation of the portfolio cannot exceed the standard deviation on bonds. Equality would be achieved when $\beta = 1$ and the portfolio consisted entirely of bonds. In this case the expected return on the portfolio is the same as that expected for bonds. Consider what would be the case if $\beta = 0$?

The above relationships can be represented diagrammatically (see Figure 4.8). The OA_i lines show the possible combinations of interest and risk available at the time—each higher line represents a higher rate of interest. These are a diagrammatic representation of the relationship expressed in

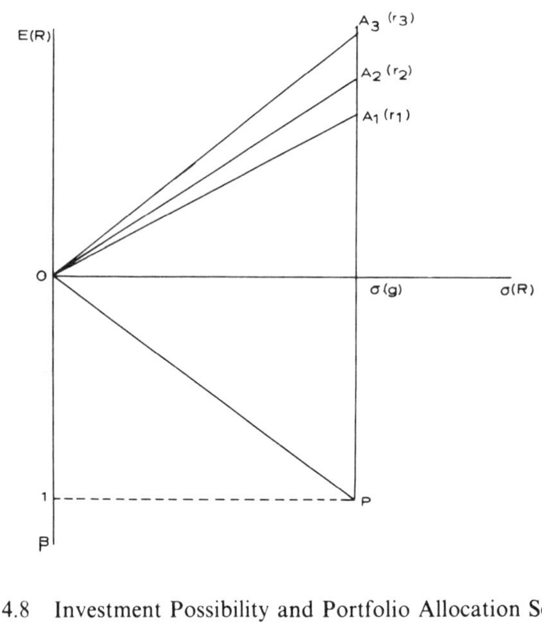

Figure 4.8 Investment Possibility and Portfolio Allocation Schedules

equation (4.30). If $\sigma(R) = \sigma(g)$, then $E(R) = r$; and when $\sigma(R) < \sigma(g)$, then $E(R) < r$.

The OP line gives the proportion of wealth allocated to bonds and relates this to the riskiness of the portfolio. This illustrates the relationship expressed in equation (4.29). If $\beta = 1$, then $\sigma(R) = \sigma(g)$; and $\beta < 1$ when $\sigma(R) < \sigma(g)$.

To summarise:

$$\beta = \frac{\sigma(R)}{\sigma(g)} = \frac{E(R)}{r} \tag{4.31}$$

The exact combination of expected risk and return on the portfolio depends on the proportion of wealth held in bonds. From this it follows that both return *and* risk are maximised when all wealth is held in the form of bonds, i.e. $\beta = 1$. The OA_i lines therefore show the *opportunities* open to the investor.

In order to identify the point on the opportunity locus that the investor will actually choose we need to know his attitudes to return and risk. These may be summarised by a set of indifference curves – representing combinations of expected return and risk between which the individual is indifferent, i.e. they have the same utility. If we assume, as we did above, that the average investor likes a positive return but dislikes risk, and that as risk and return rise, his aversion to the latter rises more than his preference for the former, this will generally result in *risk-aversion*. This case is illustrated in Figure 4.9.

The first case illustrated, where the maximum $\sigma(R)$ is $\sigma(g)_1$, shows that a rise in interest rates from r_1 to r_2 will increase *both* the proportion of wealth held in the form of bonds *and* the utility of the investor. The demand for money schedule for such an individual would be a continuous downward-sloping line, convex to the origin. The second case illustrated, where the maximum risk on the portfolio is restricted to $\sigma(g)_2$, shows that a similar portfolio choice and increase in utility could be obtained if the subjective appreciation of the risk associated with bonds was reduced to $\sigma(g)_2$ from $\sigma(g)_1$ while keeping the expected return at r_1. Although it is not included in this model, we should also note that an increase in uncertainty surrounding the planned holding period, e.g. doubts that bonds might have to be exchanged for money before desired, will also have effects similar to asset price uncertainty.

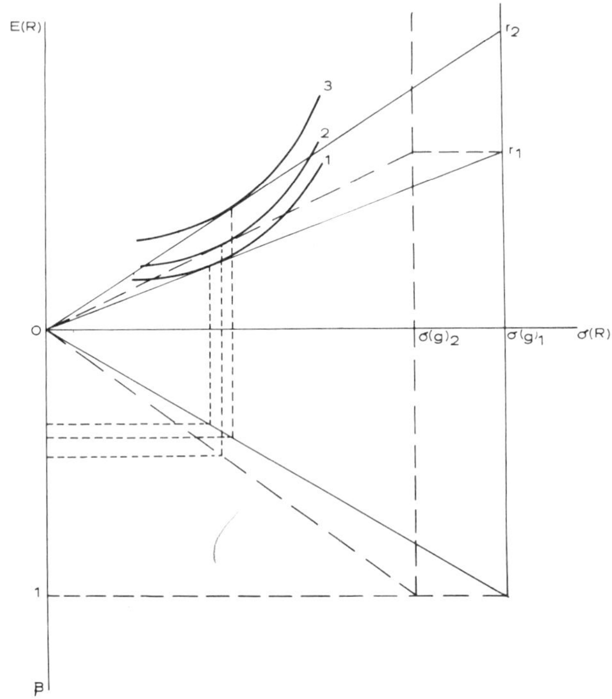

Figure 4.9 Normal Risk-aversion

It is possible that an individual could be so risk-averse that an increase in the expected rate of interest could actually result in a reduction in bond holdings. Such a possibility is illustrated in Figure 4.10. In this case the indifference curves will be relatively steep so that the income or wealth effect of the change $(b-c)$ is negative and exceeds, in absolute terms, the substitution effect $(a-b)$. The implication of this, that an increase in wealth would cause investors to reduce their money holdings, suggests that this will not represent the general case. In addition the effect of an increase in the rate of interest on bonds is to reduce the value of existing bond holdings, and therefore the stock of financial wealth. This influence will be reflected in the effect of changes in wealth on the demands for money and bonds. This is an indirect route through which an increase in the rate of interest might be

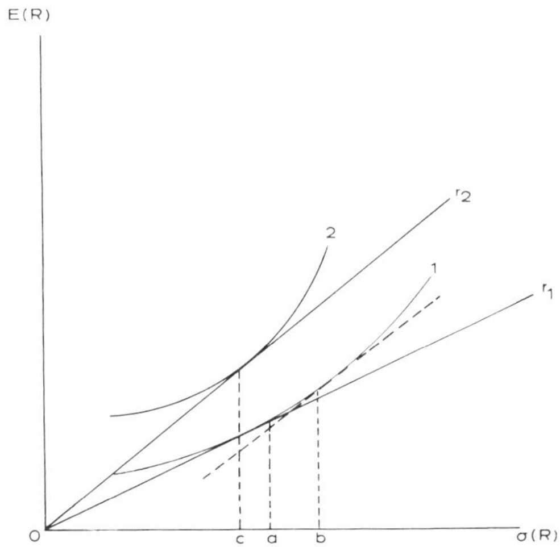

Figure 4.10 Extreme Risk-aversion, where the Wealth Effect exceeds the Substitution Effect

expected to reduce the demand for money. We shall have more to say about the likely effects of wealth revaluations resulting from interest-rate changes in Chapter 6.

Support for the assumption of risk-aversion is to some extent provided by the wide use of insurance. We find that this becomes a rational action if the individual has a diminishing marginal utility of income or wealth, i.e. if each successive unit of wealth adds less to total welfare than its predecessor, as, for example, is shown in Figure 4.11. With such a utility function the certainty of having W_2 will be valued more highly than a 50 per cent probability of either W_0 or W_1, even though the expected level of wealth is identical. This is illustrated in Table 4.1. As can be seen, insurance which guarantees $W_2 > W > W_3$ is preferable to $E(W_2)$ with these probabilities. In addition it should be clear that a utility function which exhibited increasing marginal utility, i.e. the slope of the function increased as we moved to the right, would not result in the individual taking out insurance. In that case a 50 per cent probability of either W_0 or W_1 would be valued more highly than W_2. This illustrates the close association between risk-aversion and diminishing marginal utility of wealth.

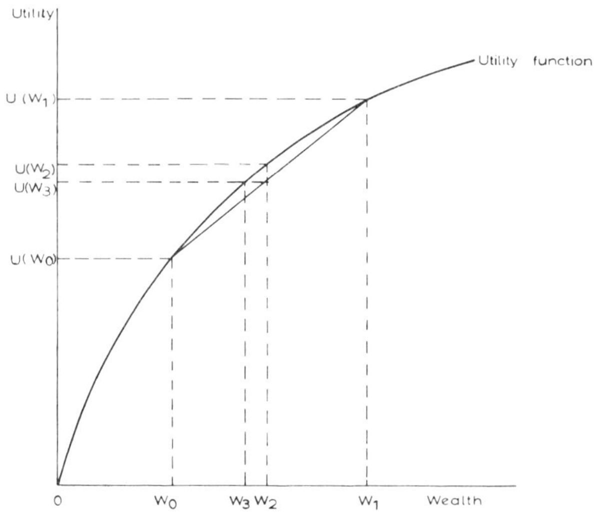

Figure 4.11 The Value of Insurance in the Face of Diminishing Marginal Utility of Wealth

Table 4.1 The Utility of Wealth

Wealth	*Utility*
W_0	$U(W_0)$
W_1	$U(W_1)$
W_2	$U(W_2)$
$0.5W_1 + 0.5W_0 = W_2$	$0.5U(W_1) + 0.5U(W_0) = U(W_3)$ and $U(W_3) < U(W_2)$

One way of deriving indifference curves in terms of the expected mean and the standard deviation of the rate of return is by assuming that the individual has a quadratic utility function. The simplest approach is to assume that the return on the portfolio (R) is the only source of income for the individual, and that his utility function takes the form

$$U = a + bR - cR^2 \tag{4.32}$$

which exhibits diminishing marginal utility, i.e.

$$\frac{dU}{dR} = b - 2cR = \text{marginal utility} \tag{4.33}$$

and

$$\frac{d^2U}{dR^2} = -2c$$

so marginal utility is reduced as R increases. This creates a problem, for there comes a point, when $R > b/2c$, where utility is actually reduced by any increase in R, which is hard to justify, at least for the typical investor. It is therefore necessary to restrict the analysis to that area of the function where $R < b/2c$. If this seems somewhat restrictive, it is worth noting that the same general model can be derived by assuming a normal distribution of expected returns (Tobin, 1965).[5]

The variance of the expected return, σ_R^2, can be derived as follows:

$$\begin{aligned}\sigma_R^2 &= E[R - E(R)]^2 \\ &= E\{R^2 - 2RE(R) + [E(R)]^2\} \\ &= E(R^2) - 2E(R)E(R) + [E(R)]^2\end{aligned}$$

which simplifies to

$$\sigma_R^2 = E(R^2) - [E(R)]^2$$

Rearrangement gives

$$E(R^2) = \sigma_R^2 + [E(R)]^2 \qquad (4.34)$$

The expected value of utility, $E(U)$, is obtained by taking the expected value of the whole function given in (4.32):

$$\begin{aligned}E(U) &= E(a + bR - cR^2) \\ &= a + bE(R) - cE(R^2)\end{aligned}$$

since the expected value of any constant is its actual value. Substituting for $E(R^2)$ from equation (4.34) shows that expected utility depends positively on the expected return, and negatively on the variance of that return, i.e.

$$E(U) = a + bE(R) - c[E(R)]^2 - c\sigma_R^2 \qquad (4.35)$$

which is exactly the relationship required by the analysis.

The indifference curves represent the offsetting changes in the components of equation (4.35) required to maintain a constant expected utility. These can be derived by differentiating (4.35) and setting the result equal to zero:

$$dE(U) = [b - 2cE(R)]dE(R) - 2c\sigma_R d\sigma_R = 0 \quad (4.36)$$

so that

$$\frac{dE(R)}{d\sigma_R} = \frac{2c\sigma_R}{b - 2cE(R)} \quad (4.37)$$

which gives the slope of the indifference curve.

With $c < 0$, as has been assumed, the slope will be positive since the denominator, $b - 2cE(R)$, represents the marginal utility resulting from an increase in the rate of return, i.e. $\partial E(U)/\partial E(R)$, which has been restricted to be positive. The fact that the indifference curves will be concave upwards is demonstrated by the second derivative also being positive, i.e. the expected return increases by more than its standard deviation:

$$\frac{d^2E(R)}{d\sigma^2} = \frac{2c[(dE(R)/d\sigma)^2 + 1]}{a - 2cE(R)} \quad (4.38)$$

Alternative indifference configurations can be obtained by defining different utility functions. For example, an individual with a quadratic utility function who receives increasing marginal utility from each successive addition to his wealth will positively enjoy risk. In this case the utility function will be concave upwards and the indifference curve will be concave downwards. Such a utility function would be obtained by making $c > 0$ in equation (4.32), in which case the slope of the derived indifference curve (4.37) would now be negative (downward-sloping) and so would be the second derivative (the slope would be increasingly negative). This case is illustrated in Figure 4.12.

It is not impossible that such behaviour might be observed over some small range of values, but it is hard to imagine that it represents the general case. And, of course, if the individual is completely indifferent to risk, so that expected utility is linearly related to expected return only, the indifference curves will be a set of horizontal straight lines. In that case only bonds will be held and no money.

These different possibilities are no more than those that exist for any micro-choice theoretic behaviour, and it seems re-

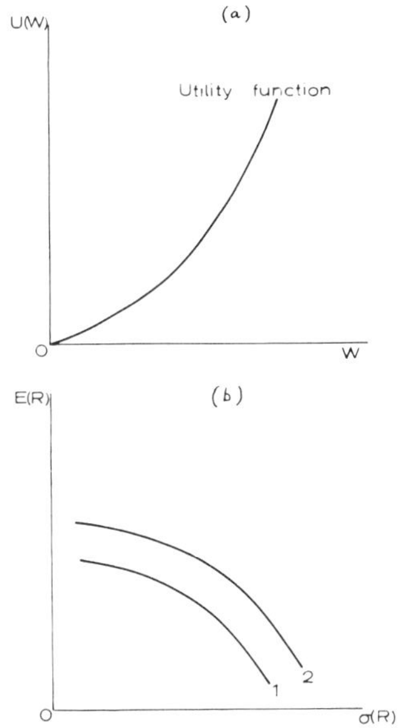

Figure 4.12 (a) A Utility Function exhibiting Increasing Marginal Utility; (b) The Indifference Map that is Derived from such a Function

asonable to assume that risk-aversion is the *normal* case, so that individuals will typically diversify their portfolios, and an increase in expected return will result in an increase in the proportion of the portfolio devoted to bonds. While there are always likely to be certain people who will adopt apparently irrational behaviour, we might anyway expect these largely to offset each other. This analysis therefore supports an aggregate demand for money schedule that is a smooth, continuous, downward-sloping function of the rate of interest.

Although this approach has been presented as an extension of Keynes's speculative demand for money, it is not really the same thing. The analysis justifies a demand for money in terms of rational utility-maximising decisions in the face of *risk*. It provides a rationalisation of individual behaviour, and the argument is not framed in terms of speculative activity. The objective really is to take account of uncertainty, i.e. unpredictability, but in order to make the theory manageable, uncertainty has been reduced to risk by assigning finite probabilities to all conceived outcomes. As a result of this theoretical development, the interest-elasticity of aggregate liquidity preference now has a firmer foundation on individual behaviour.

The theory is highly simplified in that it makes many assumptions we may not expect strictly to hold in reality, for example that unmeasurable uncertainty can be approximated by risk which can be measured. There is also a problem as regards the choice of a measure of risk, as the standard deviation is a symmetrical measure of dispersion about the mean, and it may be that this is an inappropriate assumption to make. If, for example, the probability of loss exceeds the probability of gain, i.e. the distribution is negatively skewed, then the standard deviation will underestimate the risk involved. In the case of a positive skew the standard deviation will overestimate the risk involved. In addition two distributions with the same measure of mean, dispersion and skewness may still be sufficiently different to affect significantly any portfolio choices that are made.

The more usual statement of this problem is that the analysis is restricted to the first two *moments* of the distribution.[6] Many attempts have been made to improve on this situation, but so far no simple alternative has resulted in a generally acceptable improvement. Moreover, as we shall see in Chapter 5, most of the empirical work on the demand for money has proceeded without even a symmetrical measure of risk.

As with Keynes's speculative demand, this portfolio approach has been criticised as only explaining the choice between capital-safe and capital-uncertain assets, and need not necessarily explain the choice between non-interest-bearing money and bonds. The criticism is, however, misleading since there exists a category of bank deposits bearing a competitive rate of interest which is included in broad definitions of the money stock. Too often, what is called 'money' is not defined and this can lead to confusion. If interest-bearing deposits exist which can be transferred to current account at zero pecuniary cost, then no one will hold speculative/investment balances on current account beyond that dictated by the transactions and precautionary needs associated with financial transactions.

Consequently we might expect portfolio demand to apply only to the choice between interest-bearing deposits and bonds.

Possible definitions of what constitutes 'the money stock' may change over time depending on the form and sophistication of the financial system. The definition of money thought to be most important is likely to depend on the importance one attaches to money in influencing the rest of the economy, particularly prices. We shall see in the next chapter that, when it comes to estimating demand for money functions, the actual definition of money employed is critically important in specifying the empirical form to be tested.

It has sometimes been suggested that there should be a single theory to explain *the* demand for money which incorporates all of the motives so far discussed. The previous argument would, however, suggest that this is not the case. It may be that any theory of broad money holdings should be all-embracing, but it is hard to justify such an approach for narrow money balances. No such general theory of broad money holdings has been developed in the rigorous manner of the separate theories discussed above, though, as we shall see, Friedman's reformulation of the quantity theory can be interpreted as a generalisation of a portfolio approach to include the total demand for money (broadly defined).

Friedman's Reformulation of the Quantity Theory

Keynes's theory of the demand for money was specifically designed to apply at the macroeconomic level. The extension of the quantity theory by Milton Friedman (1956) can also be seen in this light. Not only is it developed to apply at a macroeconomic level, but it can also be interpreted, in a superficial sense, as an extension of Keynes's theory.

Friedman treats the demand for money in the same way as the demand for any asset yielding a flow of services, where 'the conception of assets is as broad as the conception of expenditures' (Friedman and Meiselman, 1964, p. 218). Anyone holding money has to forgo the services of the alternative assets he could buy with the money.

These forgone yields (both subjective and objective) measure the *opportunity cost* of holding money. The normal demand theory assumption is made, that there exist diminishing marginal rates of substitution between assets, so that the more of any asset held, the less valuable its marginal services relative to the services yielded on other assets become. Equilibrium is established where the marginal rates of substitution are equalised and there is no advantage to be gained from a further division of one's wealth. Friedman's objective is to identify the major costs involved.

Obviously there is a constraint on the total quantity of assets that may be held by any individual, and this must be given by his wealth. Wealth to Friedman, however, is not simply the aggregation of all stocks of physical and financial assets, but includes human wealth as well, i.e. the present discounted value of the income-earning capacity embodied in an individual's ability to produce. A person can sell a claim on this potential income stream and hold the proceeds in money. Wealth is therefore viewed as the present value of the discounted flow of permanent income, Y^p, permanent income because it is maintainable income which is important; so

$$W = \frac{Y^p}{r}$$

The major alternatives to money-holding which Friedman considers are bonds, equities and physical goods. Other important influences are the ratio of non-human to human wealth, and subjective tastes and preferences. Each of these factors is considered in turn.

Bonds

As we have already seen above, the yield can be divided into two parts:

(i) coupon payment, r_b; and
(ii) any capital gain or loss resulting from a rise, or fall, in the price of the bond

$$\frac{1}{r_b}\frac{dr_b}{dt}$$

so that the total yield $= r_b - \dfrac{1}{r_b}\dfrac{dr_b}{dt}$.

Equities

In this case the yield can be separated into three different parts:

(i) a constant nominal amount, r_e, which would be paid as long as there is no inflation;

(ii) any divergence from this rate due to inflation – complete compensation is assumed, i.e. the return is assumed to keep pace with inflation:

$$\frac{1}{P}\frac{dP}{dt}$$

(iii) an adjustment for any change in the nominal price of the equity over time

$$\frac{1}{r_e}\frac{dr_e}{dt}$$

analogous to the capital gain adjustment on bonds.

$$\text{Total yield} = r_e + \frac{1}{P}\frac{dP}{dt} - \frac{1}{r_e}\frac{dr_e}{dt}.$$

Physical goods

The yield on these is similar to that on equities except that the return is in kind rather than in money, and like equities this is also a function of changes in the price level. Because the yield is in kind and not measurable in money terms, it is assumed that the real yield is constant so that the nominal yield will be determined by the rate of inflation plus the constant real yield:

$$\frac{1}{P}\frac{dP}{dt}$$

Wealth

The budget constraint, Y/r.

The ratio of non-human to human wealth, h

This is included because the markets in human and non-human

wealth are very different. A high degree of substitution is assumed between items of non-human wealth, *nhw*, but very imperfect markets in human wealth, *hw*, and only limited substitution between categories. The major exception is investment in education at the sacrifice of higher current earnings, or at the cost of some existing asset:

$$h = \frac{nhw}{hw}$$

Tastes and preferences, u

These are mainly assumed to be fixed for empirical work. However, Friedman does expect the demand for money to rise with the degree of geographical mobility (e.g. increases in war time), or with increases in *uncertainty*.

Bringing all these variables together we can write an implicit demand for money function as:

$$Md = f\left(P;\, r_b - \frac{1}{r_b}\frac{dr_b}{dt};\, r_e + \frac{1}{P}\frac{dP}{dt} - \frac{1}{r_e}\frac{dr_e}{dt};\, h;\, \frac{Y}{r};\, u\right) \tag{4.39}$$

P is included because the demand for money, or any other asset, is deemed to be a *real* demand, being valued in terms of current goods and services that could be purchased.

The next step is to simplify the model still further. There are three explicit rates of interest in the equation – the general rate, r, plus the specific rates, r_b and r_e, and in addition the unobservable returns on physical assets and human wealth. The simplest way to take the unobservable rates into account is to assume that they vary directly with the observed rates, and since r, the general rate, can be interpreted as a weighted average of all the other rates, it can also be assumed that its influence is fully accounted for by the inclusion of r_b and r_e.

Then, 'if there [were] no difference of opinions about price movements and interest movements, and bonds and equities were equivalent except that the former are expressed in nominal units' (Friedman, 1956, p. 57), then *arbitrage*[7] could be relied upon to ensure that

$$r_b - \frac{1}{r_b}\frac{dr_b}{dt} = r_e + \frac{1}{P}\frac{dP}{dt} - \frac{1}{r_e}\frac{dr_e}{dt} \tag{4.40}$$

And if interest rates are stable, or their proportional rates of change are equal, this can be reduced to

$$r_b = r_e + \frac{1}{P}\frac{dP}{dt} \tag{4.41}$$

which can then be interpreted as follows: the nominal 'money' rate, given by r_b, is equal to the 'real' rate plus the percentage rate of change of prices. This is an interesting interpretation, but we should note the assumptions that underlie it. In addition Friedman points out that it is really the *expected* rate of inflation that is important and therefore expectations may differ; consequently 'we cannot suppose [this equation] to hold; indeed one of the most consistent features of inflation seems to be that it does not' (Friedman, 1956, p. 57).

The function is assumed to be homogeneous of degree one in prices and income, because the demands are real and are therefore 'independent in any essential way of the nominal units used to measure money variables' (Friedman, 1956, p. 58).

The simplified equation can be written:

$$M^d = f\left(P;\ r_b;\ r_e;\ \frac{1}{P}\frac{dP}{dt};\ h;\ u;\ Y\right) \tag{4.42}$$

The model was first presented in the spirit of the old quantity theory and as an alternative to the Keynesian approach to the demand for money. However, Patinkin claimed that the model had more in common with Keynes than the old quantity theory: 'What Friedman has actually presented is an elegant exposition of the modern portfolio approach to the demand for money which . . . can only be seen as a continuation of the Keynesian theory of liquidity preference' (Patinkin, 1969, p. 47). Even Friedman (1956, p. 73) has himself since observed that the reformulation was 'much influenced by the Keynesian liquidity analysis'.

The similarity with the portfolio approach is worth noting, but it is important also to be aware of the form of the underlying portfolios assumed. In the final simplified form it makes a lot of sense to interpret Friedman's equation as an extension of Keynes's approach, putting emphasis on wealth as such, and on inflation as an important determinant of the demand for money. However, the underlying approach is very different; the debate turns on what money is in fact directly substitutable for. Monetarists view money as a direct substitute over a wide range of assets. So the interest-elasticity of money with respect to any particular asset is likely to be low. Friedman and Meiselman (1964) went so far as to claim that the mechanism is so complicated and rates so diverse (and anyway not measurable) that it cannot be hoped to even approximate the demand for money by employing one or two measured interest rates. In the limit the demand for money is directly related to Y alone.

Each particular theory carries with it implications for the interest-elasticity of the demand for money and the interest-elasticity of investment. If real assets and financial assets are poor substitutes, while within the sub-set of financial assets there is very high substitutability, then a rise in money supply will have,

(i) a small effect on interest rates; and
(ii) hardly any effect on investment.

As we saw above in Chapter 3, the quantity theory and monetarism can be interpreted as exclusively concerned with the determination of the price level *in the long run.* This interpretation is fully justified by many of Friedman's later statements (see, for example, Friedman, 1968). In the short run, changes in the supply of money from that demanded may result in short-run changes in real variables, which can be substantial and long-lasting, depending on the adjustment of expectations. The 'reformulation', however, was not clear on this. While it is possible to relate nominal income to the supply of money, 'it tells us nothing about how much of any change in Y is reflected in real output and how much in prices. To infer this requires bringing in outside information, as, for example, that real output is at its feasible maximum, in which case any increase in money would produce the same or larger percentage increase in prices; and so on' (Friedman, 1956, p. 62). This open assumption became a weakness as soon as the model achieved some form of academic respectability, and the later emphasis on the long-run inflationary implications seems to have been a reaction to this.

5. ESTIMATING THE DEMAND FOR MONEY

Empirical studies of the demand for money have mainly been conducted in the past under the assumption that there was a general theory of the demand for money which was applicable regardless of the particular definition of money employed. This, however, is not the case, and the actual definition of money should have important implications for the relevant form of the demand function. The first three sections of this chapter are concerned with general arguments, while the fourth considers how these need to be amended to take account of a specific definition of money. The first section summarises the general arguments likely to appear in a demand function, together with some of the problems associated with the attempt to identify particular variables. The second section deals briefly with the identification problem encountered in trying to estimate any demand equation employing single-equation techniques, and the third section introduces simple models of lagged adjustment; an understanding of such models is essential to be able to interpret the demand studies that have been published. In the fourth section it is argued that the actual definition of money employed needs to be taken into account in specifying any demand for money relationship. The final section contains a survey of recent empirical evidence for the United Kingdom. Appendix 5.1 contains a summary table of results obtained in demand for money studies in the United Kingdom, and a list of the major studies is contained in Appendix 5.2.

A General Discussion of the Specification and Data

In Chapter 4 we were able to identify a number of important potential influences on the demand for money. However, as we shall see below, only a very limited number of these have actually been employed in empirical tests. To summarise, the main influences are:

(i) The expected level of transactions, generally proxied by income or expenditure. If there is uncertainty about the expected future income stream, then the variance of the level of transactions about its expected value will also be important.

(ii) The level (and possibly the variance) of the stock of wealth.

(iii) The expected price level. It is possible that the rate of inflation might also have an independent influence (apart from lagged adjustment to price changes). (This is explained below.)

(iv) The expectations of relative yields on non-monetary assets, generally restricted to the rates of return on alternative financial assets.

(v) The availability of alternative assets. As far as financial assets are concerned, this depends on the sophistication of the financial system.

(vi) The variance or standard deviation of the rates of interest about their expected value, as a measure of the risk involved in holding marketable securites.

(vii) The length of the planned holding period.

(viii) The subjective and objective transactions costs involved in switching between money and non-monetary assets.

(ix) The market structure, in particular payments conventions and the integration, and form, of industrial production.

(x) The number of individuals in the economy and household formation.

(xi) The distribution of income both between the personal and company sectors and between individuals (or households).

As we have already seen, not all of these factors have been adequately considered even at the abstract theoretical level. Some, for example the costs of transactions and availability of assets which are embodied in the institutional structure, may reasonably be considered to be fixed over time, as long as the period covered is not too long. We might expect these to remain stable over time, and even to move together. Some work has been undertaken to identify the effect of the development of financial institutions on the demand for money (e.g. Cagan and Schwartz, 1977) but it remains an area about which little is known and much remains to be done.

A larger problem, at least in the short term, concerns the usual assumption that uncertainty is fixed over time, and the complete lack of knowledge of the planned holding periods which should affect our *a priori* expectations. The things that cannot be measured are left out, with the result that the majority of the subjective considerations thought to be most important at the theoretical level are absent from the empirical work.

In empirical work we can only employ the *ex post* data which are available, and there are obvious problems when these are employed to represent *ex ante* expectations. It is not always clear exactly what the *ex post* data employed actually represent, and one inevitably ends up testing two theories at the same time:

(i) that the demand for money is related to particular expectational variables, e.g. expected interest rates or permanent income, in a particular way; and,

(ii) that expectations are formed in a certain way.

As if these problems were not enough, the data are not always particularly reliable.[1] As a result something less than perfect explanatory power is the best that can be hoped for.

On top of all this there are some potentially important problems raised by the general use of seasonally adjusted data. The use of seasonally adjusted data has recently been questioned by a number of economists (e.g. Wallis, 1974; and Hendry and Mizon, 1978). The argument is essentially that while it may be useful to adjust seasonally a single data series, in order to isolate its underlying trend, this does not justify the separate seasonal adjustment of each variable in a regression. As far as a *relationship* is concerned, it is only residual seasonality in the error term, u, that needs to be removed. In other words it should not be automatically assumed that people make decisions in terms of seasonally adjusted data, and even if they do (to some extent) it is not clear what sort of seasonal adjustment procedure they might employ. The removal of all systematic seasonal variation in each of the data series prior to estimation necessarily assumes that such variation in the dependent variable is independent of any similar variation in the explanatory variables. It is not only the attempt to explain the seasonality of the dependent variable that is important, in addition the separate adjustment of times series may itself introduce distortion into the regression estimates. This is likely to make it particularly difficult to identify the 'true' lag structure. Wallis (1974) has shown that seasonal adjustment methods can often be approximated by a lag polynomial filter. The relationship between series can therefore be distorted because series are incorrectly adjusted, separate filters are applied to different series, and some series are not adjusted at all. If it is only residual seasonality in the error term which is of concern, then, if series have to be seasonally adjusted, the same filter should be applied to all time series in the regression (Hendry and Mizon, 1978) but this should only be done if the original error term itself follows a seasonal pattern. In general, however, it is suggested that attempts should be made to model the seasonal behaviour rather than filter it out.

The most usual reply to this argument is that the seasonal adjustment procedures are really far more sophisticated than is suggested. In particular they do far more than filter out a fixed seasonal pattern; they also allow the seasonal pattern to vary over time, and take account of various changes in timing, e.g. of holidays, and in the pattern of tax payments, that otherwise need to be modelled explicitly.

The choice between using seasonally adjusted and unadjusted data is not always clear, and is anyway likely to depend on the particular problem under consideration. In fact most empirical estimation is undertaken employing seasonally adjusted data. The reason for this is probably no more than that is how most economic times series are presented and interpreted. In addition it also means it is one less problem to be considered. That, however, only ignores the problem; it does not necessarily provide a solution.

These sorts of considerations have encouraged some empirical researchers to adopt a 'positive' approach to economics. In the pejorative sense in which this description was applied by Kaldor (1970) an acceptable empirical result, i.e. one with good statistical qualities, is given more emphasis than the underlying theoretical structure – which may in fact be virtually non-existent. The alternative argument is that the job of theory is not only to suggest tests but also to check the plausibility of statistical findings. In this view it is easy to discover a statistical correspondence given enough attempts at finding it, and employing a variety of lag formulations, but that does not necessarily imply that it is economically significant.

This argument, that theory should be given greater weight than empirics, is obviously important, but is actually as open to abuse as an obsession with t statistics and coefficients of determination. If there are alternative theories, then there needs to be some empirical way of distinguishing between them, though naturally great care must be taken in setting up such tests. What this argument really illustrates is that it is not possible to test any theory in isolation; there needs to be some alternative against which to compare the results. No econometric test is ever conclusive: what might be considered a good fit for one class of tests may well prove inadequate for another; there is no *absolute* proof. Even a perfect fit over the present estimation period does not rule out the possibility of refutation by data becoming available in the future.

The Identification Problem

The problem with identification concerns the reliability with which it is possible to isolate the individual coefficients in the money demand function. While it is easy to specify a relationship between the quantity of money and various economic variables, this does not in itself guarantee that its estimation will identify a *demand* function. It is a problem that arises when estimating any demand or supply relationship. The usual argument can easily be demonstrated diagrammatically. Consider the examples shown in Figure 5.1. The actual shape of the money-supply function is not important. What is necessary to trace out a demand curve is that supply changes while demand stays fixed. If the demand function shifts about while supply is fixed, then single-equation estimation will identify the supply schedule (see Figure 5.2). Alternatively, both curves could be changing so that any single-equation estimate traces out a hybrid with no economic significance (see Figure 5.3).

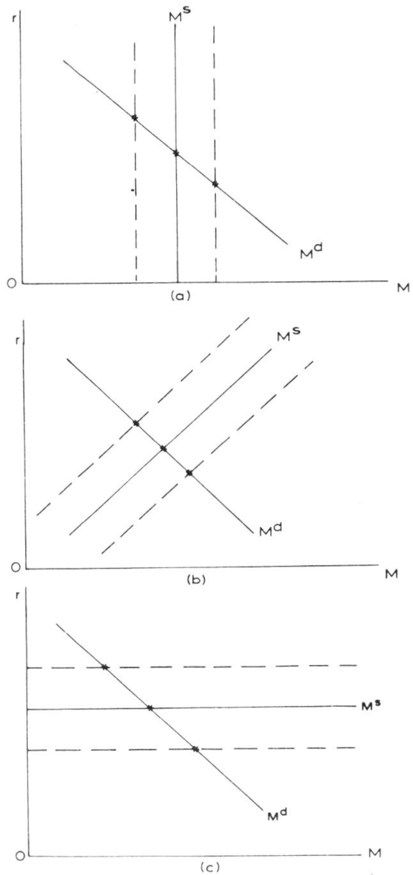

Figure 5.1 Identifying Money Demand

Demand functions have nearly always been estimated employing single-equation estimation techniques with the stock of money as the dependent variable, e.g.

$$M^d = f(Y, P, r) \tag{5.1}$$

This approach is only really justifiable in the particular circumstances in which the monetary authorities control the rate of interest, allowing the stock of money to be determined by demand, and make no attempt to influence independently

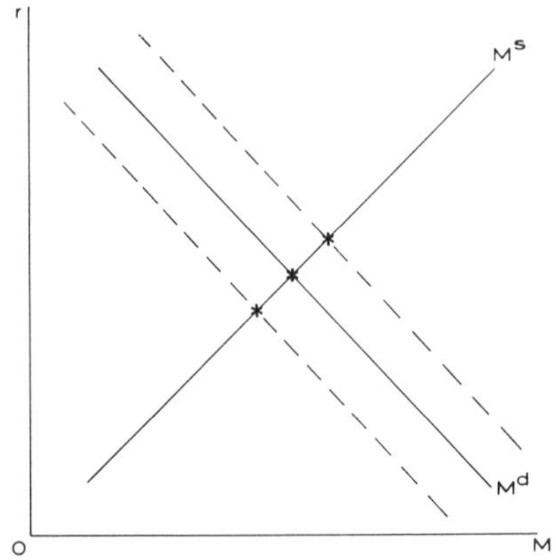

Figure 5.2 Identifying Money Supply

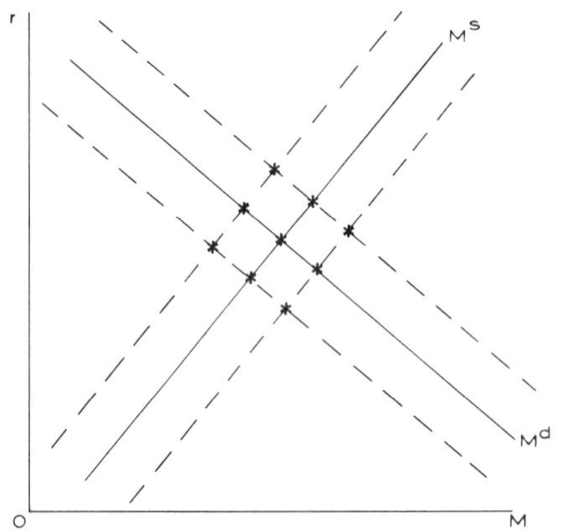

Figure 5.3 Hybrid Money Demand and Supply

the supply of money, i.e. the case illustrated in Figure 5.1(c). Although the demand function might still be identified if money supply is directly controlled (see Figure 5.1(a)), the market in fact determines the rate of interest, and it is this that should really become the dependent variable.

In fact, although we have drawn the demand function

against the rate of interest it may be that both the rate of interest and the supply of money are determined independently of the demand for money. In that case some other variable, upon which the demand for money depends, will have to adjust in order to restore equilibrium in the money market. The most obvious candidate would be the price level. The demand functions drawn above against the rate of interest are for given values of all other behavioural influences. If the price level changes, for example, this will have the effect of shifting the demand schedule when drawn against the rate of interest (or any other variable). Whichever variable adjusts in response to changes in supply, in order to restore equilibrium, this should become the dependent variable, since it is this variable which the error term is related to.

It is possible that unless great care is taken in specifying the simultaneous system of equations to be estimated that even recognising these interrelationships may not succeed in identifying a separate demand function. This is because in a period of disequilibrium, with lags in the adjustment of actual money holdings to their desired, equilibrium, value, in response to an exogenous supply disturbance, a variety of variables may absorb part of the adjustment. Friedman (1968), for example, suggests that in the short run real income/output may increase in response to an increase in the money supply, but not in the long run.

Lags

The great majority of empirical demand for money studies have employed lags as an important element in the equation specification. It is therefore necessary to be aware of the types of models that have actually been tested.

In principle lags are very simple to understand. It is fairly reasonable that there may be lags in the formation of expectations, or in the adjustment to equilibrium. The easiest way to incorporate such lags would be simply to include lagged values of the explanatory variables. There are, however, costs involved, and these are the loss of degrees of freedom (essentially the number of data observations in excess of the number of explanatory variables) and the degree of multicollinearity introduced; after all, the lagged values of many time series will be statistically correlated with the current, or other past, values of the same series. However, by restricting the actual pattern the lag can follow it is possible to reduce this cost considerably. It is therefore important to have some understanding of at least the more widely used for these approaches. And, of course, these techniques are generally applicable over a much wider area of economics than just the demand for money.

When discussing the different approaches to lag estimation it will also be convenient to discuss general specifications, and give examples from U.K. demand for money studies of the types of equations that have been estimated. A summary of results obtained is given in Appendix 5.1 below.

Partial adjustment

This is probably the most common assumption employed to justify lags in demand functions. Justification for partial adjustment can be provided in a variety of ways: for example, in terms of habit preference, uncertainty regarding the reliability of information or costs of adjustment.

The argument is that there is some desired nominal money balance (M^*) which depends upon expected income (or wealth), Y^e, prices P^e, and expected interest rates, R^e, where expectations are represented by current values, Y, P and R, and there is a partial adjustment of actual money balances, M, to this desired level. Furthermore, this relationship is assumed to be log linear in form, so taking logarithms, where the logarithms of the variables are written in lower-case letters, we can write:[2]

$$m^* = a_0 + a_1 y + a_2 p - a_3 r \tag{5.2}$$

$$m - m_{-1} = \lambda(m^* - m_{-1}) + u \tag{5.3}$$

where u is the stochastic error term, generally assumed to have zero mean and constant variance, and λ is the constant coefficient of adjustment. The model implies geometrically declining lag weights and therefore results in an identical final estimation equation as would be obtained by applying the

Koyck (1954) scheme directly. Substitution of (5.2) into (5.3) gives:

$$m = \lambda a_0 + \lambda a_1 y + \lambda a_2 p - \lambda a_3 r + (1 - \lambda)m_{-1} + u \quad (5.4)$$

When estimated in log linear form the individual coefficients, b_i, give estimates of the short-run elasticities:

$$m = b_0 + b_1 y + b_2 p - b_3 r + b_4 m_{-1} + u \quad (5.5)$$

The long-run coefficients, a_i, are obtained by setting $m = m_{-1}$, which results in dividing the respective b_i, b_0 to b_3, by λ, i.e. $1 - b_4$. For example,

$$a_1 = \frac{b_1}{1 - b_4}$$

The average length of the lag (see Griliches, 1967) is given by

$$\frac{b_4}{1 - b_4} = \frac{(1 - \lambda)}{\lambda}$$

There have in fact been very few early studies in the United Kingdom which have actually published estimates for an equation like (5.4); two such attempts were made by the Bank of England (see Goodhart and Crockett, 1970; and Price, 1972).[3] The first of these was estimated for *per capita* money balances, but in both cases the results were disastrous, with a negative income-elasticity and very unstable coefficients. The explanation of these results was put down to the high correlation between income and prices.

Because of this statistical problem real income and the price index have often been combined, i.e. to give nominal income. Equations of this type have been estimated, for example, by Goodhart and Crockett (1970) and Artis and Lewis (1976). A more common solution to this problem has been to invoke the *a priori* assumption of unit price elasticity and employ it as a constraint in the estimation process. It is therefore assumed that the desired relationship applies to real balances:

$$(m - p)^* = a_0 + a_1 y - a_3 r \quad (5.6)$$

With partial adjustment of *real* balances, the final estimating equation is

$$(m-p) = \lambda a_0 + \lambda a_1 y - \lambda a_3 r + (1-\lambda)(m-p)_{-1} + u \quad (5.7)$$

Equations of this type have been widely estimated, e.g. by Goodhart and Crockett (1970), Laidler and Parkin (1970) and Artis and Lewis (1976).

It is generally assumed that the long-run price-elasticity of the demand for money should be unity, on the grounds that economic rationality implies the absence of money illusion. However, although it may seem to be a reasonable assumption to make, it can be no more than that.[4] We may well expect interest rates to influence the level of investment; that does not relieve us of the necessity to test that assumption.

Even if we do accept the assumption of a unit price-elasticity, it would still seem unrealistic to assume instantaneous adjustment to any price changes, as is implied by equation (5.7). Such an assumption is obviously inconsistent with the assumption of lagged adjustment to real income and interest-rate changes. This conflict can be reconciled by assuming a nominal demand function which is homogeneous of degree one in prices:

$$m^* = a_0 + a_1 y + p - a_3 r \quad (5.8)$$

which combined with the partial adjustment of *nominal* balances (equation (5.3)) gives:

$$m = \lambda a_0 + \lambda a_1 y + \lambda p - \lambda a_3 r + (1-\lambda)m_{-1} + u \quad (5.9)$$

This can be rewritten as:

$$m = \lambda a_0 + \lambda a_1 y + p - (1-\lambda)p - \lambda a_3 r + (1-\lambda)m_{-1} + u$$

The equation to be estimated can therefore be written as:

$$(m-p) = \lambda a_0 + \lambda a_1 y - \lambda a_3 r + (1-\lambda)(m_{-1} - p) + u \quad (5.10)$$

The possibility of lagged adjustment to price changes has very rarely been allowed for in demand studies specified in real terms. And this is not only true for the demand for money, as is revealed from an inspection of most equations explaining consumption in real terms. One of the few demand for money studies to incorporate such an influence was by Hacche (1974).[5]

An alternative way of allowing for lagged adjustment to price changes is to include the rate of inflation as a separate explanatory variable in an equation with lagged real balances. In this case it is necessary to test whether that is the only reason for the inclusion of inflation, or whether it also has some independent effect. This is because equation (5.10) can be rewritten as:

$$(m-p) = \lambda a_0 + \lambda a_1 y - \lambda a_3 r - (1-\lambda)(p - p_{-1}) + (1-\lambda)(m-p)_{-1} + u \quad (5.11)$$

Adaptive expectations

So far we have continued to assume that the lags in the demand for money equation are explained simply by the partial adjustment of actual balances to their desired level. It should, however, be remembered that the relevant behavioural relationships are expressed in terms of expected values. Only if expectations can be encapsulated in current values will the model outlined prove reliable. Alternatively we could allow for lags in the formation of expectations by assuming that expectations are extrapolated from the past. The simplest, and most usual, assumption is that the expectation formation mechanism is identical for all explanatory variables, i.e.[6]

$$x^e = \alpha \Sigma (1-\alpha) x_{-1} \quad (5.12)$$

Writing the demand function to incorporate an error term:

$$m = a_0 + a_1 y^e + a_2 p^e - a_3 r^e + v \quad (5.13)$$

results in a final equation identical in appearance to equation (5.4):

$$m = \alpha a_0 + \alpha a_1 y + \alpha a_2 p - \alpha a_3 r + (1-\alpha) m_{-1} + u \quad (5.14)$$

but with the apparently important difference that the error term is now autocorrelated:

$$u = v - (1-\alpha) v_{-1}$$

However, this distinction is somewhat misleading since it depends crucially on the assumption that v was itself a white noise error term. Given that we have no *a priori* knowledge about the error term, this must remain an empirical question and will not enable us to distinguish between the two separate hypotheses of partial adjustment or adaptive expectations. The theoretical error structures that may be derived should therefore be treated with caution, depending as they do on the starting conditions assumed.

Lags in expectations and adjustment

An obvious development would be to combine lags in adjustment with lags in the formation of expectations, which results in (writing β in place of λ):

$$\begin{aligned} m &= \alpha\beta a_0 + \alpha\beta a_1 y + \alpha\beta a_2 p - \alpha\beta a_3 r + [(1-\alpha) \\ &\quad + (1-\beta)]m_{-1} - (1-\alpha)(1-\beta)m_{-2} + u \qquad (5.15) \\ &= b_0 + b_1 y + b_2 p - b_3 r + b_4 m_{-1} - b_5 m_{-2} + u \qquad (5.16) \end{aligned}$$

where $u = v - (1-\alpha)v_{-1}$.

The results from estimating an equation of this type are given in Coghlan (1978). A similar equation was also estimated by Laidler and Parkin (1970) but without any lags in the formation of interest-rate expectations. In this case the equation was estimated in real terms but without any lagged adjustment to price changes or lags in the formation of price expectations. The actual equation estimated was therefore

$$\begin{aligned} m - p &= b_0 + b_1 y - b_3 r + b_4 r_{-1} + b_4 (m-p)_{-1} \\ &\quad - b_5 (m-p)_{-2} + u \qquad (5.17) \end{aligned}$$

where $b_3 = a_3\beta(1-\alpha)$.

Models with unrestricted lags

The existence of lags can be justified in many ways, including the formation of expectations, costs of adjustment, habit preference and lags in the availability of information (or uncertainty about its reliability); they may also simply reflect lags in adjustment in other markets. The actual form of the lag expected is likely to be affected by the rationalisation adopted, and *a priori* there seems little justification for imposing any rigid formula. In fact, most demand for money studies have assumed that an identical lag applied to all explanatory variables, whereas we might expect different lags to apply to each of the explanatory variables. It might therefore seem more appropriate to adopt a more flexible, general approach in which the lags are freely estimated. Lags in adjustment may still turn out to be the same for each of the explanatory variables, but at least then they will not have been imposed from the outset.

The great advantage of Koyck-type lags is that they permit the estimation of long lags very economically – simply by including the lagged dependent variable. The cost of introducing the possibility of more flexible lag patterns is the loss of degrees of freedom, and the increased possibility of multicollinearity. This was a problem with the earlier demand for money studies, which were severely constrained by the short runs of data available.

The lag patterns that have been suggested above may all be thought of as specific forms of rational distributed lags (Jorgenson, 1966), which are any lag structure that can be written as:

$$P(L)H = Q(L)G + R(L)F \tag{5.18}$$

where $P(L)$, $Q(L)$ and $R(L)$ are polynomials in the lag operator L, and H, G and F are variables.

The Koyck, single lag equation may therefore be written as a rational lag of the form $P(L) = Q(L)$ where $P(L) = [1-(1-\lambda)L]$ and $Q(L) = \lambda a$. The double lag equation of the form

$$H = aG + bH_{-1} + cH_{-2} + u \tag{5.19}$$

can alternatively be written as

$$H = \frac{a}{1-bL-cL^2}G + v \tag{5.20}$$

where b and c satisfy the following restrictions:

$$0 < b < 2$$
$$1 - b - c > 0$$
$$b^2 \geqslant -4c$$

This approach is very flexible and can obviously allow for

different lag patterns on each of the independent variables, e.g.

$$H = \frac{a_0 + a_1(1 - \lambda_1 L)G + a_2(1 - \lambda_2 L)F}{1 - bL - cL^2} + u \qquad (5.21)$$

Rational lags of this type have been estimated for the United Kingdom by Price (1972) and Coghlan (1978).[7] Price had difficulty in accurately identifying individual coefficients. This undoubtedly resulted from the restricted data available at the time. The other attempt was rather more successful, employing the extended data set available in 1977. These results must still be tentative, but they did provide strong evidence that the lags on the various behavioural determinants in demand for money equations are not identical. For example, the following equation was reported in Coghlan (1978):

$$\begin{aligned} m = \; & \underset{(3.80)}{0.379y} \; \underset{(2.17)}{-0.216y_{-3}} + \underset{(6.05)}{1.326p_{-1}} \; \underset{(5.73)}{-2.069p_{-2}} \\ & + \underset{(4.57)}{1.675p_{-3}} \; \underset{(3.53)}{-0.816p_{-4}} \underset{(5.16)}{-0.048r} \; \underset{(18.62)}{+0.838m_{-1}} \end{aligned}$$

which implies the lag patterns shown in Figure 5.4.[8]

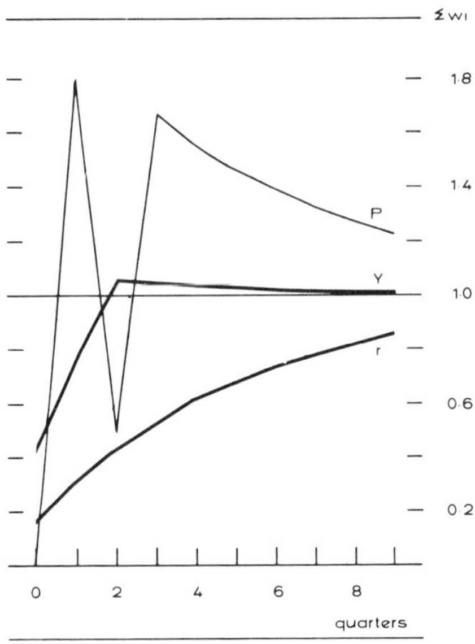

Figure 5.4 Cumulative Lag-adjustment Weights

A further possibility is that the lags in adjustment are not constant and should therefore be endogenised to allow for variable speeds of adjustment. In this respect it might be that the size of any exogenous change, and consequently the size of adjustment necessary to achieve equilibrium, will directly affect the *speed* of adjustment. For example, we might expect the unusually large changes in the price level that have taken place in recent years to have resulted in a speeding up of the adjustment process. In practice the effect is not so clear cut, and it is also possible that the associated rapid inflation would have the opposite effect. Again, the existence of such a mechanism must be an empirical question, though there are no published results incorporating variable speeds of adjustment.

The Importance of the Definition of Money

Even if we accept the restricted forms usually adopted in demand for money studies, it is still necessary to decide on exactly which variables to include and their precise definition. Most studies have tended to assume that there was a general specification which was applicable regardless of the actual definition of money employed. In fact this is not the case, and the estimation approach should be crucially dependent on whether money is defined narrowly or broadly.

A wide definition of money, eg. SterlingM3 would need to take account of speculative, or portfolio, demands for money.[9] This would seem to require the inclusion of long-term rates of interest plus some measure of the expected risks involved. As it is, most studies have not included any measure of risk, though Artis and Lewis (1976) did derive a measure for inclusion in their equations. A short-term rate of interest should also be required, since the broad definition must also encompass the transactions demand – unless, that is, the interest-rate elasticity of the transactions demand almost entirely reflects substitution between current and deposit accounts. This is in fact a fairly reasonable assumption to make. It is also a virtual necessity on practical grounds, since a broad demand for money equation should also include an own rate on those deposits contained within the definition of money. Moreover, we should expect both income and wealth to prove important explanatory variables.

The major problem that is likely to be encountered with broad definitions of money concerns the high degree of simultaneity we should expect between demand and supply. This means that the non-simultaneous estimation procedures generally employed are unlikely to identify a demand relationship except in exceptional circumstances. In addition, if we recognise that money provides a residual store of purchasing power, so that the stock of money serves as a store for *disequilibrium* balances, it may not even be possible to observe a demand schedule directly. This possibility is dealt with in greater detail in Chapter 10.

It may reasonably be assumed that the demand for money narrowly defined, e.g. M1,[10] is predominantly determined by transactions, and to some extent precautionary needs, and that speculative motives are not important. This approach means that we should expect short rates on closely competing assets to be more relevant than long rates on less-liquid assets. It also means that measures of expected capital loss, which portfolio theory suggests significantly affect the demand for money, will not in this case be relevant. Moreover, the 'income' variable should naturally be selected to represent expected transactions requirements. Taking a broader view of portfolio allocation, we might still expect total wealth to be included in the demand specification, but this is not necessary.

From an empirical viewpoint, the most important characteristic of narrow money holdings is the high probability (i) that they will be determined by demand, and (ii) that simultaneous-equation bias is at a minimum, thereby justifying the use of non-simultaneous estimation techniques employing money as the dependent variable. M1 consists of currency and private-sector sight deposits with the banking sector, both of which are free from supply constraints; for a formal discussion of this question, see Artis and Lewis (1976). Currency is supplied upon demand, and banks accept all money placed with them on current account, usually without payment of interest. Moreover, to the extent that money acts as a buffer stock, such balances are more likely to be held in the form of interest-bearing deposits rather than on current account. As regards the problems of simultaneity, it seems most unlikely that money-market interest rates should be determined by the stock of, or change in, M1 balances. Naturally, if interest rates were varied in an attempt to control M1, this could introduce simultaneous bias into any attempt to estimate single-equation demand functions, but without necessarily changing the underlying relationship. But the authorities have not attempted to control M1, and single-equation estimation seems appropriate for this exercise.

Most of the earlier demand for money studies included real income only in *per capita* terms. This procedure was probably made necessary by the limited data available in order to obtain a significant coefficient. While this might be reasonable for households' money holdings, these are not distinguished separately in the data. Statistics breaking down M1 balances either between sectors or between interest-bearing and non-interest-bearing deposits have been available only since 1975, and these show that only about two-thirds of M1 balances are held by the personal sector; furthermore, this sector includes not only individuals but also unincorporated businesses, non-profit-making bodies and private trusts. Even if we assume that households hold 75 per cent of all personal-sector M1 balances (which is probably on the high side), that still leaves them holding only 50 per cent of total M1. Deflating aggregate money balances by the number of people, or the number of households, therefore seems to be a rather arbitrary assumption.

The definition of money is also important for the way in which the interest rate is entered into the demand function. For example, consider the possibilities shown in Table 5.1. The first assumption is considered neutral in that it implies a constant elasticity, which is the same assumption generally made for the other explanatory variables. This might not be an unreasonable starting assumption for the demand for both narrow and broad money balances. The second assumption, however, is exactly the opposite of Keynes's assumption that the interest-elasticity would increase at low rates of interest, and therefore seems inapplicable to the estimation of a function explaining holdings of broad money balances. On the other hand, it does seem a reasonable alternative to the constant-elasticity as-

Table 5.1 Alternative Interest Rate Assumptions

Assumption	Elasticity	Variable
(i) 'neutral', constant elasticity	$-\alpha$	$\ln R$
(ii) elasticity	$-\alpha\left[\frac{R}{1+R}\right]$	$\ln(1+R)$
varies directly with R	$\rightarrow -\alpha$ as $R \rightarrow \infty$ $\rightarrow 0$ as $R \rightarrow 0$	
(iii) elasticity	$-\frac{\alpha}{R(1+R)}$	$\frac{1}{\ln(1+R)}$
varies inversely with R	$\rightarrow 0$ as $R \rightarrow \infty$ $\rightarrow -\infty$ as $R \rightarrow 0$	

sumption in the case of the demand for money narrowly defined. The third alternative might be a good assumption in the case of a broad money definition which includes some form of speculative balances.

Summary of Empirical Results

At the end of the 1960s the evidence seemed to suggest that a stable demand for money, as a function of a few variables, had been identified. The general view was probably best stated by Laidler (1971), who claimed that 'this evidence for Britain certainly points to the existence of a stable demand-for-money function in that economy. For the United States the evidence is overwhelming, and for Britain it is at the very least, highly suggestive.' In September 1971 'Competition and Credit Control' was introduced and, in the years that followed, the demand for money functions which had previously been estimated failed to forecast at all accurately. This was interpreted as meaning that the previously reliable, stable demand functions had broken down. This 'breakdown', however, refers only to the *estimation* of single-equation demand functions, and does not exclude the possibility that a stable but unidentified demand function actually existed. All at once it seemed we had moved from a situation in which the demand for money had been reliably and accurately estimated to a new environment where the money stock no longer exhibited these stable characteristics.

It is important to recognise that the earlier demand for money studies in the United Kingdom, upon which the conclusion of stability was based, employed a wide variety of definitions of money, interest rates, income, wealth, lag structures and estimation periods. Moreover, these differences had important implications for the results obtained, but not, it seemed, for the United States. Laidler (1971, p. 95), for example, noted that 'perhaps the aspect of the British results that separates them most strongly from the American is their sensitivity to small changes in the specification of the function fitted . . . . Why the sensitivity of results to specification should be so much more marked for Britain than for the United States is clearly a question worth further investigation.' One possible explanation of such sensitivity could be the presence of multicollinearity between the independent variables, though, as we have argued above, we should expect certain systematic variations which should be explicable in terms of the variables employed.

For example, higher interest-elasticities were observed for the long rate of interest than for the short rate, and these have generally been explained in terms of the greater variability in short rates than in long rates (Goodhart and Crockett, 1970). In addition the wider the definition of money employed (i.e. the wider the range of interest-bearing deposits/assets included), the lower the interest-elasticity expected. Apart from these 'statistical' observations, there was very little, if any, concern with the actual definition of money employed. The theoretical basis from which empirical tests were developed, and the interpretation of the results obtained, seemed independent of whether money was defined narrowly or broadly.

Although the problems encountered in trying to explain movements in monetary aggregates are commonly expressed in terms of the 'breakdown' of the demand for money, this more correctly refers to the inability to estimate, or forecast, the demand for money over the 1970s on the basis of a single, economically reliable, equation. However, if money does serve as a buffer stock, it may well be that the numbers we observe do not represent points on a demand schedule. It is therefore important to remember that any references to the breakdown of the demand for money only refer to *the estimation of non-simultaneous single-equation demand functions*, implying that the money stock is necessarily demand-determined. Such a finding is fully consistent with the view that the *actual* demand for money is a stable function of relatively few variables, but that non-simultaneous estimation techniques fail to identify it.

Evidence that simple demand functions for both M1 and M3 had broken down was provided by Artis and Lewis (1974 and 1976), who reported (1974, p. 241) that 'the standard demand function simply does not fit the experience of 1971 and 1972', adding that 'the forecasting ability of this equation (in common with alternative equations of the same general character that we tested, whether for M1 and M3) is quite good for 1971, but disastrously bad for 1972 and the first two quarters of 1973'.

This conclusion is repeated in their later, more extensive, study (Artis and Lewis, 1976: see pp. 153 and 157). These results encouraged the conclusion that there had been a *general* breakdown of single-equation demand functions. Artis and Lewis concluded that there was a stable demand function, but that there had in fact been substantial excess supply over the early 1970s. At a superficial level the complete failure to estimate any form of stable demand for money function provides them with strong support for their excess-supply argument. This is because the failure cannot be put down simply to the improvement in competition within the wholesale money markets facilitated, and encouraged, by 'Competition and Credit Control'. A more considered view suggests, however, that the discovery of a stable demand for M1 need not weaken their argument. Although they do end up concluding that the evidence supports their hypothesis of an exogenous supply (by implication for both M1 and M3), it is also recognised (Artis and Lewis, 1976, pp. 157 and 161) that strong arguments can be put forward to support the view that M1 is demand-determined. It should not be surprising, nor is it incompatible, for M1 to be demand-determined while at the same time M3 is perhaps partially supply-determined.

An alternative rationalisation of the experience over the

1970s was given by Hacche (1974, p. 295), who found that the 'M1 equation had performed fairly satisfactorily and . . . there seemed little reason to conclude that there had been structural change in the determination of the narrow money stock'. On the other hand, single-equation estimates of M3 (in aggregate and when divided into personal- and company-sector balances) failed to forecast into the 1970s. The performance of the M3 demand function was, however, substantially improved when the rate of interest on certificates of deposit was included from 1971(4) in order 'to reflect the shift in the competitiveness of interest-bearing money'. Most of the subsequent controversy has surrounded the broad definition of money, and Artis and Lewis (1976, p. 150) doubted whether the procedure proposed above really provided a genuine solution to this problem. In any case these equations, including that for M1, broke down when the period was extended further into the 1970s.

The claim of breakdown is not really as dramatic as it might appear at first sight. A possible reconciliation of the apparent divergence between the earlier claims for stability and the evidence of more recent empirical studies may be provided by recognising a qualitative difference in the nature of the evidence. The earlier studies, with only limited data available, obtained equations which had a good statistical fit and a fairly low interest-elasticity. When compared with the more extreme Radcliffian claims of an unstable relationship, and a potentially infinite interest-elasticity, it was reasonable to claim that a stable demand function could be estimated. However, when those same equations were examined for internal stability, e.g. by Artis and Lewis, they failed the test. But now the criteria for comparison had changed. Moreover, the traditional M3 relationship really did seem to break down, and this is likely to have coloured the interpretation of the less obvious evidence for M1.

So far there has been no success in re-estimating a demand function for M3. A possible explanation for this failure lies in the argument that was made above regarding the neglect of the possibility that the money supply has been determined independently of the demand for money; this will be discussed in much greater detail in Chapter 10. There has, however, been a recent study (Coghlan, 1978) which did present estimates for a stable M1 demand function. The estimated coefficients for income, prices and the short-term interest rate all have the correct sign, reasonable long-run values and the majority of adjustment is completed quite quickly (see above, p. 126). Furthermore, these lags do not follow a simple Koyck pattern, though it is easy to see how such approximations might provide an apparently reasonable explanation, at least so long as no more realistic alternative was considered. However, the forecasting performance of the simpler distributed lag models was rather poor, and considerably worse than the models incorporating more flexible lags. In addition the flexible model satisfied fairly rigorous tests for stability.

This last study had the advantage of a longer data period than was available for the earlier studies, and also data with greater independent variation. This, however, does not guarantee that the estimates will stay fixed in the future. Behavioural relationships do not remain immutable but adapt to developments in the financial, industrial and political environment, and to factors which are probably not included in standard demand equations – and may not even be capable of satisfactory inclusion. In addition the data employed in all these studies were seasonally adjusted, and seasonal-adjustment factors frequently change. For this reason, and because of the general updating and amendment of data, it might be expected that the estimates may be changed. After all, any statistical inference can only be as good as the data available; the most one can hope for is to make the best use of the data that do exist.

Hamburger (1977) has argued that in fact a better measure of the opportunity cost of holding M1 balances, at least up to 1971, was given by the three-month eurodollar rate. The evidence for this conclusion is based on an M1 equation that has been estimated up to 1971 but which then breaks down. It is true that given the simple lag model the eurodollar rate does give a better fit for the earlier period than does any domestic short rate, but not when the data period is extended. A possible interpretation is that in a system of fixed exchange rates, and administered interest rates, the eurodollar rate did provide an accurate measure of the cost of holding M1 balances, but that the recent change to a more flexible exchange rate, and market-determined interest rates, has modified this relationship. This argument seems very hard to justify in terms of economic behaviour, but the limitations on data availability are probably sufficient to prevent any definitive conclusion being reached. It is also worth noting that there are still fairly wide differences between the movements of domestic short rates and the eurodollar short rates. For present purposes it is perhaps sufficient to conclude that the domestic short rates, the local authority three-month rate and the Treasury bill rate, are preferable to the eurodollar rate at the moment. In any case, employing the domestic rates for the full period does not result in large residuals occurring through the 1960s or early 1970s.

In conclusion, it is possible to derive theoretically plausible arguments for the existence of a stable demand for M1 balances that is estimable employing non-simultaneous estimation techniques. Moreover, there is reasonable evidence that such an equation does exist (even if we can never be entirely sure that it has been completely correctly estimated). It is, however, much less clear that we should be able to estimate a demand function for M3, particularly employing single-equation, ordinary least squares, methods. This asymmetry in treatment illustrates an important point that there is no general theory of the demand for money which is applicable regardless of the definition of money employed. This point is worth emphasising, if only because it has so often been ignored.

Appendix 5.1 Demand for Money Studies in the United Kingdom – Summary of Results

Author	*Data*	*Money*	*Interest rate*	*Interest-elasticity*[c]	*Income variable*	*Income-elasticity*[c]	*Price*
Kavanagh and Walters	Annual: 1880–1961	Broad	Long	−0.31(−0.22)[a]	G.N.P.	1.149	—
	1926–61	Broad	Long	−0.50(−0.25)[a]	G.N.P.		—
Crouch	Quarterly: 1954–65	London Clearing Banks Deposits (total)	Long	−0.50	G.N.P.	1.08	—
Fisher	Quarterly: 1955(I)–1967(II)	Narrow	Short	−0.11	P.D.I.	0.686	—
		Broad	Short	—	P.D.I.	0.742	—
		Narrow	Long	−0.30	P.D.I.	0.686	—
		Broad	Long	—	P.D.I.	0.742	—
Goodhart and Crockett	Quarterly: 1955(III)–1969(III)/1963(II)–1969(III)[b]	Narrow	Short	−1.05	G.D.P.	1.25	—
		Narrow	Long	−0.80	G.D.P.	1.09	—
		Broad	Short	−0.09/−0.21[b]	G.D.P.	0.77/1.50[b]	—
		Broad	Long	−0.35/−0.51[b]	G.D.P.	1.09/1.89[b]	—
Laidler and Parkin	Quarterly: 1955(III)–1967(IV)	Broad	Short	−0.008	G.D.P. (perm.)	0.68	1*
Laidler	Annual: 1900–65	Broad	Long	−0.570	G.D.P.	0.795	1*
	1900–13	Broad	Long	−0.268	G.D.P.	1.241	1*
	1920–38	Broad	Long	−0.448	G.D.P.	0.793	1*
	1946–65	Broad	Long	−0.739	G.D.P.	0.684	1*
Price	Quarterly: 1964(I)–1970(IV) (*persons*)	Broad	Short	—			
		Broad	Long	−0.30	G.D.P.	2.29	0.90
	Quarterly: 1964(I)–1970(IV) (*companies*)	Broad	Short	−0.36			
		Broad	Long	—	G.D.P.	2.77	0.41

Hacche	Quarterly: 1963(IV)–1971(III)	Narrow	Short	−0.081	T.F.E.	0.391	1*
			Long	−0.184			
		Broad	Short	−0.091	T.F.E.	0.450	1*
			Long	—			
	Persons	Broad	Short	—	P.D.I.	0.927	1*
			Long	−0.069			
	Companies	Broad	Short	−0.067	T.F.E.	0.511	1*
			Long	−0.197			
	Quarterly: 1963(IV)–1972(IV)	Narrow	Short	−0.062	T.F.E.	0.697	1*
			Long	−0.206			
		Broad	Short	—	T.F.E.		1*
			Long	—			
	Persons	Broad	Short	—	P.D.I.	1.081	1*
			Long	−0.110			
	Companies	Broad	Short	−0.044	T.F.E.	2.206	1*
			Long	−0.696			
	Quarterly: 1963(IV)–1972(IV)	Broad	Short	−0.248	T.F.E.	0.995	1*
			Long	—			
			own rate	0.537			
	Companies	Broad	Short	—	T.F.E.	1.003	1*
			Long	−0.345			
			own rate	0.568			
Artis and Lewis	Quarterly:						
	1963(II)–1970(IV)	Narrow	Long	−0.26	G.D.P.	0.77	—
	1963(II)–1971(IV)	Narrow	Long	−0.39	G.D.P.	0.95	—
	1963(II)–1973(I)	Narrow	Long	−0.66	G.D.P.	1.24	—
	1963(II)–1970(IV)	Broad	Long	−0.47	G.D.P.	1.42	—
	1963(II)–1971(IV)	Broad	Long	−0.52	G.D.P.	1.48	—
	1963(II)–1973(I)	Broad	Long	−3.00	G.D.P.	4.27	—

Appendix 5.1 – *continued*

Author	*Data*	*Money*	*Interest rate*	*Interest-elasticity*[c]	*Income variable*	*Income-elasticity*[c]	*Price*
Hamburger	Quarterly: 1963(II)–1971(I)	Narrow	Short[e] Long[e]	−1.20[f] −1.07[f]	G.D.P.	0.672	—
Coghlan[g]	Quarterly: 1964(I)–1976(IV)	Narrow	Short	−0.300	T.F.E.	1.008	0.709

G.N.P. = Gross National Product
G.D.P. = Gross Domestic Product
P.D.I. = Personal Disposable Income
T.F.E. = Total Final Expenditure

(a) From the same equation estimated in first differences.
(b) Results for money on a broad definition for both M2 and M3 respectively.
(c) These are the long-run elasticities.
(d) Here only the results of the standard approach are summarised, and not the attempts to provide an improved specification.
(e) In this case the short rate is the three-month eurodollar rate, and the long rate is the dividend–price ratio on ordinary shares.
(f) These are not the interest-elasticities, but the elasticity times one plus the rate of interest divided by the rate of interest.
(g) This is only one result from the tables presented, but given the evidence of stability discovered it does adequately summarise the results obtained.

* Price elasticity of unity imposed.

Appendix 5.2 Demand for Money Studies in the United Kingdom – References

A. J. Brown, 'Interest, Prices and the Demand for Money', *Oxford Economic Papers*, 1939.

A. M. Khusro, 'An Investigation of Liquidity Preference', *Yorkshire Bulletin of Economic and Social Research*, 1952.

H. F. Lydall, 'Income, Assets and the Demand for Money', *Review of Economics and Statistics*, 1958.

N. J. Kavanagh and A. A. Walters, 'The Demand for Money in the U.K., 1877–1961: Preliminary Findings', *Bulletin of the Oxford University Institute of Economics and Statistics*, 1966.*

L. De Alessi, 'The Demand for Money: A Cross Section Study of British Business Firms', *Economica*, 1966.

R. L. Crouch, 'A Model of the U.K.'s Monetary Sector', *Econometrica*, 1967.

D. Fisher, 'The Demand for Money in Britain: Quarterly Results, 1951–67', *Manchester School*, 1968.

C. A. E. Goodhart and A. D. Crockett, 'The Importance of Money: Some Results for the U.K.', *Bank of England Quarterly Bulletin*, June 1970.*

D. E. W. Laidler and J. M. Parkin, 'The Demand for Money in the U.K., 1955–67: Preliminary Estimates', *Manchester School*, September 1970.*

D. E. W. Laidler, 'The Influence of Money on Economic Activity: A Survey of Some Current Problems', in *Monetary Theory and Monetary Policy in the 1970s*, ed. G. Clayton, J. C. Gilbert and R. Sedgwick (London: Oxford University Press, 1971).

L. D. D. Price, 'The Demand for Money in the United Kingdom: a Further Investigation', *Bank of England Quarterly Bulletin*, March 1972.

M. J. Artis and M. K. Lewis, 'The Demand for Money: Stable or Unstable?', *Banker*, March 1974.

G. Hacche, 'The Demand for Money in the United Kingdom: A Further Investigation', *Bank of England Quarterly Bulletin*, September 1974.

M. J. Artis and M. K. Lewis, 'The Demand for Money in the United Kingdom: 1963–1973' *Manchester School*, June 1976.

M. J. Hamburger, 'The Demand for Money in an Open Economy: Germany and the United Kingdom', *Journal of Monetary Economics*, January 1977.

R. T. Coghlan, 'A Transactions Demand for Money', *Bank of England Quarterly Bulletin*, March 1978.

*Reprinted in *Readings in British Monetary Economics*, ed. H. G. Johnson *et al.* (Oxford: Oxford University Press, 1972).

6. BALANCE-SHEETS AND FLOWS OF FUNDS

This chapter has two objectives. The first is to relate flow-of-funds accounts to balance-sheets and the national income/expenditure accounts. These relationships are illustrated by analysing simplified accounts of the six sectors identified in the flow-of-funds tables. The second objective is to demonstrate the reduction in risk attainable through portfolio diversification. This last section is somewhat technical, but the principle is important since it helps explain the significance of financial intermediaries, a topic we shall be returning to in Chapter 8.

Flows of Funds

This section discusses the construction and use of sectoral balance-sheets and flows of funds. The construction of sectoral balance-sheets for the United Kingdom is discussed at length by Revell (1967), Revell and Roe (1971) and Roe (1971). Balance-sheets reveal the total, and distribution, of assets and liabilities *at any point in time*, 'and show the position which the economy has reached as the result of its entire past activity' (Revell, 1967, p. 3). They consist not only of past transactions in assets and liabilities but also any accumulated revaluations of marketable assets and liabilities.

On the other hand, national income and expenditure accounts consist of the current transactions which go to make up national income. In order that financial accounts should be comparable, only current transactions in assets and liabilities are included. Flow-of-funds accounts, or sources and uses statements, are obtained by first differencing the balance-sheets and subtracting any capital gains.

The balance-sheet for a typical sector will take the following general form:

Balance-sheet

Assets	*Liabilities*
A_1	L_1
A_2	L_2
$\vdots$	$\vdots$
A_n	L_m
R	NW
K	

where A_i = the stock of each financial asset included in the portfolio and valued at the purchase price, L_i = the stock of each financial liability issued by the sector and valued at the sale price, K = the stock of real assets valued at the purchase price, R = net revaluations of assets and liabilities (including the depreciation of real assets), and NW = net worth. Each financial asset can alternatively be thought of as the liability of another sector. Net worth is obtained as a residual and ensures that the two sides of the balance-sheet add up. It is equal to the total of all assets less the total of all liabilities:

$$NW = K + R + \sum_{1}^{n} A_i - \sum_{1}^{m} L_i \tag{6.1}$$

This is an example of a *consolidated* balance-sheet as opposed to a *combined* balance-sheet. The latter also shows financial relationships within the sector, whereas the former aggregates these out. By first differencing the items in the balance-sheet, and subtracting any capital gains/losses (including depreciation), we obtain the flow-of-funds accounts or sources and uses statement. This gives the transactions in assets and liabilities over the period:

Flow of funds

Assets	*Liabilities*
ΔA_1	ΔL_1
ΔA_2	ΔL_2
$\vdots$	$\vdots$
ΔA_n	ΔL_m
ΔK	$\Delta NW - \Delta R = S$

The change in net worth minus the change in revaluations has been redefined as the saving, S, of the sector in question. If the change in the capital stock, gross investment, was also excluded, this would leave only the financial flows. Investment has been retained here in order to illustrate those transactions which add to the balance-sheet (wealth), as conventionally defined, as compared with those transactions which represent current consumption and do not therefore represent a flow of services in the future. Strictly speaking, these transactions should be equal to current income less consumption – as opposed to expenditure on what are generally referred to as 'consumption goods'. For example, food which is stored is as much wealth (as long as it remains edible) as any other asset. Although this would seem to be conceptually the more reasonable distinction, information available (i.e. the published data) is only in the form of broad categories of expenditure.

In order to illustrate the importance of flows of funds, and the way they fit into the income/expenditure framework, it will be helpful to examine the simplified flows between the six sectors defined in the official flow-of-funds accounts (Bank of England, 1978). We begin by defining the balance-sheets for the six sectors.

Assume that each sector issues a single type of liability which is held as an asset by each of the other five sectors, except for the public and overseas sectors, which in addition issue cash. Cash issued by the public sector, Q, is assumed to be held by all other sectors, but cash (including gold) issued by the overseas sector, EQ, is only held by the public sector. Although certain institutions are allowed to hold foreign currency, this last assumption is approximately correct. The exchange of foreign for domestic currency is managed by the Exchange Equalisation Account, created in 1931 after the United Kingdom left the gold standard. For the moment, each domestic sector is also assumed to hold some real assets, K. Finally, because the flow-of-funds accounts require the cancellation of any revaluations, these are assumed away from the beginning.

To summarise, a typical sector, i, within the private sector will hold cash plus real assets plus the liabilities of $n-1$ other sectors, where $n = 6$ in this case. Sector i also issues liabilities which are held by the other $n-1$ sectors, i.e.

Sector i	
Assets	*Liabilities*
Q_i	
K_i	
$\sum_{j=1}^{n-1} {}_jL_i$	$\sum_{j=1}^{n-1} {}_iL_j$
	S_i

Each non-cash financial liability, L, is prefixed by the letter presenting the sector to which the loan was made and suffixed by the sector making the loan. For example, personal-sector holdings of bank deposits (plus any other money lent to the banking sector by the personal sector) is represented as BLP. This enters the personal sector's balance-sheet as an asset and the bank sector's balance-sheet as a liability. The illustrative balance-sheets for each of the six sectors are given in Table 6.1.

As should be obvious, all financial liabilities are also an asset to someone else. Each financial claim is therefore a link between two economic units. There is a problem with the equity issues of companies, since the purchasers become the owners of the company. How then do they owe debts to themselves? However, if we want to identify a separate company sector, it is necessary to interpret equities as the debts of companies.

The next stage is to first difference these balance-sheets to obtain the flows of funds. These can then be combined with the income and consumption expenditures of the various sectors to give total current transactions. In order to simplify the exposition, and to concentrate attention on the fundamental characteristics of the system, we shall assume that all income accrues to the personal and company sectors, and that the financial institutions hold no real assets. In this way we can emphasise the intermediary function performed by the financial sectors. It also assumes that in aggregate those economic activities under public-sector control do not make a profit.

The notation is simplified by writing flows (changes in stocks) with lower-case letters. For example, 'ΔCLP' becomes 'clp'. To start with, it is also convenient to net out inter-sector

Table 6.1 Sectoral Balance-sheets

Personal sector (P)			Company sector (C)	
Assets	Liabilities		Assets	Liabilities
QP			QC	
CLP	PLC		PLC	CLP
BLP	PLB		BLC	CLB
NLP	PLN		NLC	CLN
GLP	PLG		GLC	CLG
OLP	PLO		OLC	CLO
KP	SP		KC	SC
Banking sector (B)			**Non-bank financial intermediaries (N.B.F.I.s) (N)**	
Assets	Liabilities		Assets	Liabilities
QB			QN	
PLB	BLP		PLN	NLP
CLB	BLC		CLN	NLC
NLB	BLN		BLN	NLB
CLB	BLG		GLN	NLG
OLB	BLO		OLN	NLO
KB	SB		KN	SN
Public sector (G)			**Overseas sector (O)***	
Assets	Liabilities		Assets	Liabilities
EQ			QO	EQ
PLG	GLP	QP	PLO	OLP
CLG	GLC	QC	CLO	OLC
BLG	GLB	QB	BLO	OLB
NLG	GLN	QN	NLO	OLN
OLG	GLO	QO	GLO	OLG
KG	SG			SO

* Partial balance-sheet showing position with respect to the United Kingdom only.

non-cash transactions. So for the personal sector, net financial transactions with the banking sector are

$$blp - plb$$

which is then written as

$$bp$$

This *net* transaction enters the banking sector's accounts as *pb*, i.e. it is the same quantity with the sign reversed.

Personal sector

We begin with the personal sector. Identity (6.2) below simply says that personal-sector income, *yp*, is distributed between income-tax payments, *tp*, consumption and investment expenditure, *xp* and *kp*, and transactions in assets and liabilities with the other five sectors:

$$xp + kp + qp + cp + bp + np + gp + op \equiv yp - tp \quad (6.2)$$

This identity can be further simplified by aggregating together all financial transactions to give the net acquisition of financial assets, $\text{N.A.F.A.}_{\cdot p}$:

$$xp + kp + \text{N.A.F.A.}_{\cdot p} \equiv yp - tp \quad (6.3)$$

Company sector

Identity (6.4) below presents a very similar situation for the company sector except that in this case there are no consumption expenditures:

$$kc + qc + pc + bc + nc + gc + oc \equiv yc - tc \quad (6.4)$$

And again the financial transactions can be aggregated together to give

$$kc + \text{N.A.F.A.}_{\cdot c} \equiv yc - tc \quad (6.5)$$

Banking sector and N.B.F.I.s

The two financial sectors are taken together. In both cases income and capital expenditure are relatively small, and have been assumed to be zero for the present illustrative purposes:

$$qb + pb + cb + nb + gb + ob \equiv 0 \quad (6.6)$$
$$qn + pn + cn + bn + gn + on \equiv 0 \quad (6.7)$$

Identities (6.6) and (6.7) state that changes in financial assets are equal to changes in financial liabilities for the banks and

N.B.F.I.s taken individually:

$$\text{N.A.F.A.}_b \equiv 0 \tag{6.8}$$

$$\text{N.A.F.A.}_n \equiv 0 \tag{6.9}$$

Public sector

The public sector's net increase in financial *liabilities*, identically equal to the public sector's financing requirement, P.S.F.R., is equal to the excess of total public-sector expenditure, xg and kg, over total revenue – taxes on the income of the personal and company sectors, tp and tc, and on expenditures, te:

$$\begin{aligned} xg + kg - tp - tc - te &\equiv q - eq - pg - cg - bg - ng \\ &\quad - og \\ &\equiv q - eq + gp + gc + gb + gn \\ &\quad + go \\ &\equiv \text{P.S.F.R.} \end{aligned} \tag{6.10}$$

where $q = \sum_i qi, \quad i = p, c, b, n, o.$

If transactions in financial *assets*

$$eq + plg + clg + blg + nlg + olg \equiv \Delta\text{F.A.}_g$$

are transferred to the left-hand side of the identity, leaving only the increase in financial *liabilities*

$$q + glp + glc + glb + gln + glo \equiv \Delta\text{F.L.}_g$$

on the right-hand side, this defines the public sector's *borrowing* requirement, PSBR.

$$\begin{aligned} xg + kg - tp - tc - tc + \Delta\text{F.A.}_g &\equiv \Delta\text{F.L.}_g \\ &\equiv \text{P.S.B.R.} \end{aligned} \tag{6.11}$$

The borrowing requirement is taken to be the most important indicator of public-sector policy by those who consider the stock of money to be of fundamental importance to general economic activity (see Brittan, 1971, ch. 4; and Bank of England, 1978, part 2). The P.S.B.R. shows the total amount the public sector has to borrow to cover all of its financial commitments. To the extent that the public sector is unable, or unwilling, to borrow funds from the non-bank private sector it must borrow from the banking sector, and this results in an increase in the money supply. This relationship is made clear in Chapter 10.

Overseas sector

Finally, the net acquisition of financial assets by the overseas sector is equal to the negative of the balance of payments on current account, C.A.:

$$qo - eq + po + co + bo + no + go \equiv -\text{C.A.}$$
$$\text{N.A.F.A.}_o \equiv -\text{C.A.} \qquad (6.12)$$

Or, alternatively, the change in foreign-currency reserves is identically equal to the balance on current account plus the net acquisition of domestic (U.K.) assets by the overseas sector, N.A.U.K.F.A._o, i.e.

$$eq \equiv \text{C.A.} + qo + po + co + bo + no + go$$
$$\equiv \text{C.A.} + \text{N.A.U.K.F.A.}_o \qquad (6.13)$$

Adding each of the six sectors together yields the following identity:

$$yp + yc \equiv xp + kp + kc + xg + kg - te + \text{C.A.} \qquad (6.14)$$

Aggregating income flows together to give y, private-sector capital expenditures to give k, and also both types of government expenditure to give g, allows us to simplify this expression to

$$y \equiv x + k + g - te + \text{C.A.} \qquad (6.15)$$

which can then be rewritten, using more familiar notation, as

$$Y \equiv C + I + G - \text{T.E.} + \text{C.A.} \qquad (6.16)$$

All of the financial transactions have now dropped out and we are left with a definition of what I would like to call gross national income (G.N.I.) measured at factor cost. This represents the country's command over resources, and is made up of all incomes accruing to the United Kingdom from whatever source, and for whatever reason, less all transfers, whether they be taxes, profits, subscriptions or gifts.

If we wish to identify the output of the economy as measured by gross domestic product (G.D.P.), i.e. only incomes earned in the United Kingdom, it is necessary to subtract all foreign income flows (gifts, transfers, etc.) not earned from the sale of goods from Y, and also from C.A. The external component of the accounts then becomes the balance of exports, X, and imports, Z, of goods and services only, i.e.

$$\text{G.D.P.} \equiv C + I + G - \text{T.E.} + X - Z \tag{6.17}$$

So while for a closed economy, in aggregate, saving, S, must always be equal to investment, I,

$$S \equiv I \tag{6.18}$$

for any sector (or individual economic unit) this need not be true, and, in fact, will practically never be true:

$$Y_i - C_i \equiv S_i$$

$$S_i - I_i \equiv \Delta F_i \equiv \Delta \text{F.A.}_{\cdot i} - \Delta \text{F.L.}_{\cdot i}$$

The sectoral flows given above have been quite involved but even these are extreme simplifications and have stopped far short of the extensive financial interrelationships that actually exist between the various sectors. There is no single one-way flow of funds from one sector to the others, which is an impression one might get by only looking at figures for the final net positions. In particular, because the personal sector is generally in surplus it can easily be overlooked that it is also a substantial borrower.

The variety of financial flows within the domestic economy is summarised in Figure 6.1. This illustrates the complexity of financial relations, showing not only the main connections between the financial sector and the other sectors of the economy, but gives some indication of the interrelatedness existing between intermediaries.

Portfolio Diversification and the Reduction of Risk

The objective of this section is to demonstrate that it may be possible to reduce the risk on a portfolio of assets below that

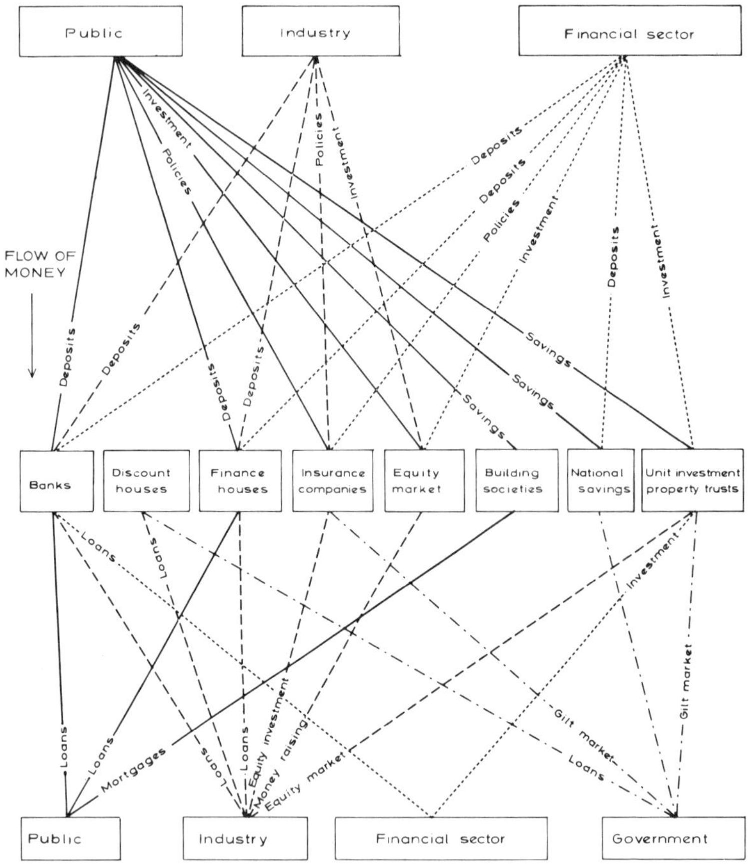

Figure 6.1 Domestic Inter-sectoral Flows of Funds

Reproduced from *Financial Services Review 1972–73* (London: Gower Press, 1972)

associated with each of the assets held. At first sight this may seem surprising, and it is a possibility which helps explain the importance of financial institutions, and the gains from the professional management of portfolios. It is really only an extension of the portfolio analysis of the demand for money of

Chapter 4. For a more detailed treatment see Levey and Sarnat (1972) and Francis and Archer (1971).

The rate of return on the portfolio (r_p) will be equal to the rate of return on each of the assets weighted by the proportion held in the portfolio:

$$r_p = \sum_{i=1}^{n} a_i r_i \tag{6.19}$$

for n assets. If either $a_i = 0$, i.e. the asset is not included in the portfolio, or $r_i = 0$, i.e. the asset yields no return, the product $a_i r_i = 0$.

The expected rate of return on the portfolio will simply be the expected rate of return on each asset weighted by the proportion of the asset in the total portfolio:

$$E(r_p) = \sum_{i=1}^{n} a_i E(r_i) \tag{6.20}$$

The variance of the portfolio return (σ_p^2) is obtained by squaring the sum of all deviations of returns from their expected value and taking the expected value:

$$\sigma_p^2 = E[r_p - E(r_p)]^2 \tag{6.21}$$

The important thing to realise about this expression is that the variance (and therefore the risk) of the portfolio is not simply a weighted average of the individual variances on each of the returns. The covariance, or correlation, between each of the asset returns also plays a crucial role. This can be illustrated by expanding (6.21) for an example consisting of only two assets, i.e. $i = 1, 2$:

$$\sigma_p^2 = E[(a_1 r_1 + a_2 r_2) - E(a_1 r_1 + a_2 r_2)]^2$$

Because the expected value of a constant is the constant, this can be rearranged as

$$\sigma_p^2 = E\{a_1[r_1 - E(r_1)] + a_2[r_2 - E(r_2)]\}^2 \tag{6.22}$$

Expanding (6.22) by squaring the expression within the brackets gives

$$\sigma_p^2 = a_1^2 E[r_1 - E(r_1)]^2 + a_2^2 E[r_2 - E(r_2)]^2 + 2a_1 a_2 E\{[r_1 - E(r_1)][r_2 - E(r_2)]\} \tag{6.23}$$

The final expression in (6.23) is nothing more than the covariance between the returns on the two assets, i.e.

$$\text{cov}(r_i, r_j) \equiv \sigma_{ij} \equiv E\{[r_i - E(r_i)][r_j - E(r_j)]\} \quad (6.24)$$

If $i = j$ (6.24) reduces to the variance of the return on a single asset, i.e. the covariance of the return on an asset with its own return is the variance of the return. Therefore, (6.23) can be rewritten as

$$\sigma_p^2 = a_1^2\sigma_1^2 + a_2^2\sigma_2^2 + 2a_1a_2\sigma_{12} \quad (6.25)$$

which is equivalent to

$$\sigma_p^2 = \mathrm{a}_1\mathrm{a}_1\sigma_{11} + \mathrm{a}_2\mathrm{a}_2\sigma_{22} + 2\mathrm{a}_1\mathrm{a}_2\sigma_{12}$$

This formula can be generalised for any n assets so that

$$\sigma_p^2 = \sum_{i=1}^{n}\sum_{j=1}^{n} a_i a_j \sigma_{ij} \quad (6.26)$$

The double summation sign need not cause concern: (6.26) can be rewritten as

$$\sigma_p^2 = \sum_{i=1}^{n} a_i \sum_{j=1}^{n} a_j \sigma_{ij}$$

and each of the summations can be expanded in turn.

There is a problem with using the covariance of returns in that it is related to the units of measurement employed, and therefore does not tell us anything beyond the sign of the relationship between returns. The use of the correlation coefficient (R_{ij}) between asset returns removes this element of arbitrariness and provides a measure of the relationship between variables that is free from any dependence upon the unit of measurement.

The coefficient of correlation is obtained quite simply by dividing the covariance by the standard deviations of the two returns:

$$R_{ij} = \frac{\sigma_{ij}}{\sigma_i \sigma_j} \quad (6.27)$$

from which it follows that the covariance can be written as

$$\sigma_{ij} \equiv R_{ij}\sigma_i\sigma_j \quad (6.28)$$

The correlation coefficient is restricted to values between $-1 \leqslant R_{ij} \leqslant +1$. A value of $+1$ means that the returns are perfectly positively correlated, i.e. they move in the same direction at the same time; -1 means that they are perfectly negatively correlated, i.e. they vary inversely; 0 means they are uncorrelated, unrelated.

(6.28) can now be substituted for σ_{ij} in (6.26), and the example with two assets will become

$$\sigma_p^2 = a_1^2 R_{11}\sigma_1^2 + a_2^2 R_{22}\sigma_2^2 + 2a_1 a_2 R_{12}\sigma_1\sigma_2$$

where $R_{12} = R_{21}$. And since the return on any security is perfectly positively correlated with itself, i.e. $R_{11} = R_{22} = 1$, this reduces to

$$\sigma_p^2 = a_1^2\sigma_1^2 + a_2^2\sigma_2^2 + (2a_1 a_2\sigma_1\sigma_2)R_{12} \tag{6.29}$$

The expression in parentheses will be positive as long as both of the two assets are included in the portfolio, i.e. $a_1 > 0$ and $a_2 > 0$, and neither of the assets has a certain return, i.e. $\sigma_1 > 0$ and $\sigma_2 > 0$.

Given these conditions it must be true that the smaller is R_{12} the smaller will be σ_p^2. To see this we shall consider the three extreme cases where $R_{12} = +1, 0$ and -1. It is first necessary to derive the optimal portfolio weights. Because we are restricting the portfolio to only two assets, the proportions of each in the portfolio must add up to unity, i.e.

$$a_1 + a_2 = 1$$

so that

$$a_2 = 1 - a_1$$

If we substitute for a_2 in (6.29), we obtain:

$$\sigma_p^2 = a_1^2\sigma_1^2 + (1 - a_1)^2\sigma_2^2 + [2a_1(1 - a_1)\sigma_1\sigma_2]R_{12} \tag{6.30}$$

In order to obtain the optimal proportions for the first asset (i.e. the asset proportions which minimise the risk) we need to differentiate (6.30) with respect to a_1, and set the result equal to zero:

$$\frac{\partial \sigma_p^2}{\partial a_1} = 2a_1\sigma_1^2 - 2\sigma_2^2 + 2a_1\sigma_2^2 + 2\sigma_1\sigma_2 R_{12} - 4a_1\sigma_1\sigma_2 R_{12} = 0 \tag{6.31}$$

This can be simplified to give

$$a_1 = \frac{\sigma_2^2 - \sigma_1\sigma_2 R_{12}}{\sigma_1^2 + \sigma_2^2 - 2\sigma_1\sigma_2 R_{12}} \tag{6.32}$$

And because $a_2 = 1 - a_1$:

$$a_2 = 1 - \left(\frac{\sigma_2^2 - \sigma_1\sigma_2 R_{12}}{\sigma_1^2 + \sigma_2^2 - 2\sigma_1\sigma_2 R_{12}}\right) = \frac{\sigma_1^2 - \sigma_1\sigma_2 R_{12}}{\sigma_1^2 + \sigma_2^2 - 2\sigma_1\sigma_2 R_{12}} \tag{6.33}$$

We can now return to consider the question of how the correlation between expected returns affects the risk of the portfolio.

Perfect positive correlation, $R_{12} = +1$

Substituting unity for R_{12} in (6.29), the expression for the variance of the return on the portfolio, gives:

$$\sigma_p^2 = a_1^2\sigma_1^2 + a_2^2\sigma_2^2 + 2a_1a_2\sigma_1\sigma_2$$

which reduces to

$$\sigma_p^2 = (a_1\sigma_1 + a_2\sigma_2)^2$$

so that the standard deviation (the square root of the variance) is

$$\sigma_p = a_1\sigma_1 + a_2\sigma_2 \tag{6.34}$$

With asset returns perfectly positively correlated the standard deviation of the portfolio is linearly related to the proportions in which the assets are held. The risk on the portfolio therefore simply reflects the risk associated with each individual return times the proportions in which assets are held.

Zero correlation, $R_{12} = 0$

In this case (6.29) reduces to

$$\sigma_p^2 = a_1^2\sigma_1^2 + a_2^2\sigma_2^2 \tag{6.35}$$

and the optimal asset proportions, (6.32) and (6.33), become

$$a_1 = \frac{\sigma_2^2}{\sigma_1^2 + \sigma_2^2} \tag{6.36}$$

$$a_2 = \frac{\sigma_1^2}{\sigma_1^2 + \sigma_2^2} \tag{6.37}$$

Substituting (6.36) and (6.37) into (6.35) yields

$$\sigma_p^2 = \left\{\frac{\sigma_2^2}{\sigma_1^2 + \sigma_2^2}\right\}^2 \sigma_1^2 + \left\{\frac{\sigma_1^2}{\sigma_1^2 + \sigma_2^2}\right\}^2 \sigma_2^2$$

which becomes

$$\sigma_p^2 = \frac{\sigma_1^2\sigma_2^2(\sigma_1^2 + \sigma_2^2)}{(\sigma_1^2 + \sigma_2^2)^2}$$

and simplifies to

$$\sigma_p^2 = \frac{\sigma_1^2\sigma_2^2}{\sigma_1^2 + \sigma_2^2} \tag{6.38}$$

The next step is to discover whether the variance of the portfolio will be less than the lowest variance on any individual asset, eg, σ_1^2; i.e. is

$$\sigma_p^2 < \sigma_1^2$$

Substituting for σ_p^2 from (6.38):

$$\frac{\sigma_1^2\sigma_2^2}{\sigma_1^2 + \sigma_2^2} < \sigma_1^2$$

Since σ_1^2 and σ_2^2 are both positive, this can be simplified to

$$\sigma_1^2\sigma_2^2 < \sigma_1^2(\sigma_1^2 + \sigma_2^2)$$

or

$$\sigma_1^2\sigma_2^2 < \sigma_1^4 + \sigma_1^2\sigma_2^2$$

Subtracting $\sigma_1^2\sigma_2^2$ from both sides gives

$$0 < \sigma_1^4$$

or

$$0 < \sigma_1$$

Therefore, as long as the standard deviation of the return on each asset in the portfolio is positive – an assumption already made – the portfolio variance will be less than the lowest asset variance. Obviously if there is an asset with zero variance about the expected return, it will be impossible to reduce the variance of the portfolio below zero.

An alternative, more intuitive, way of deriving the same result is as follows. (6.38) can be rearranged slightly as

$$\sigma_p^2 = \sigma_1^2 \left\{\frac{\sigma_2^2}{\sigma_1^2 + \sigma_2^2}\right\}$$

Given that both $\sigma_1^2 > 0$ and $\sigma_2^2 > 0$:

$$0 < \frac{\sigma_2^2}{\sigma_1^2 + \sigma_2^2} < 1$$

which means that σ_p^2 must be some proportion of σ_1^2 (and σ_2^2), i.e.

$$\sigma_p^2 < \sigma_1^2 \text{ and } \sigma_2^2$$

Perfectly negative correlation, $R_{12} = -1$

The variance of the return on the portfolio becomes

$$\sigma_p^2 = a_1^2\sigma_1^2 + a_2^2\sigma_2^2 - 2a_1a_2\sigma_1\sigma_2$$

This reduces to

$$\sigma_p^2 = (a_1\sigma_1 - a_2\sigma_2)^2 \quad (6.39)$$

and the optimal asset proportions (6.32) and (6.33) become:[1]

$$a_1 = \frac{\sigma_2}{\sigma_1 + \sigma_2} \quad (6.40)$$

$$a_2 = \frac{\sigma_1}{\sigma_1 + \sigma_2} \quad (6.41)$$

Substituting (6.40) and (6.41) into (6.39) gives:

$$\sigma_p^2 = \left\{ \frac{\sigma_1\sigma_2}{\sigma_1+\sigma_2} - \frac{\sigma_1\sigma_2}{\sigma_1+\sigma_2} \right\}^2$$

which reduces to

$$\sigma_p^2 = 0 \tag{6.42}$$

So if rates of return on assets are perfectly negatively correlated, it will be possible to choose a portfolio with zero risk, i.e. an absolute certainty of return, even though there is a positive return and variance on each of the included assets.

We have now succeeded in demonstrating a very important result. Risk on a portfolio can be reduced by diversification as long as returns are not perfectly positively correlated. The lower the correlation coefficient between the returns on any two securities, i.e. R moving from $+1$ through 0 to -1, the smaller the risk will be on a portfolio containing these two assets.

Although it requires a statement of the obvious, it is perhaps worth pointing out that risk on the portfolio is only minimised if the optimal, minimum variance, weights are chosen. This in turn suggests that some form of detailed analysis will be required in order to identify that combination of assets providing the lowest risk for the portfolio for any given, desired, return. The role and importance of financial institutions will be considered in Chapter 8. For the moment it is sufficient to recognise that financial intermediation can be justified in terms of the reduction in risk made possible by the pooling of risks and the provision of professional fund management.

Before concluding this chapter it should be emphasised that the composition of a portfolio is based on the expectation of returns and the expected variances and covariances of these returns. If the covariances turn out to be very different from those expected at the time the assets were purchased, the risk on the portfolio may become unacceptably high. This is an argument which brings attention to the interrelatedness of financial institutions and markets. It may be that under normal circumstances two assets have a high negative covariance, whereas the collapse of a financial intermediary, or a major change in the general economic environment, may cause all rates to rise together. It is therefore possible for the risk associated with a particular portfolio to change quite dramatically.

7. THE FUNCTIONS OF FINANCIAL MARKETS

We began by examining the role of money in the economy. The next stage, given the existence of money, is to consider the function of financial markets. It is all too easy to accept the existing institutional structure we observe without understanding its significance, or indeed questioning whether it is even necessary. Moreover, there is a fairly natural tendency to associate financial markets with financial intermediation. That is not really surprising given the quantity of funds that flow through these institutions; after all, the great majority of financial transactions are conducted via a financial intermediary of one sort or another, at least in developed economies. However, from an expositional point of view it is convenient to separate out the function of financial markets – the exchange of financial claims and the part played in that process by financial intermediaries. The importance of the financial institutions is therefore considered separately in the next chapter.

In the absence of financial intermediaries all financial transactions must necessarily take place directly between ultimate borrowers and lenders of funds. Money does exist, in the form of notes and coins issued by the government, and is assumed to be kept at whatever level is desired by the private sector, i.e. the government responds passively to the demand for cash, substituting the proceeds for other forms of debt.

The following discussion begins with the basic reasons for, and sources of, financial flows. This is followed by a demonstration of the welfare gains resulting from the introduction of financial markets, both with and without the possibility of productive investment. The chapter ends with a brief summary of the financial relationships existing between surplus and deficit units.

The Demand for and Supply of Finance

The need for financial markets arises because of the separation of saving and investment decisions. In general those individuals and/or institutions who want to invest are not the same as those who wish to save, or those who have accumulated excess money balances as the result of past saving.

We can define the allocation of a current flow of income by an economic unit as follows:

$$Y_i - C_i \equiv S_i \tag{7.1}$$

i.e. for any economic unit, i, income, Y_i, minus consumption, C_i, must equal saving, S_i. And

$$S_i - I_i \equiv \Delta\text{F.A.}_{\cdot i} - \Delta\text{F.L.}_{\cdot i} \tag{7.2}$$

i.e. saving, S_i, less investment, I_i, must equal net accumulation of financial assets ΔF: that is, transactions in financial assets, $\Delta\text{F.A.}_{\cdot i}$, less transactions in financial liabilities, $\Delta\text{F.L.}_{\cdot i}$.

Identity (7.2) can be written as

$$Y_i - C_i - I_i \equiv \Delta\text{F.A.}_{\cdot i} - \Delta\text{F.L.}_{\cdot i} \tag{7.3}$$

or

$$Y_i - E_i \equiv \Delta F_i \tag{7.4}$$

where E_i represents total expenditure.

Aggregating over all economic units (and assuming a closed economy with no external claims) the changes in financial asset holdings net out resulting in the familiar national income accounting identity:

$$Y \equiv C + I \tag{7.5}$$

Obviously, if each individual or institution always invested his saving, or did not save, there would be no exchange of financial claims, and no financial markets would exist. This is, however, quite clearly not the case and the aggregate relationship (7.5) conceals a whole infrastructure of financial interrelationships which need to be recognised explicitly if we are to understand how the economy functions. It is in fact a weakness of the so-called Keynesian models that they start from the aggregate income/expenditure indentities and fail to give sufficient attention to the financial infrastructure which is a crucial part of the economic behaviour underlying these identities.

The next step is to consider the means through which finance may be obtained, the sources from which it may be supplied, and the implications of these various alternatives. Any economic unit (individual or institution) which spends in excess of its current income ($E_i > Y_i$) we shall call a deficit unit, while an economic unit spending less than its current income ($Y_i > E_i$) is called a surplus unit. The distinction is therefore drawn in terms of current flows rather than the state of the economic unit's balance-sheet.

(1) There are essentially four ways in which an individual deficit unit may obtain finance *in excess of its current income*:

(i) borrowing, i.e. selling a new financial liability;
(ii) selling an existing financial asset from its portfolio;
(iii) selling a real, tangible, asset; and
(iv) employing existing cash balances.

(2) In the first three cases the finance will ultimately be provided out of:

(i) current saving by surplus units; and
(ii) running down the existing stock of cash balances held by some other economic unit.

We shall consider the implications of each of these alternatives in turn:

Borrowing (1i). Finance is obtained by increasing the stock of financial assets. This is done by issuing *primary* securities; these are new securities being sold for the first time. The ease with which these liabilities can be sold will depend upon a number of important factors. The most important single factor is likely to be the economic viability of the deficit unit. This will depend on expectations of its future income flow and the existing stock and distribution of its debt: in short its ability to repay, as seen by its creditors. In addition the financial position of the rest of the economy is relevant, i.e. the income flow, stock of wealth, liquidity, existing level of debt outstanding, general market conditions, the period of the loan, and if not very short, the existence and efficiency of any secondary market in such debt.

Selling a financial asset (1ii). Finance is obtained without increasing the stock of financial assets. This is achieved through a *secondary* market dealing in second-hand liabilities. The ability to finance expenditures this way depends upon the deficit unit possessing a stock of marketable financial assets which it can sell. Naturally the quality and marketability of the assets are important, but, in this case, the unit's own financial standing (economic viability) will not be a factor governing the availability of finance.

Selling a real asset (1iii). The case of selling an existing capital asset in order to purchase a new one is similar to case (1ii) above except that the market will generally be much narrower, and quite possibly non-existent.

In talking about the ease with which an asset can be sold quickly without losing any of its capital value we are referring to its *liquidity*. The liquidity of many assets will vary over time. When house prices are rising rapidly, and are expected to continue to do so, houses may become a highly liquid asset. This, however, is not generally the case: selling times and prices will, vary and transactions costs can be very high. The term 'liquidity' is generally restricted to that group of assets which can be converted to cash at little or no cost (in time or money), or loss of capital value.

Having looked at the ways in which a deficit unit may go about obtaining finance, we now turn to consider the implications of the various possible sources of finance. The source from which the finance is provided is in fact unlikely to affect the individual deficit unit (unless it is employing its own currency reserves), but it will make a lot of difference to the aggregate economy.

Current saving (2i). In this case the flow of finance simply represents the diversion of currently earned income from the recipients who wish to save to others who wish to spend. This will not result in an increase in aggregate income but is necessary to prevent it from falling – which would be the result if surplus units desired to hold their savings as idle cash balances.

Cash balances (1iv and 2ii). If existing cash balances are employed to finance expenditures, directly or indirectly, this represents a more efficient use of the existing money stock, a rise in the velocity of circulation of money, and an increase in aggregate income. This is true in aggregate but not for any individual economic unit, as a rundown of cash balances in one part of the economy may be matched by an increase elsewhere.

The Importance of Financial Markets

We now turn to examine the economic significance of financial markets. Two basic models are employed for this purpose; in the first case the form of saving is restricted to financial transactions only with no possibility for real investment, while the second example admits this latter possibility. In both cases it is assumed that there are no existing capital goods, or no markets in these goods, so that it is not possible to obtain finance by selling real assets.

Financial transactions only

For the purposes of comparsion we start by supposing that there are no financial markets. The decision period is restricted to a two-period choice set, the present and the future. Each economic unit is assumed to have a positive cash flow in each period, and the objective is to allocate this so as to maximise the unit's utility. This will obviously depend upon the unit's subjective time preference for expenditure. However, while expenditure may be postponed from period one to period two, the opposite is not possible. It is not possible to save future income for spending in the present.

Figure 7.1 measures expenditure in the first period (E_1) along the horizontal axis and the second period's expenditure (E_2) along the vertical axis. The trade-off between present and future expenditure for any single economic unit is measured by

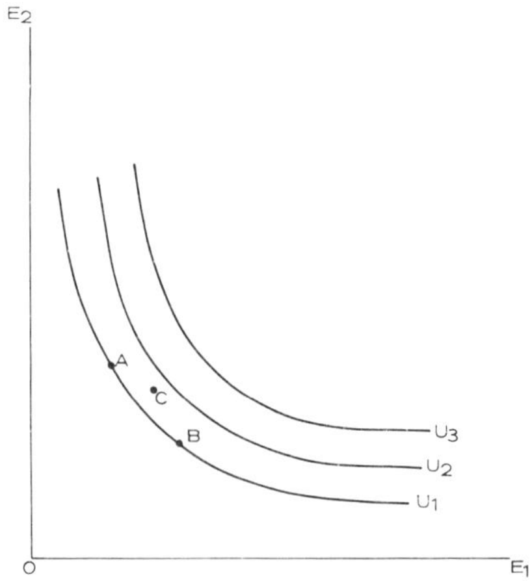

Figure 7.1 Indifference Curves illustrating Relative Preferences between Present and Future Expenditure

the set of indifference curves applicable to that particular unit. These curves are drawn under the assumption of diminishing marginal returns to expenditure in one period in terms of the other, i.e. they are convex to the origin. Obviously the objective is to get on to the highest indifference curve possible.

The economic unit is therefore indifferent between those combinations of current and future expenditure represented by *A* and *B* since they both lie on the same curve. However, point *C* is preferable to both as it lies above and to the right of U_1. For this same reason all points along the indifference curve U_2 are preferred to all points along U_1 (and to *C*).

We can now superimpose particular cash flows on to this utility map, and see in what ways funds will be allocated. Consider the two examples shown in Figures 7.2 and 7.3. In these figures:

OC_1 = cash flow in period 1.
OC_2 = cash flow in period 2.
$OA_2 = OC_2 + OC_1$ = the maximum cash available in the second period if all current income is saved.
$B_0 A_2$ = the budget constraint (the locus of all possible

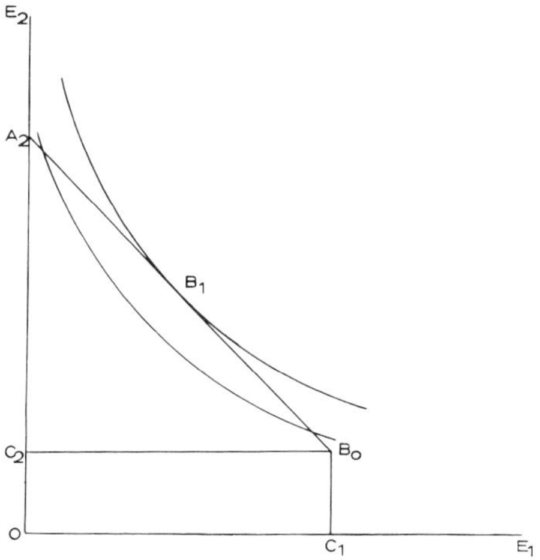

Figure 7.2 Saving in the First Period in order to get on to a Higher Indifference Curve

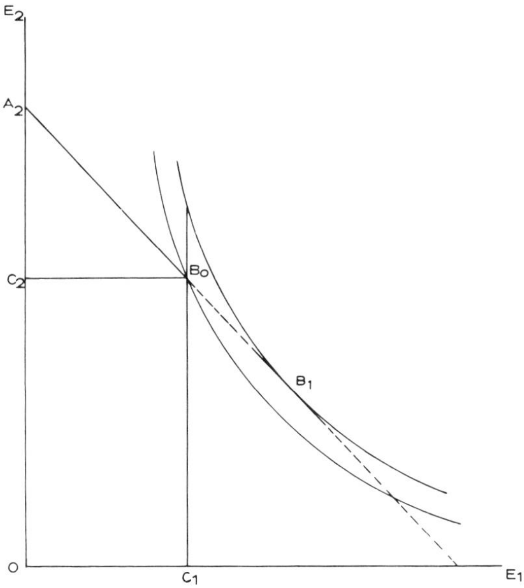

Figure 7.3 Inability to Save Second-period Income in the First Period to get on to a Higher Indifference Curve

expenditures over the two periods given the assumed cash flows). The slope of this line is given by $C_2A_2/C_2B_0 = C_2A_2/OC_1 = OC_1/OC_1 = 1$, i.e. it is a 45° line.

B_1 = maximum utility attainable, given by the tangency between the budget line and an indifference curve.

Figure 7.3 illustrates what can happen given a different distribution of cash flows. In this case if borrowing were possible, utility would be maximised, at B_1, by consuming more in the first period and less in the second. This, however, is not possible in the absence of financial markets. The introduction of financial markets may permit an improvement in both of these positions.

In the first case the income unconsumed in period 1 can be invested and so earn a return, thereby resulting in a steeper budget line (see Figure 7.4). Here:

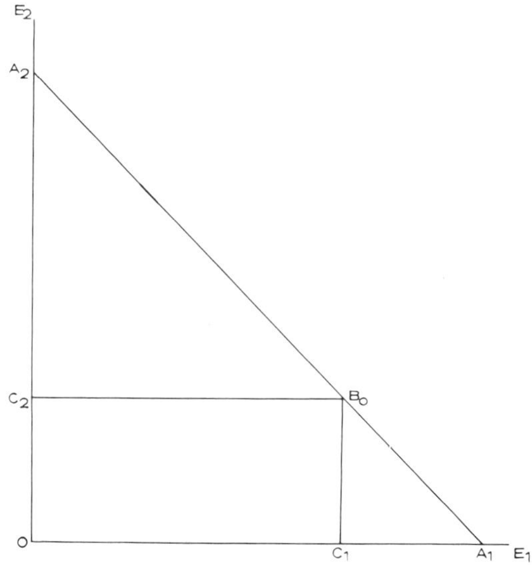

Figure 7.4 Budget Line with a Rate of Interest

$$OA_2 = OC_2 + OC_1(1+r)$$
$$OA_1 = OC_1 + \frac{OC_2}{1+r}$$

where r is the single rate of interest on both borrowing and lending.

The slope of the budget line $= 1 + r$:

$$\frac{C_2A_2}{C_2B_0} = \frac{C_2A_2}{OC_1} = \frac{OC_1(1+r)}{OC_1} = 1 + r$$

which means that it is now possible to get on to a higher indifference curve than before.

The second case is the more important. By borrowing at interest rate r it should be possible to get on to a higher indifference curve (see Figure 7.5). In this case the economic unit borrows C_1D_1 in the first period and pays back $C_2D_2 = C_1D_1(1+r)$ in the second period, thereby lifting the constraint of current income from current expenditure and allowing expenditure to follow the time path desired. Note that because borrowing is not costless the budget line is steeper than before (the slope is $1 + r$ again), so that a lower indifference curve is attainable than if borrowing were costless.

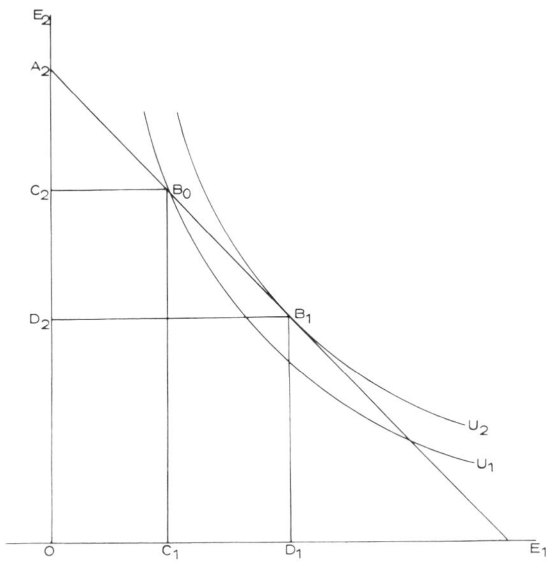

Figure 7.5 How the Ability to Borrow can Improve Welfare

To summarise, this demand for and supply of funds can be explained in the following terms:

(1) *Different cash flows and an identical indifference map* (see Figure 7.6). Given the utility map and the slope of the budget line, X will want to borrow $C_1^x D_1$ in the current period and Y will want to lend $C_1^y D_1$. The need for financial markets arises simply out of divergent cash flows.

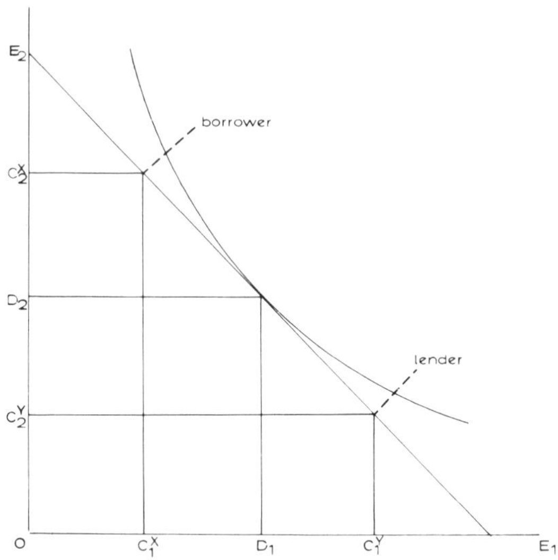

Figure 7.6 Different Cash Flows and Identical Utility Maps where X and Y are different Economic Units with different Cash Flows

(2) *Different trade-offs between current and future expenditure.* Assume identical cash flows OC_1 and OC_2 but different indifference schedules (see Figure 7.7). From the diagram X would neither borrow nor lend, Y has a strong preference for current expenditure and would borrow (tangency to the right of the initial budget allocation), and Z has a strong preference for future expenditure and would lend (tangency to the left of the initial budget allocation).

We are here concerned with the behaviour of individual economic units and are assuming r to be given exogenously. In aggregate r must be determined in the market in order to equate the supply of and demand for finance.

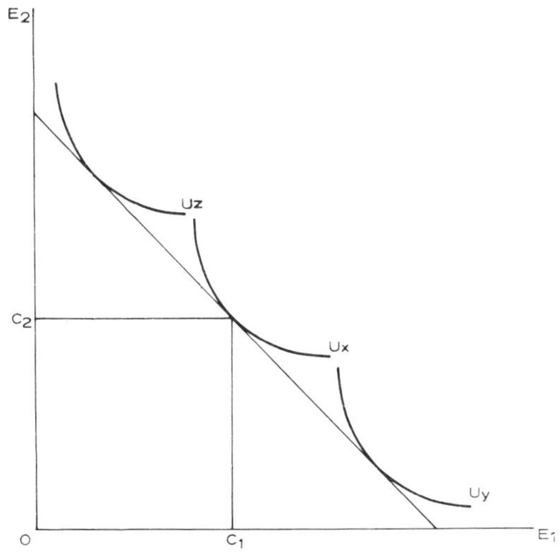

Figure 7.7 Identical Relative Cash Flows, Different Expenditure Patterns

Introducing the possibility of productive investment

Assume that an economic unit has an income in the current period of OA_1 (Figure 7.8). If he spends all of it in this period, he will have no income in the second period. Maximum return in this two-period model is obtained if all the current income is invested at an average yield, a, giving $OA_2 = OA_1(1+a)$.

In Figure 7.8 current income is given by OA_1. Investment is measured from A_1 towards O. The curve A_1A_2 is the 'production-possibility frontier' depicting those investments yielding the highest return at each level of production. As the quantity of investment increases, so diminishing marginal returns are assumed to set in. As we move from A_1 towards O so average and marginal returns decline. The average return is measured by a straight line from A_1 to a point on the curve, while the marginal return, e, at that point will be measured by a line tangent to the curve. It is reasonable to assume that no one will invest beyond the point where the average return, a, becomes zero. This point is obtained by drawing a 45° line from A_1 to the production-possibility locus; all investment opportunities will lie to the right of this line. The assumption of profit

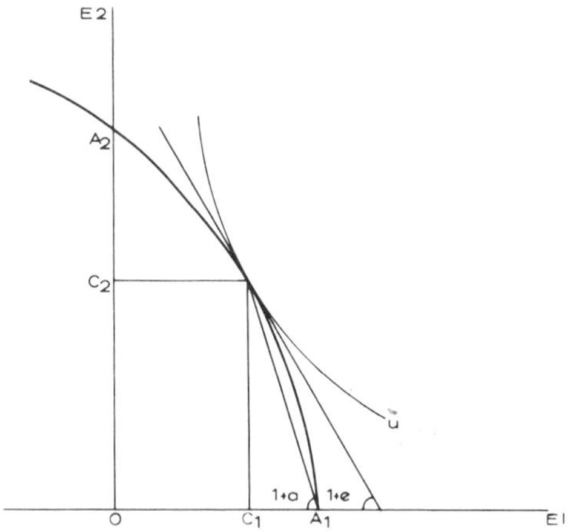

Figure 7.8 Production-possibility Frontier and Investor Preferences

maximisation would restrict investment to the right of a 45° line tangent to the possibility frontier, i.e. at a positive *marginal* return.

The production-possibility frontier is extended over into the negative quandrant in order to show that potential production opportunities are likely to exist for an individual unit beyond the limit imposed by current income. This, in fact, is not only likely but will represent the more usual case, where opportunities for profitable investment exist way beyond that which may be financed out of current income. If it is possible to have a negative current income, i.e. through borrowing, it will generally be possible to attain a higher point on the production-possibility frontier.

High entrepreneurial ability is likely to be associated with a steep production-possibility curve and a strong preference for investment, i.e. a tangency to the left of A_2. It is, however, still possible to demonstrate the advantages of financial markets without these 'negative' income possibilities. We shall therefore begin by assuming tangency in the positive quandrant, and only after that consider the other possibility.

In the absence of financial markets investment will be determined by the tangency of the economic unit's indifference curve with the production-possibility frontier. In the case illustrated in Figure 7.8 investment is equal to A_1C_1, current expenditure is OC_1, and future income is $OC_2 = A_1C_1(1+a)$.

If we now introduce a financial market with a single borrowing and lending rate of r, this increases the possibilities open to the economic unit. Whether any particular unit will lend or borrow depends upon its relative time preference of consumption and the rate of interest. Consider the two cases shown in Figure 7.9 and 7.10.

In the first example (Figure 7.9) unit X is assumed to have a preference for future consumption (but, for the moment, still within the constraints imposed by its current income and production possibilities). The diagram illustrates the equilibrium situation both with and without financial markets, i.e. with and without the ability to borrow and lend.

Without a financial market;

$$\begin{aligned}
&\text{investment} = A_1C_1\\
&\text{present consumption} = OC_1\\
&\text{future consumption} = OC_2 = A_1C_1(1+a)
\end{aligned}$$

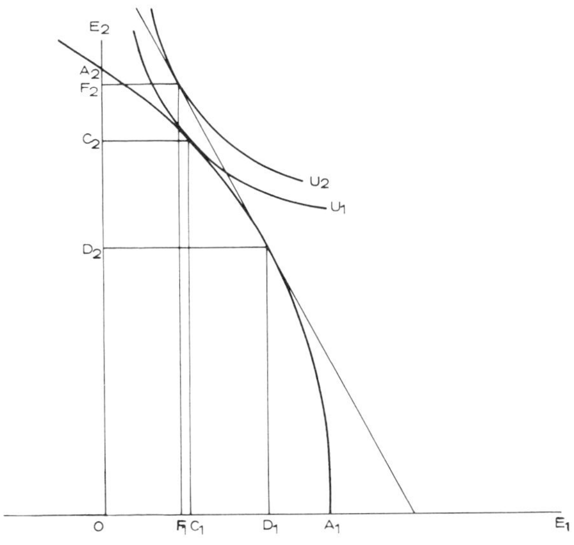

Figure 7.9 Real and Financial Investment Opportunities: Unit X – Relative Preference for Future Consumption

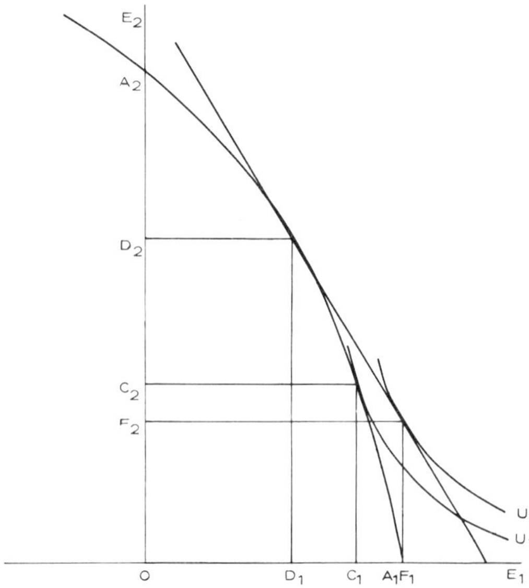

Figure 7.10 Real and Financial Investment Opportunities: Unit Y – Relative Preference for Present Consumption

With a financial market:

investment = A_1D_1
lending = D_1F_1
present consumption[1] = OF_1
future consumption = $OF_2 = A_1D_1(1+a) + D_1F_1(1+r)$, with $a > r$.

So with preferences strongly weighted towards future consumption, and no financing constraint, we should expect investment to be *reduced*. This is because in the absence of financial markets investment will continue at low marginal returns. The introduction of financial markets enables a higher return to be gained on the marginal pound so that investment will not proceed beyond the point where $e = r$. There is no reason why this investor should accept a return below r since he can lend his money at this rate.

The second example (Figure 7.10) illustrates the opposite

case; here unit Y is assumed to have a relative preference for present consumption.

Without a financial market:

investment $= A_1C_1$
present consumption $= OC_1$
future consumption $= OC_2 = A_1C_1(1+a)$

With a financial market:

investment $= A_1D_1$
borrowing $= D_1F_1$
present consumption[1] $= OF_1$
future consumption $= OF_2 = OD_2 - D_2F_2$, where $OD_2 = A_1D_1(1+a)$ and $D_2F_2 = D_1F_1(1+r)$, with $a > r$.

Therefore, when preferences are strongly weighted towards present consumption we should actually expect investment as well as present consumption to be increased. In this case borrowing takes place to finance both investment and consumption at the expense of future consumption.

It is therefore quite possible, in such a perfect world without any prior financial constraints, for the quantity of real investment to be reduced as a result of the introduction of a financial market. Such a general conclusion would, however, be misleading in that it fails to take account of a crucial aspect of financial markets – the lifting of financial constraints. However, even the present examples illustrate an unambiguous increase in welfare in the economy, with both units being able to get on to higher indifference curves. Before introducing financial constraints on investment possibilities, it is instructive to recapitulate on the welfare gains resulting from the existence of financial markets *and* productive opportunities.

In Figure 7.11 the economic unit is assumed to have an income of OA_1. In the absence of any productive opportunities but with financial markets the unit's future income possibilities are restricted to A_1A_3, resulting in a much lower utility level than can be achieved given actual productive possibilities.

Maximum welfare with financial markets only is at B_1, while welfare level B_2 is attainable when only the possibility of real investment exists. However, for the same initial income and

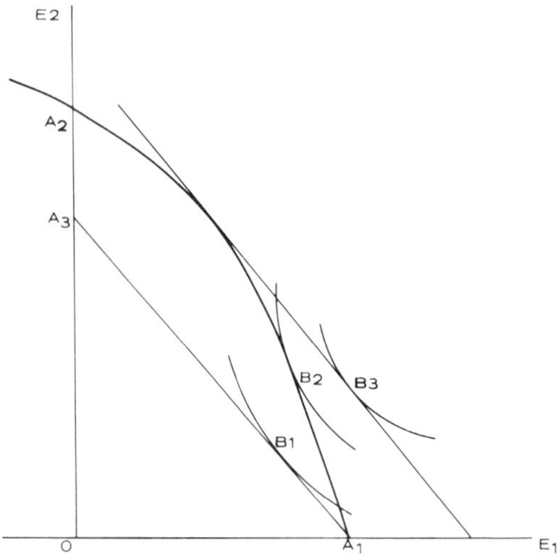

Figure 7.11 Welfare Gains from Productive Opportunities

both financial and real investment opportunities the welfare level B_3 may be achieved.

In such a model each economic unit will generally hold three different types of asset/liability: cash for transactions purposes, real assets and a private debt instrument.

Having demonstrated that financial markets have an important role to play even when no financial constraints exist, it is now time to admit such constraints into the analysis. In general it seems reasonable to assume that entrepreneurial members of society, the innovators or risk-takers, will not also be those with vast current incomes. And it is exactly because the potential savers are different from the potential investors that financial markets will be important in increasing the quantity of investment. We may also suppose that the production-possibility frontier is steeper for the innovator than for the saver, precisely because entrepreneurial ability is not evenly distributed between units.

Suppose we have the situation depicted in Figure 7.12, where the economic unit's investment is constrained at a high marginal return through lack of currently available funds. We

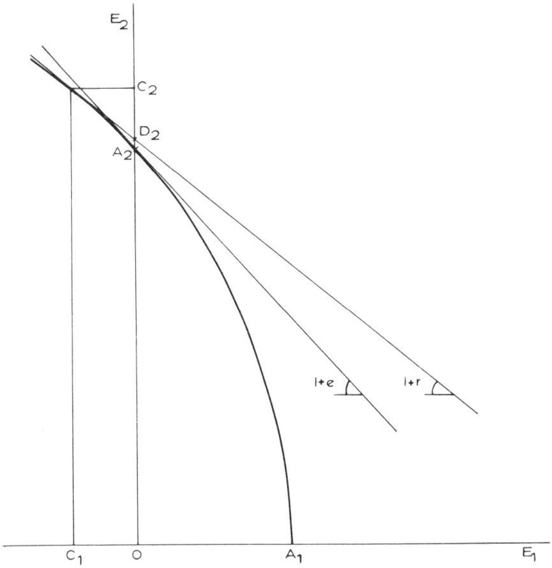

Figure 7.12 Increasing Investment by Removing a Financing Constraint

assume that this economic unit has a current income of OA_1, so that the maximum he can invest is OA_1, to give a future income of OA_2. Assume, however, that in the absence of financial constraints he is prepared to invest almost to the point where the marginal return is reduced to zero. The introduction of a financial market, with $r < e$, will enable this economic unit to borrow money in the present and expand its real investment. The constraint imposed by current income is thereby removed.

Without a financial market:

investment $= OA_1$
present consumption = nil
future consumption $= OA_2 = OA_1(1+a)$

With a financial market:

investment $= C_1A_1$
borrowing $= OC_1$
present consumption = nil
future consumption $= OD_2 = OC_2 - D_2C_2$ where

$OC_2 = A_1C_1(1+a)$ and $D_2C_2 = OC_1(1+r)$, with $a > r$.

The existence of financial markets enables money to be channelled to more productive and more satisfying uses than when expenditures are limited to current income or accumulated saving. In addition investment will be increased to the extent that the ability to borrow removes a constraint on available financial resources.[2]

The gain in efficiency is somewhat similar to the gains to be made when money is introduced into a barter economy. In both cases the necessity for the existence of a dual coincidence of wants has been removed. In the barter-economy situation it no longer becomes necessary for the person wishing to buy something to be able to make or obtain the particular commodity desired by the partner in the exchange. The acts of buying and selling are separated and facilitated through the intermediation of money.

The existence of financial markets means that the ability to take advantage of profitable opportunities (defined broadly to include the services of capital assets, e.g. houses) is separated from the need to finance such expenditures out of current income. The existence of financial intermediaries takes the process much further, and by more closely matching the individual needs of the borrowers and lenders facilitates an improved flow of finance from surplus to deficit units. This will be considered in Chapter 8.

Summary of Financial Relationships

Finance flows from the surplus units to deficit units and the government provides the currency required for current transactions purposes. These relationships are summarised in Figure 7.13, which illustrates the balance-sheet and flow-of-funds position for each type of unit.

The arrows show the relationship existing between holdings of financial claims, and it is not necessary for there to be flows in these directions in each period. For example, the government need not add to the currency stock in each period if the volume of transactions is not growing. We are, however, assuming in this simple presentation that history repeats itself, that the

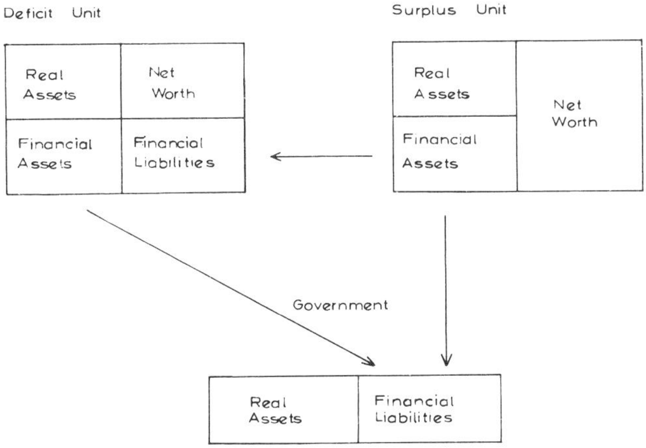

Figure 7.13 Flow-of-funds and Balance-sheet Positions without Financial Intermediaries[3]

stock and flow relationships between surplus and deficit units remains in the same direction, i.e. once a surplus (deficit) unit always a surplus (deficit) unit. This need not necessarily be true. An economic unit currently in surplus and lending could also have accumulated debts; or, since we are aggregating over types of unit, some currently surplus units could still have liabilities incurred in the past.

The deficit units will generally be characterised by large holdings of real assets and with financial liabilities in excess of financial assets. The typical surplus unit will have financial assets well in excess of financial liabilities (in this case assumed to be zero), and generally a high net worth. This means that deficit units have balance-sheets very similar to business firms, while that for surplus units is representative of the household sector. This is not to suggest that business firms never lend or that households never borrow, but that their *net* positions follow this pattern.

Figure 7.13 illustrates the point that has been central to this section: that the existence of financial markets enables the process of investment to be separated from the process of saving. This is critically important to the development of an advanced industrial society.[4] However, borrowers and lenders generally desire certain characteristics in the debts they issue or hold which in the absence of financial intermediaries will tend to be irreconcilable. This would indicate that welfare and efficiency should therefore be further improved, and the growth rate increased, through the introduction of financial intermediaries, and it is to this topic that we now turn.

8. FINANCIAL INTERMEDIATION

In this section we turn to consider financial intermediaries, the part they play in the transmission of funds, and how thereby they contribute to the growth and prosperity of the economy. Apart from examining the importance of financial intermediation for the rest of the economy, we shall also briefly consider the portfolio composition and operation of the financial institutions. This is a considerable subject covering a wide area, and the discussion must necessarily be severely compressed. The aim is not to provide a detailed rundown of the institutional structure; this has been done elsewhere (see Revell, 1973). Rather, the intention is to consider the basic significance of financial intermediation for the economy in general, and the general behavioural principles governing the intermediaries' portfolio options.

The Role of Financial Intermediaries

In order to understand the importance of financial intermediaries, it is necessary to consider the various financial requirements of borrowers and lenders. In both cases the need for security predominates, but the achievement of the same aim on each side of the transaction will tend to be impossible in the absence of financial intermediaries.[1]

Borrowers. It is assumed that the representative deficit unit wishes to borrow to finance the purchase of durable capital goods yielding a flow of services into the future. The most obvious example is productive investment, but the purchase of a house or flat is an equally good example. The unit will therefore generally wish to borrow a relatively large amount, for a reasonably long period, at as low a rate of interest as possible.

Lenders. Lending is considered to be typically out of current saving. People (and institutions) save in order to provide for the future – about which there is some uncertainty. They wish (i) to ensure a regular flow of income for themselves and their dependants in the future – this they do by accumulating savings in the present and by insurance; and (ii) to be able to take advantage of profitable opportunities, or have a reserve to meet any unforeseen contingencies. These objectives will require the spreading of risk and the maintenance of a fair degree of liquidity. In addition much saving will be done in small amounts.

This division should not be taken to suggest that in reality borrowers and lenders form two separate, compartmentalised, groups. The presentation is adopted simply to emphasise the desired characteristics of any financial claim from each side of the transaction. An economic unit might well engage in both borrowing and lending, and will have these different preferences depending upon which type of transaction is involved. We might suppose a representative individual who will borrow a large capital sum in order to purchase a house, who will insure his life and property, and who will also lend money to a bank or building society. In each of these activities he will desire certain of the characteristics that have been described. There is no single transaction which is likely to achieve all of the individual's objectives, and without the benefit of intermediaries the reconciliation of these desires will be difficult, if not impossible, to achieve. It can only be by chance that potential deficit and surplus units will meet and agree terms acceptable to both of them.

The existence of financial intermediaries can be justified in terms of the three main functions they perform, thereby providing an at least partial reconciliation of these divergent requirements.

(1) They collect the small savings of the surplus units and parcel them up into larger packages for the deficit units. An alternative way of thinking about this would be the breaking down of large loans into smaller parcels more acceptable to the surplus units. This is a basic function of all financial intermediaries.

In performing this role an intermediary can greatly reduce transactions costs by taking advantage of economies of scale in the collection of information and portfolio management. By lending through the intermediary the individual can obtain the benefits of reduced risk available from portfolio diversification (see Chapter 6). This will be the case even if the time scale of the borrowing and lending remains unaltered, i.e. there is no gain in liquidity to the lender. It will be very difficult for a surplus unit with only a small amount of money to lend to be able to diversify this investment, and then only at a high cost. The financial intermediary with control over much larger resources, and much greater information, will be able to diversify its lending at a greatly reduced marginal cost.

(2) They provide insurance services. An insurance company can insure against individual risks while matching its assets to the actuarial expectation of its contingent liabilities. All this means is that, while certain specific events cannot be known about, the population of such events may be perfectly predictable. For example, it is not possible to predict who will die in any one year (assuming no direct involvement) but it is fairly easy to estimate approximately the total number of deaths. Once an outcome becomes predictable, it becomes insurable (the principle is identical to the reduction of risk in a diversified portfolio). It is, however, worth emphasising that risk is only reduced if the events are independent. Moreover, while the pooling of risks will reduce the chance of extreme loss, some loss will become almost certain – and this will have to be paid for.

The importance of insurance comes from the fact that although catastrophic events like early death, fire, etc., have only a remote chance of occurring, when they do the effect is devastating. Those left behind are likely to be suddenly and dramatically worse off, so although the statistical probability of such events may be very low, they will generally be disproportionately weighted in the individual's utility function. This type of behaviour conforms to Shackle's (1955) view that because of general uncertainty people cannot assign fixed probabilities to all possible outcomes but wish instead to avoid the worst possibilities. Losses carry a greater weight in their utility function than do gains.

One way of offsetting the more extreme possibilities is to accept a lower mean income in the present, and spend the difference on providing insurance against such events. In addition an individual may wish to maintain his level of income after retirement, and this, too, must be at the expense of a lower mean current income. It is in meeting this need that pension funds have come to play an increasingly important role.

It is worth considering in somewhat greater detail the way in which the pooling of risks reduces the possibility of individual loss. Suppose that the risk of any individual's house burning down is 10 per cent and that the market value of that house, and all houses, is £10,000. The expected value of the house is, therefore, only £9000, with an expected loss of £1000. The standard deviation, σ, of such a binomial distribution is given by

$$\sigma = \sqrt{npq} \tag{8.1}$$

where n = the number of houses, p = the probability of them burning down, and $q = 1 - p$ is the probability of them not burning down. In this case

$$\sigma = \sqrt{1 \times 0.1 \times 0.9} = 0.3$$

which in monetary terms means that there is an expected deviation of £3000, i.e. 30 per cent of £10,000, around the expected value of £9000.

However, that does not really represent the actual possible outcomes facing the individual. He will either end up with a house worth £10,000 or nothing at all. If a number of households come together in order to pool the risk, the total risk will rise as n rises, but the *average* risk, σ/n, will become much smaller:

$$\frac{\sigma}{n} = \frac{\sqrt{npq}}{n} \tag{8.2}$$

This is illustrated in Figure 8.1.

Average risk is reduced by the pooling of risks, but some risks become more and more certain as the numbers rise. So for twenty-five individuals the average risk of loss due to their houses burning down is reduced from 30 per cent to 6 per cent.

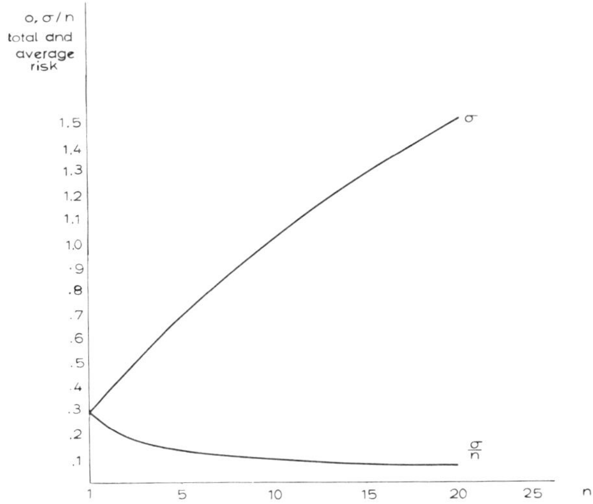

Figure 8.1 Relationship between Total and Average Risk

But more important still is that this can now be treated as a statistical probability. By being prepared to accept almost certain losses ranging from £1060 to £940, the house-owners can eliminate the possibility of complete loss with which they were previously faced. While the actual risks involved may have been somewhat exaggerated in this simple example, the gains resulting from risk insurance are clear.

In performing their insurance function, insurance companies and pension funds also provide in the process longer-term finance to industry. This group of financial institutions are the major holders of equity debt. Since 1945 the personal sector has steadily run down its equity holdings, and this has been substantially taken up by the insurance companies and pension funds.

(3) The archetypal function of financial institutions is concerned with changing the form, the *transmutation*, of the financial claims flowing from borrowers to lenders. Consequently the performance of this function is generally referred to as the 'transmutation effect' of financial intermediaries. This they do in order to match more closely the needs and desires of the separate surplus and deficit units.

By providing more liquid (in some cases, e.g. banks, highly liquid) assets for the surplus unit to hold, they are able to attract very small, temporary, savings which would otherwise not be available for investment. The liquidity is provided once more by the effect of pooling the savings, and obtaining funds from a large number of largely independent sources. This advantage will accrue to all popular deposit-taking institutions, e.g. building societies. Banks, however, have an additional advantage, particularly if they are very large, few in number, and operate over a wide area. This derives from the use of chequeing accounts as money in order to make final payment. A deposit withdrawn to make a payment is very likely to be deposited back in a bank. Even if the deposit is not returned to the same bank, the existence of a small number of large banks of approximately similar size, and covering the same area, means that gains and losses are likely on average to net out. This implies that there will be fairly high negative covariance between at least some deposits; and negative covariance greatly reduces risk (see Chapter 6) and therefore improves liquidity.[2]

It is perhaps worth while emphasising the structure of trust upon which this liquidity is based. Banks are only able to provide perfect liquidity because of their expectation that deposits withdrawn will be fairly quickly returned. On the other hand, depositors only hold transactions balances with the banks because they expect cheques drawn on these accounts to be settled immediately. The provision of liquidity depends upon an act of faith in the behaviour of other individuals and institutions in the economy. If these expectations were to change suddenly, liquidity would disappear. In order, therefore, to maintain trust in the system some form of liquid reserves will be required as well as a lender of last-resort facilities.

Because of the way in which expectations can change and decisions become interdependent, stability is required at all points in the system. This can only be assured if fairly close *prudential* control is observed over all institutions in the market. The success of each individual institution depends, in part, upon maintaining the stability of the whole system, and the stability of the system depends upon maintaining the stability of each separate institution.

The Effect of Financial Intermediation on the Level of Capital Accumulation

We have already seen that the existence of financial markets results in an increase in the welfare of society by enabling borrowing and lending to take place. Also, by removing the necessity for all expenditures to be self-financed, out of current or accumulated income, the level of investment, and thereby the wealth of the community, should be increased. The question we now turn to concerns the way in which financial intermediation may further increase investment and wealth. This is done by considering the costs (so far ignored) involved in transmitting funds from surplus to deficit units.

The model we shall develop in order to demonstrate the advantages of intermediation is based upon the particular characteristics of financial markets and the preferences of both deficit and surplus units. The objective is to understand the process involved, and in particular the role played by financial intermediaries in the development of an economy. The argument is presented in terms of the costs involved in financing investment, and this clearly illustrates the likely gains resulting from financial intermediation.

The costs of obtaining finance can be usefully divided into two separate categories:

(i) the costs of internal finance – out of current and past income; and
(ii) the costs of external finance – borrowing.

These are now considered in turn.

Costs of internal finance (C.I.F.)

These costs are essentially those involved in waiting, the postponement of investment. Some finance will be available as a result of waiting. By forgoing present consumption an economic unit may be able to accumulate the finance to pay for investment. The costs involved are the objective costs of missed investment opportunities and lower productivity relative to more modern production methods; and subjective in the sense of frustration resulting from being unable to invest as and when desired. These costs will rise with the quantity of finance required: the more that is required, the longer the waiting period; and the longer the postponement, the greater the cost.

We can therefore plot a cost schedule for internally financed investment (see Figure 8.2). *This must set the maximum cost that any economic unit will be prepared to pay for its finance*. We cannot expect it to pay more to another unit than the cost of providing the funds itself. This naturally represents the cost of finance in the absence of financial markets.

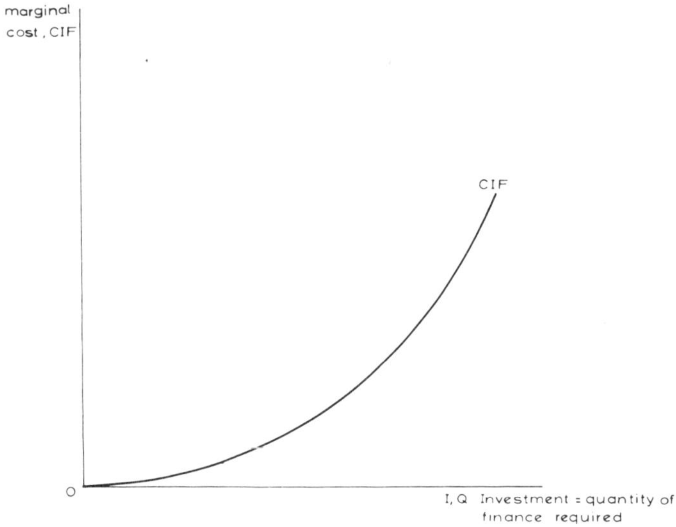

Figure 8.2 Costs of Internal Finance

This in effect provides us with a supply schedule for funds. If we restrict the analysis to investment in real productive capital, the demand function will be determined by the production possibilities available. It gives the marginal return, R, resulting from any given quantity of investment, and is represented by the *D* schedule in Figure 8.3. Of course, as investment increases the stock of capital this will have the effect (*ceteris paribus*) of depressing current investment demand. No attempt has been made to include this feedback from investment to the demand curve. We can either interpret the model as illustrating the differences that the availability of finance makes to the investment outcome *at any particular point in time*; or, alternatively, we can take a longer-term view but assume that such depressing forces are offset by the development of technology. It would anyway be strange to ignore the advancement of technology since we are interested in the role that finance plays in development, and a major force behind development and growth must surely be technological development. Equilibrium is established at *B* with cost *Oa* and quantity of investment financed internally *OA*.

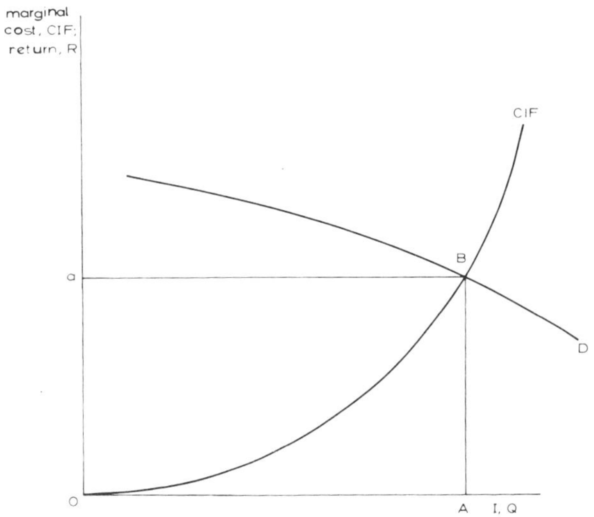

Figure 8.3 Demand for and Supply of Finance

Costs of external finance (C.E.F.)

The alternative to waiting to accumulate savings is to borrow the money, and this will entail costs of a different kind. These schedules can be drawn relative to the C.I.F. curve (see Figure 8.4). They show the quantity of *additional* finance available for a particular market structure and at any given cost.

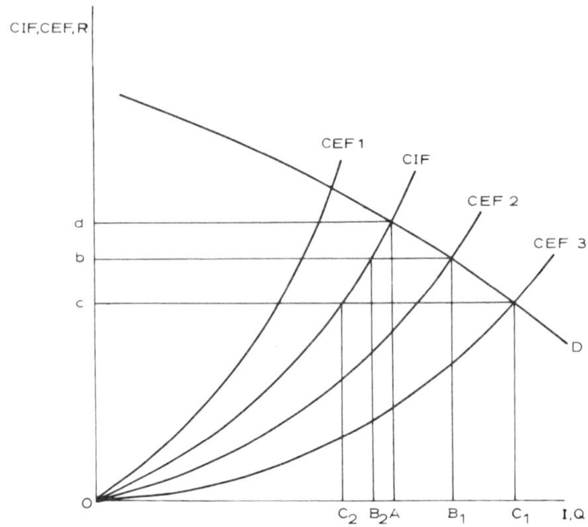

Figure 8.4 The Effects of Financial Intermediation on the Cost and Availability of Finance

The costs of borrowing will also rise with the quantity of finance required, and are related to the search needed to locate potential lenders, the persuasion needed to get them to actually lend, and the return they require to offset the risk and loss of liquidity involved. These costs will depend upon the financial structure in existence. A number of C.E.F.curves can therefore be drawn relative to the C.I.F. curve, each depending upon the actual financial system operating. These can be ranked bearing in mind what has been said above regarding the requirements of borrowers and lenders, and the role played by financial intermediaries.

(C.E.F. 1). This is the most costly system in which to obtain external funds, the case where there are no financial intermediaries or secondary markets for securities. In this situation the ultimate borrower, user, of the funds has to locate potential lenders himself. This could be an expensive operation both in terms of time and money; and even if he locates possible sources of funds, he may be unable to negotiate acceptable terms. It is likely that lenders will only have small amounts to lend, or even if they have access to large-scale funds, they may not wish to lend them to a single enterprise. Potential lenders will be interested in the liquidity of the liability they accept as an asset, as well as its return, and in the absence of markets for trading second-hand securities this must be guaranteed exclusively by the deficit unit. This will be difficult, and generally impossible, to do given a long-run commitment of funds.

The conflicts between borrowers and lenders will loom large in any such transactions, and the costs may well in many, if not most, cases exceed those of waiting and accumulating internally generated funds.

(C.E.F. 2). Finance will become easier to obtain with the introduction of secondary markets for securities – for example the stock exchange as a market for second-hand equities. In this case finance can be provided without the surplus unit commiting its funds permanently. Given the continued profitable operation of the firm, the surplus unit will be able to withdraw its money at the going price – as long, that is, as its equity holding does not form too large a proportion of the total outstanding. Ultimately the liquidity, and value, of the equity, or debt, depends upon the viability of the deficit unit, but now other market forces will also be important, and, most importantly, the ability to repay upon demand may cease to be a dominant consideration. Such secondary markets are only likely to exist for the debt issue of large, respectable, borrowers, e.g. large industrial firms and the government, the debt generally being held by the more wealthy surplus units. But even given these limitations the cost of finance should be reduced and availability improved.

(C.E.F. 3). The introduction of financial intermediaries will greatly reduce the costs of finance. The large-scale operations will be more efficiently handled by professional managers, and security will be improved. The assets of the surplus units will be more liquid, while lending to the deficit units can represent a fairly long-run commitment. As a result the large-scale savers will probably lend more, and more importantly, small-scale savings will be attracted into productive use. By more closely matching the portfolio requirements of the various borrowers and lenders, the financial intermediaries greatly improve the conditions under which finance is made available.

The introduction and profitable operation of a new financial intermediary may generally be interpreted as the provision of a service more efficiently than had been done previously, or even providing a service that had not existed before. This should therefore result in an increase in the availability of finance and a reduction in its cost.

This schematic presentation may be summarised in Figure 8.4 with the C.E.F. lines showing the additional funds available at each cost.

Oa and *OA* are the same as for Figure 8.3, and represent the cost and quantity of finance in the absence of financial markets. To be strictly accurate, the existence of financial markets should shift the schedule for internal finance to the right. Savings can now earn a return, and this will reduce the length of time required to accumulate any given amount. This complication is ignored for the purposes of the present exposition.

The introduction of a secondary market for financial securities will result in a number of changes. In the new system:

Ob = cost of finance
OB_1 = total investment = total finance
OB_2 = internal finance
$B_1 B_2$ = external finance

The addition of financial intermediaries, thereby changing the characteristics of financial claims, will result in a further expansion of investment and finance, e.g.

Oc = cost of finance
OC_1 = total investment = total finance
OC_2 = internal finance
$C_1 C_2$ = external finance

It is therefore possible to see how the introduction of financial intermediation will reduce the cost of finance and increase the quantity of finance and investment. The more sophisticated the form of financial intermediation, i.e. the greater the variety of different requirements catered for, and the more efficiently the business is conducted, the more the C.E.F. schedule will shift to the right, i.e. the greater the reduction in cost and the increase in quantity.

Financial markets and institutions come into existence in response to pressures resulting from deficiencies in the existing structure. The development of an economy requires and generates a complex set of demands for, and potential supplies of, finance. It should not be possible to describe the process of economic development without first understanding the underlying financial structure that facilitates and motivates this development. This is a continuing process; it does not come to an end at any particular stage but continues to change with the development process. It is a mistake to ignore financial institutions when considering either the development of industrial economies, or the present structure of the so-called 'advanced' countries.

It also needs to be recognised that the financial institutions existing at any one time reflect the history and traditions of the countries within which they operate. We should not expect all institutional arrangements to be identical throughout the world, or think that the adoption of foreign practice would result in the same system. The principle, however, will be the same. As outlined here, financial institutions will develop in response to pressures made apparent through the market. If there is no demand for the service of the intermediary, then it will not come into existence. It seems likely that the development of financial institutions and markets will play a more important role in facilitating economic growth than any other financial variable, e.g. interest rates or the money supply. Indeed, the model outlined here indicates that the development of financial institutions is intimately tied to the expansion of the economy.

Financial Structure of Financial Intermediaries

In addition to examining the financial structure of the main intermediaries existing at any one time it is also worth while identifying the historical development of such institutions. A historical perspective is to some extent required in order to understand the present institutional structure. We are particularly concerned here with the institutions as they exist in the United Kingdom, but although there will be differences in detail the broad principles of operation are widely applicable.

Left to natural evolution the earliest type of institution likely to develop is the *bank*, in historical terms providing secure depositories for holders of precious metals, and developing into general deposit-taking institutions enabling efficient means for payment. Other forms of banking institution that develop at an early stage of the industrialisation process include the merchant banks and accepting houses, which facilitate trade by 'accepting' bills of exchange and marketing securities.

This latter section of the banking system has recently developed further in many of the more advanced industrial countries, often operating in international financial markets, e.g. the euro-dollar market. These institutions take deposits of large amounts and for reasonably long periods, three months or more. They are sometimes referred to as 'wholesale' banks, as opposed to the 'retail' banking system, which provides a means of payment mechanism.

While it is possible to distinguish clearly between these two types of business, and some economists have argued for the benefits of keeping them separate, there does seem to be a movement towards combining the two operations; this may be thought of as an improvement in economies of scale rather than in economies of specialisation. In particular, the clearing banks, the main retail banks in the United Kingdom, now offer differential rates for large-scale deposits. This has been a noticeable development in the United Kingdom since 1971, after the introduction of a new, more competitive structure for the banking sector.[3]

Within the banking sector the discount, or money, market plays a privileged, and unique, role. The discount market consists mainly of the discount houses, and we shall continue by assuming that the two are the same. The origins of the discount market lie in the days before the development of the large commercial banks, with their country-wide operations. At the time of the industrial revolution the discount market provided an essential link between the regional banks in the surplus agricultural areas and the deficit industrial areas. And the importance of the discount houses still reflects their role as bankers to the banks. Money placed at call with the discount houses by the banks is counted as a reserve asset, and this is an important mechanism through which the banks convert any excess cash into earning assets. On the other hand, when the banks are short of cash this is obtained by calling in money from the discount market. If liquidity is tight, then the discount market will be forced to seek assistance from the Bank of England by rediscounting eligible bills. This crucial 'lender of last-resort' facility is mainly operated through the discount market.

In the late 1970s practically 90 per cent of the discount houses' borrowed funds came from the banking sector, and was generally repayable on demand. The unique position of the discount houses between the banks and the Bank of England undoubtedly results in a demand for a high degree of liquidity. In addition, because the financial stability of the discount houses is central to maintaining stability of the banking sector, and the financial system in general, there is an official requirement that they maintain an extremely liquid portfolio.[4]

Liquidity is also important to the clearing banks, whose current accounts are repayable upon demand and serve as the major means of payment. The extension of the clearing banks into the wholesale deposit market, and the greater matching of assets with liabilities, has probably reduced to some extent their desired reserve holdings. However, the confidence factor associated with the use of bank accounts as a means of payment does require these banks to pay high regard to the need to meet all claims, and consequently to regard adequate liquidity as an essential requirement. And because of the high social costs of bank failure the banks are required to hold a given proportion ($12\frac{1}{2}$ per cent from September 1971) of their deposit liabilities in the form of designated reserve assets.[5] These prudential requirements are often confused with the use of reserve ratios for the purpose of control. It is possible that without an imposed reserve requirement the actual liquidity of the banking sector would be reduced, but this is not obvious.

The majority of the wholesale banking conducted by the non-clearing banks[6] is conducted with overseas residents and in foreign currencies. These operations are characterised by a high degree of matching of the portfolio, i.e. the banks tend to acquire assets of the same maturity as their liabilities and in the same currency. This matching of liabilities reduces the need for reserves, and prior to 1971 the non-clearing banks were not subject to any formal reserve requirements. In 1971 this was changed and the $12\frac{1}{2}$ per cent reserve ratio that was introduced, applied to all banks. Up to this time the majority of non-clearing bank liquidity was provided by clearing bank deposits plus short-term local authority liabilities. In certain cases it is possible that the quantity of liquid assets held has changed, though in general the ratio was always quite high; however, the composition has changed. In particular this change in reserve requirements has increased the significance of the discount market for this section of the banking system.

The United Kingdom has the most complicated banking system in the world. Traditionalists consider it to be the most advanced, while other more radical economists consider it to be an anachronism which is out of place in this more enlightened age. The main dispute centres round the operation of the discount houses, which stand as a buffer between the private banks and the central bank, either introducing flexibility into the system, or complicating the structure to an unreasonable degree, depending on one's view. Those in favour of abolishing the privileged role of the discount market favour a simpler, more direct relationship between the private banks and the central bank, reducing the number of eligible reserve assets, and adopting a cash-base system similar to that operated in West Germany or the United States.

Another important early development in any industrial market economy is the *stock market*. Its importance will to some extent depend upon the activities of the financial institutions. In the United Kingdom, where the banks have traditionally not provided longer-term finance to industry, it was a more important development than in West Germany or Japan, where the banks have been far more directly involved. But in both cases the stock exchange serves an indispensable role in providing a market for the sale of second-hand securities.

Life insurance companies and pension funds take care of the

longer-term interests of individuals for security. Essentially they borrow money from the insured person, on a contractual basis, generally guaranteeing some minimum return on the money, and payment in full in the event of certain eventualities, e.g. death, disablement, or retirement. The liabilities of the insurance companies are therefore highly illiquid, though a policy will often be accepted as collateral for a loan from another intermediary. General (non-life) insurance really provides a service rather than financial intermediation, and general insurance policies do not constitute a financial claim in the same way that life policies do. However, the business does result in a build-up of funds available for investment in financial assets.

The balance-sheet for the insurance companies and pension funds contains little that is identifiable as liquid assets. The majority of their funds are held in the form of highly illiquid assets having potentially very variable capital values but stable income flows.

The balance-sheet of unit and investment trusts is also orientated towards the longer end of the asset and liability spectrum. The objective is to provide investors with the benefits of expert portfolio management and a diversified portfolio much more cheaply than they could obtain acting individually.

The desire of individuals to own their own homes has in most industrialised countries resulted in the development of specialised institutions to provide the finance. In the United Kingdom this function is performed by the building societies, and in the United States by the Savings and Loan Associations and Mutual Savings Banks. In all cases the funds are predominantly supplied to the institutions in the form of short-term deposits or shares[7] – often liable to immediate withdrawal. These institutions are generally considered to be providing a valuable social service, and consequently enjoy certain tax advantages over other financial or industrial organisations. For example, interest on building society shares and deposits are paid net of the standard rate of tax, whereas the societies are only required to pay tax on these payments at a 'composite' rate which is somewhat less than the standard rate of tax. Their competitive advantage is further improved by the fact that as non-profit-making organisations they are not required to pay dividends over and above the interest paid on their shares and deposits. Also, borrowers from building societies are entitled to tax relief on their mortgage interest payments (up to a certain limit), thereby reducing the real cost of such borrowing.

The building society provides a good example of a specialised lending institution, and there would appear to be a pronounced imbalance between the two sides of the balance-sheet. Mortgages are a very illiquid form of lending, and shares and deposits are a highly liquid form of borrowing. Also, a large proportion of the other investments of the building societies are illiquid.

What explanations can be put forward to justify this behaviour? The traditional stability of these institutions may be some part of an explanation, as may also be the excellent security for the loan provided by the property, particularly in inflationary times. But these do not provide a complete or satisfactory explanation, and depend critically on economic conditions continuing as over the recent past. Of more importance are the large payments of capital and interest accruing to the building societies each period. These provide a regular and reliable source of funds from which to meet short-term liquidity problems. This is a very important point often overlooked in economic analysis. The expected cash flow of an individual or institution (not necessarily a building society) provides a major liquid asset which should be taken into account when making any portfolio decision.

A more recent development is the hire-purchase company in the United Kingdom, or the credit union in the United States. These institutions have developed in response to the growth of mass-produced durable goods. The availability of a wide range of durable goods, e.g. cars, televisions, washing-machines, etc., to the majority of the population created a need for finance. People do not want to have to save the total cost of the commodity before enjoying the benefit of its services. In many cases it seems more desirable to pay for the commodity while at the same time enjoying the flow of services resulting from its possession. The principle is exactly the same as with house ownership. In this case the credit or finance companies grew up in order to provide the finance.

High specialisation in lending is also observed in the case of the finance houses. On the face of it there would appear to be an imbalance between the asset and liability sides, the majority of funds being made available through deposits. In fact these deposits are not withdrawable on demand, and the majority of funds are in fact supplied from the financial and non-financial company sectors. Moreover, the close connection existing between the banks and finance houses increases the security of their overdraft borrowing.

An additional form of institution is that encouraged (or even run) by the government to supply medium- to long-term finance to industry. This is often seen as an area in which the private sector does not perform adequately. In the United Kingdom such organisations include the National Enterprise Board, Finance for Industry Limited, and, since 1976, Equity Capital for Industry Limited.

Here we have just given some indication of the variety of financial institutions that are likely to exist in any advanced industrial country, and the economic circumstances that gave them birth and nourished their growth. While it is possible to identify particular types of activity and reasons why they might be conducted by different institutions, the degree of separation varies between countries and over time. In this connection government legislation is particularly important. For example, the imposition of extensive controls on commercial banking activities in the United Kingdom in the 1960s resulted in banks creating and purchasing other institutions to carry out certain types of business. It is doubtful whether quite this degree of differentiation would have been observed without these controls. This is supported by the movement in the 1970s towards a more conglomerate banking system, offering a more comprehensive range of financial services. Tax laws will also be important in this respect, as we have already seen with regard to the operation of the building societies.

We have seen above that the actual form of activity undertaken by the financial intermediaries is an important determinant of their asset portfolios. In summary it is worth emphasising the main determinants of liquid asset holdings.

The main requirement for liquidity will be determined by uncertainty regarding the possibility of withdrawals from the intermediary, relative to the expected flow of new deposits, and the predetermined income flow from repayments of capital and interest. If the likelihood of sudden withdrawals is high, then the means to meet these demands must be available. The most vulnerable institutions are naturally those accepting deposits withdrawable upon demand; and the prime example is the commercial banks. Perfectly liquid assets will be cash and rediscountable bills in the case of the banking system, but including also bank deposits for the non-bank intermediaries.

As well as short-term variability in the inflow and outflow of funds requiring highly liquid cash reserves, there are also medium-term factors which must be insured against. For example, conditions in other markets may spill over into the intermediary's own market. The state of the economy, the stability of other intermediaries or commercial firms, etc., will therefore be important. For these reasons a higher echelon of slightly less liquid and higher-yielding assets will be held, a sort of contingency reserve of assets which can be quickly converted into cash at approximately their full capital value. These semi-liquid assets will include such things as bills and short bonds (i.e. bonds close to maturity), short-term deposits, etc.

Another factor determining liquidity requirements will be the ability, cost and ease of borrowing money at short notice to cover unforeseen circumstances. This ability is, however, likely to be tied to the past, and future expected, stability of the institution; and that will be very dependent upon preserving what is considered to be adequate liquidity. Financial intermediaries are likely to hold a spectrum of assets ranged by liquidity and yield, and the exact composition will depend upon the type of business they conduct, the liquidity of their liabilities to those holding them as assets, and the stability and size of their non-deposit cash-flow position.

Operation of Financial Intermediaries

In this section we shall briefly consider the operations of financial intermediaries in terms of the normal maximising behaviour of an individual firm. The fact that a financial intermediary is not concerned with the production of a physical commodity should not lead us to overlook the fact that as commercial enterprises they will still aim to achieve certain economic objectives. The most common assumption is that firms are profit maximisers. We may be required to amend this assumption in the real world, but that is true with respect to an examination of the behaviour of any firm.

Financial intermediaries are providing services, financial services in this case, in the same way as any other commercial enterprise; and in the same way their total operations can be examined within the general theory of the firm. The main difference is that the demand and supply schedules are more closely related than is the case for an industrial firm. The intermediary will both borrow and lend money in financial markets.

Let us start by considering a particular group of financial intermediaries offering a financial product that is in some way differentiable from any other, e.g. in terms of liquidity, benefits of availability of loans, insurance, etc. Assume that this 'industry' lends to the private sector[8] on a particular, fixed, type of contract. The demand schedule for loans facing this industry will depend upon many factors, for example the rate of interest charged compared with interest rates on other types of loans, any other terms or conditions associated with this loan as compared with the non-interest terms for other forms of borrowing, plus all other factors that will affect demand, e.g. tastes and preferences, general economic conditions, etc.

As with standard elementary demand analysis we shall concentrate on the relationship between quantity and price and assume that all other relevant variables are held constant. Given this assumption we can draw a demand curve for loans from this group of intermediaries where its elasticity will depend upon the price of this finance, i.e. the rate of interest charged, and the price and availability of substitute sources of finance. We may assume a normal downward-sloping demand curve, so that more finance is demanded at a lower price. A relative improvement in the non-interest terms on these loans will shift the demand curve up and to the right.

The supply curve of funds to the private sector will depend upon:

(i) the cost to intermediaries of borrowing funds (plus an allowance for the funds retained as part of a liquidity reserve);

(ii) the costs involved in intermediating between borrowers and lenders – operating costs (these are the costs of premises, equipment, labour, general running costs, costs of locating borrowers and lenders, and of minimising risks of default, e.g. checking security, taking out insurance, etc.); and

(iii) the costs of providing services to the borrowers or lenders, in addition to or in place of, interest-rate payments (for example, the provision of a payments mechanism by the commercial banks to holders of current-account deposits).

If we combine operating costs and service costs, these may be thought to follow the same pattern as for any productive enterprise. Average costs will initially fall, mainly due to the spreading of fixed costs, but also reflecting other economies of scale. After some point diminishing returns may be assumed to set in; one can imagine rising costs of locating borrowers and lenders, increasing costs of security, etc. This familiar cost pattern is depicted in Figure 8.5.

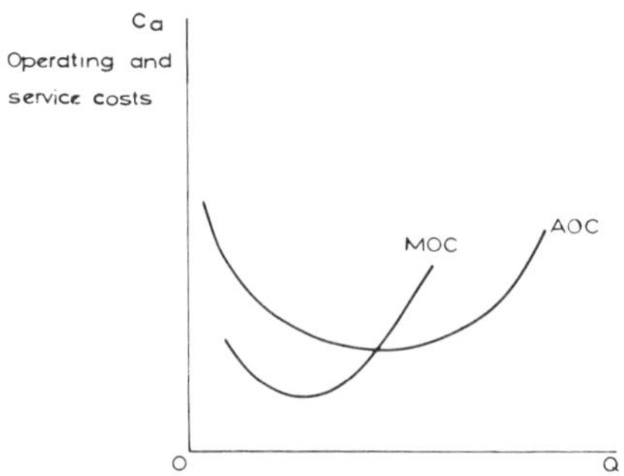

Figure 8.5 The Industry's Average Operating Cost, AOC, and Marginal Operating cost, MOC

The other cost is determined by the reward required by the rest of the private sector in order to lend money to this group of intermediaries. Again assuming that the industry borrows on a fixed contract, then we may imagine an upward-sloping supply curve of funds with respect to the interest rate offered. This private-sector supply curve will also be a function of alternative returns and liquidity/risk available, economic conditions, relative services offered, etc. In addition the cost schedule for the industry will be raised by the extent to which the intermediaries retain funds as part of their liquid reserves. For present purposes this 'cost' can be included as part of the interest payment due to lenders. For example, if 10 per cent of all borrowed money is retained in the form of non-interest-bearing reserves, then at an interest rate of 10 per cent the intermediaries have to earn 11.11 per cent just to cover the cost of holding these reserves. The actual cost schedule will therefore be 11.11 per cent above the original supply schedule. This cost schedule is given in Figure 8.6. Note that the average cost curve cuts the vertical axis. This illustrates the point that a surplus unit will generally require a positive return before it will lend any money. There is one possible exception: the services offered by a bank deposit, in terms of security and payments mechanism, may result in deposits at a zero, or even a negative, rate of interest.

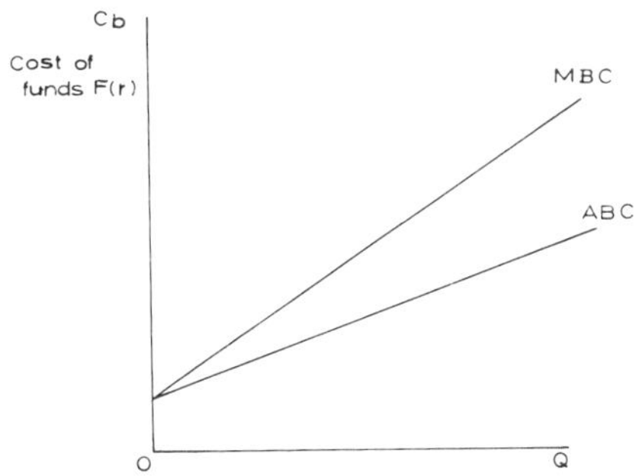

Figure 8.6 The Industry's Average Borrowing Cost, ABC, and Marginal Borrowing Cost, MBC

Figure 8.7 combines these two costs (a *vertical* summation of costs at each quantity) in order to give the total costs involved in the supply of any particular quantity of funds. It is interesting to observe that it is exactly this type of cost structure that Keynes (1936) argued set a floor to the rate of interest, rather than the concept of an infinite demand for liquidity as such – the 'liquidity trap'. Keynes (1936, p. 208) considered that 2–2½ per cent was the minimum long-term rate of interest

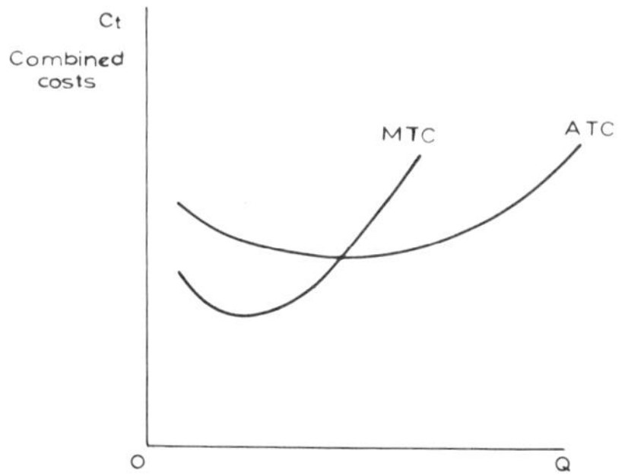

Figure 8.7 The Industry's Average Total Cost, ATC, and Marginal Total Cost, MTC

possible, set by 'the intermediate costs of bringing the borrower and ultimate lender together, and the allowances for risk, especially moral risk, which the lender requires over and above the pure rate of interest' (see also Keynes (1936, pp. 218–19) and Chapter 4).

Having obtained the cost structure we may now superimpose the average revenue curve, AR (demand curve), and the marginal revenue curve, MR, and determine the equilibrium cost and quantity of finance. This is done in Figure 8.8.

So far we have not specified the competitive structure of the industry, but this must be done before it is possible to say anything about market equilibrium. If the industry is composed of many small intermediaries and the conditions of perfect competition are met, then, under the assumption of profit maximisation, equilibrium will be established at A, where the marginal cost curve[9] cuts the demand curve, lending Oq_1 at interest rate Oc_1.

If the industry consists of a single intermediary, or of a small group acting together, it will be more relevant to suppose that equilibrium is established according to monopolistic behaviour – that is, given profit maximisation, lending that quantity of funds at which marginal cost equals marginal revenue, at a price determined by the average revenue curve at that point. In this case the quantity will be Oq_2 and price OC_2.

Although it is possible to identify different points of equilibrium according to the existing market structure, it does

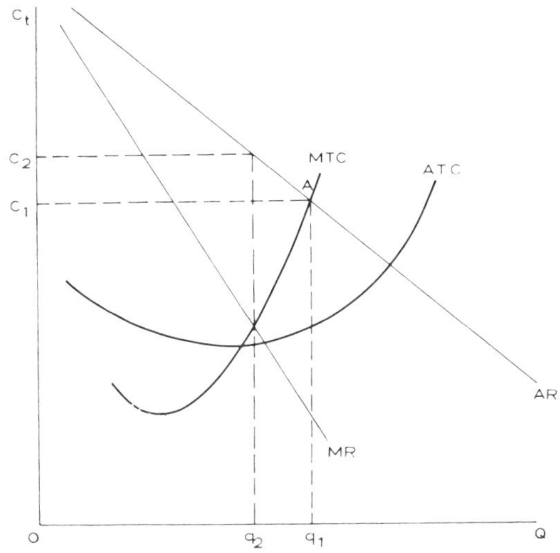

Figure 8.8 Market Equilibrium Price and Quantity

not follow from this that a perfectly competitive industry will lend more at a lower price. Before that would be valid we would require that the aggregate cost curves were identical for the two market structures, and that firms were indeed maximising profits. We shall not consider alternative market structures, but the model presented above can easily be adapted to deal with any industry structure or maximising behaviour required.

Before leaving this model it is useful to examine the effects of a general increase in uncertainty throughout the economy. Such a change will have fundamental effects on both the demand for and supply of funds.

The borrowers' demand curve will shift down as a result of increased uncertainty regarding their ability to repay loans. The supply of funds to the intermediary will be reduced, i.e. the price will rise, because of an increased desire for liquidity. This means that the cost curves will shift upwards and to the left. On top of this the intermediaries themselves are likely to desire greater liquidity, and this will increase the cost of supplying funds even more.

Such a change is shown in Figure 8.9, assuming a perfectly competitive industry. The dashed lines are the pre-change

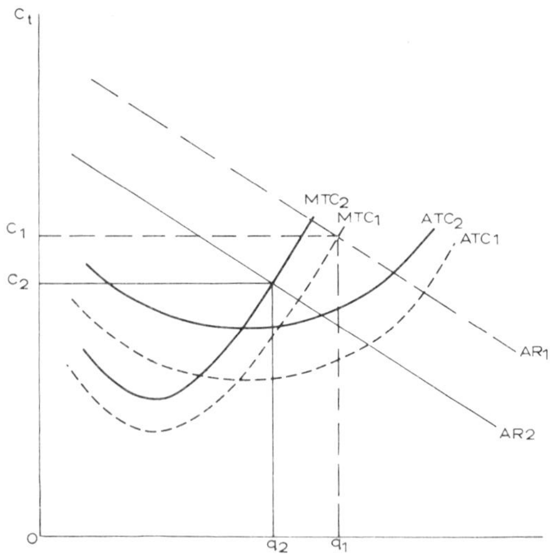

Figure 8.9 The Effects of an Increase in Uncertainty

schedules and the solid lines the post-change schedules. The quantity of loans must be reduced, but whether interest rates will fall or not will depend upon the relative shifts in the schedules and their price-elasticities. It is easy to see how an increase in uncertainty can reduce the supply of finance, and so depress the economy, even accompanied by a *fall* in the rate of interest; and, of course, there are many things that may lead to increased uncertainty, and there are anyway other 'external' influences on supply and demand. For example, an increase in the rate of interest offered by thc government would raise the cost of funds to the intermediaries and so increase costs of lending. Furthermore, in a more realistic model, including a wider range of asset holdings, this shift in relative prices would probably result in the intermediaries increasing their lending to the government; and so pushing up the cost of finance to the private sector still further.

An opposite example to the increase in uncertainty would be an improvement in the efficient operation of the financial intermediaries. In this case the movement would be in the opposite direction, with a reduction in the cost schedules.

9. THE SUPPLY OF MONEY: THE MULTIPLIER APPROACH

Having considered the broad institutional structure we now turn to examine the process through which the stock of money comes into existence. This chapter develops the traditional money multiplier model, and considers the standard criticisms that have been raised against it. The argument is developed in terms of comparative statics, i.e. a comparison of static-equilibrium positions. This is an unfortunate framework within which to discuss the *dynamic* process of money creation, particularly if we are concerned with the relationship between the supply of money and the rest of the economy. The following chapter, therefore, presents a more dynamic approach, emphasising the importance of the demand for bank credit in the money-supply process, and considering the implications of such a model for macroeconomic analysis.

Money Multiplier Models

The basic characteristic of these money-supply models is that they are based on an approach which makes the stock of money some multiple of the reserve assets defined by the monetary authorities. Examples of such models can be found in Friedman and Schwartz (1963). For the United States these reserves would be high-powered money; in the United Kingdom eligible reserve assets were redefined when 'Competition and Credit Control' was introduced in 1971. In both cases the stock in question may be referred to as the 'monetary base'. In its simplest form the multiple depends on the portfolio preferences/requirements of the banking sector and the aggregate non-bank sector. It is therefore assumed that control can be exercised through manipulation of the quantity of these reserve assets. This simple model can be set out as follows:

$$R = aD \tag{9.1}$$

i.e. banks' reserve assets, R, are some proportion, a, of their deposits, D.

$$C = bD \tag{9.2}$$

i.e. the holdings of notes and coin by the non-bank private sector, C, are some proportion, b, of their bank deposits, D.

$$P = dD \tag{9.3}$$

i.e. the private sector's holdings of eligible reserve assets, P, are some proportion, d, of their bank deposits, D.

$$D \equiv R + A \tag{9.4}$$

i.e. banks' deposit liabilities, D, are equal to their reserve assets, R, plus their advances to both the public and private sectors, A; this represents the normal balance-sheet identity for the simplified model considered here.

$$Q \equiv R + P \tag{9.5}$$

i.e. the stock of potential reserves to the banking system is held either by the banks, R, or the private sector, P.

$$M \equiv C + D \tag{9.6}$$

i.e. money, M, is defined as the sum of notes and coin, C, and bank deposits, D, held by the private sector.[1]

Substituting (9.1) and (9.3) into (9.5), and rearranging, gives:

$$D = \frac{Q}{a+d} \tag{9.7}$$

Combining (9.2) and (9.6) defines the money stock in terms of the quantity of deposits, i.e.

$$M = D(1+b) \tag{9.8}$$

and this can be reduced to an expression for money in terms of eligible reserve assets by substituting for D from (9.7):

$$M = \left[\frac{1+b}{a+d}\right]Q \tag{9.9}$$

As long as the parameters of the system (a, b and d) are fixed or known, then Q can in principle be employed to control M. In industrial terms the monetary base can be thought of as raw-material input and the multiplier as some technical coefficient of production indicating the efficiency of converting raw materials into finished products. There is no need for this technical relationship to be fixed, though that is usually the assumption made for simple pedagogic models. In principle it can be allowed to vary with relative prices and economic conditions. This approach has the great attraction of providing a simple supply example analogous to the more usual product market case.

This simple model can be made more complicated by explicitly identifying the operations of the non-bank financial intermediaries (N.B.F.I.s) separately from the rest of the non-bank private sector. The following changes must be made to the previous relationships:

$$Rb = aD \tag{9.1a}$$

i.e. bank reserves are now defined as Rb.

$$C = bDp \tag{9.2a}$$

i.e. private-sector deposits are redefined as Dp.

$$P = dDp \tag{9.3a}$$

$$D = Dp + Dn \equiv Rb + A \tag{9.4a}$$

i.e. total deposits are now divided between the N.B.F.I.s, Dn, and the rest of the private sector, Dp.

$$Q \equiv Rb + Rn + P \tag{9.5a}$$

i.e. reserves are now also held by the N.B.F.I.s, Rn.

Also, the following behavioural relationships need to be added:

$$Rn = eNp \tag{9.10}$$

i.e. N.B.F.I. reserve holdings, Rn, are some proportion, e, of their (total) receipts from the private sector, Np.

$$Dn = fNp \tag{9.11}$$

i.e. the N.B.F.I.s allocate some proportion, f, of their receipts to bank deposits, Dn.

$$Np = gDp \tag{9.12}$$

i.e. the private sector lends money to the N.B.F.I.s, Np, in some proportion, g, of its holdings of bank deposits, Dp.

Since

$$D \equiv Dp + Dn$$

this can be written as

$$D = (1 + fg)Dp \tag{9.13}$$

Substituting (9.1a), (9.3a) and (9.10) into (9.5a) gives

$$Q = aD + (eg + d)Dp$$

so that substituting for Dp from (9.13), and rearranging, gives:

$$D = \left[\frac{1 + fg}{a(1 + fg) + eg + d}\right]Q \tag{9.14}$$

Substituting (9.2a) and (9.13) into (9.6a) gives

$$M = \left(\frac{1 + fg + b}{1 + fg}\right)D$$

and the expression for money therefore reduces to

$$M = \left[\frac{1 + fg + b}{a(1 + fg) + eg + d}\right]Q \tag{9.15}$$

We have now obtained a more complicated multiplier expression than before which brings out some elements of the rest of the financial system. If $g = 0$, i.e. no deposits are placed with the N.B.F.I.s (or if e and $f = 0$, i.e. the N.B.F.I.s have no assets), the equation reduces to that obtained before, i.e. equation (9.9).

In practice, of course, there is a great variety of different financial institutions, and also a great variety of individual and company behaviour, summarised within the multiplier relationships. Any formal model necessarily involves extreme simplification, and it is only realistic to hope that one has identified broad trends in aggregate behaviour, but at least the most important ones.

It is now possible to differentiate M with respect to Q, or any of the various behavioural, or institutionally imposed,[2] parameters and thereby determine the effect, *ceteris paribus*, of such changes on the money supply. For example, it is easy to see that any increase in reserve ratios will have the effect of reducing the money supply. *Ceteris paribus*, an increase in the banks' reserve ratio will have a bigger effect than an increase in the reserve ratio of the N.B.F.I.s or the rest of the private sector. This therefore means that the banks are in a potentially more powerful position than the rest of the financial system, in that they can convert a given quantity of reserves into a greater quantity of money, and credit, than can the N.B.F.I.s.

We can also see that if the N.B.F.I.s hold all their reserves in the form of bank deposits, this actually increases the leverage of the banks. This is in fact not an unreasonable assumption to make since bank deposits will serve very well as liquid reserves, being easily transferable, and will be generally accepted as a means for the final settlement of debts. However, the real significance of this development goes beyond the actual supply of money as it may also change the velocity of circulation of the money stock. This means that a given stock of money will circulate faster, i.e. a given stock of reserves will support a much greater quantity of credit. We can imagine a *credit pyramid* of the following type:

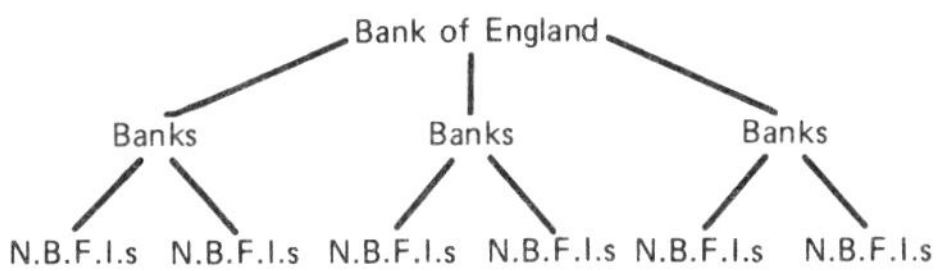

The banks hold the liabilities of the Bank of England as reserves while the N.B.F.I.s hold reserves in the form of bank liabilities. It is therefore easy to see how the introduction, or expansion, of the N.B.F.I.s may lift a restriction imposed by the limited availability of reserve assets. The question arises, however, as to the extent to which this development can counteract monetary policy, i.e. if the credit base is restricted, so restricting money supply and bank credit, can the N.B.F.I.s compensate sufficiently by attracting deposits and increasing their lending? Before answering this question, we need to consider the introduction of the N.B.F.I.s in greater detail.

The New View

Many economists have attacked the idea of a stable money multiplier and the implication that banks are essentially different from the rest of the financial sector. The most sophisticated version of this attack came from Gurley and Shaw (1955), and this was further refined and christened by Tobin (1963). Gurley and Shaw (1955, p. 521) stressed the similarities between the different financial intermediaries, and pointed out that although bank deposits were differentiable from the liabilities of other financial intermediaries, in that 'banks alone have the capacity to create demand deposits and currency', this was no reason in itself to treat banks separately. The liabilities of each group of N.B.F.I.s are equally differentiable from those of the banks and the other N.B.F.I.s. To quote Tobin (1963, p. 412), 'insurance against death is equally a feature differentiating life insurance policies from obligations of other intermediaries, including banks. It is not obvious that one kind of differentiation should be singled out for special analytical treatment.' The relevant criterion according to this view is the ability of the different groups of financial intermediaries to extend credit, and Gurley and Shaw (1955, p. 521) 'take exception to the view that banks stand apart in their ability to create loanable funds out of hand, while other intermediaries are busy with the modest brokerage function of transmitting loanable funds that are somehow generated elsewhere'. Tobin (1963, p. 273) makes the same point by condemning 'the tradition of distinguishing sharply between those assets which are and those which are not "money", and accordingly between those institutions which emit "money" and those whose liabilities are not "money"'.

There are two aspects to the 'new view' argument: (1) the multiplier approach to money-supply determination is too simple; and (2) the banks have no greater capacity for creating credit than the N.B.F.I.s. These two arguments were not separated adequately, so that consequently they became confused with each other in the 'new view'; this situation is discussed in greater detail in the first part of Coghlan (1977). They are really quite distinct, as is now shown.

(1) It was argued that the apparent ability of the banks to create a multiple expansion of credit and deposits is really an illusion dependent only on the existence of restrictions on bank operations, in particular reserve ratio requirements and limitations on the interest rates payable on certain types of deposit (see Tobin, 1963, p. 279). The argument can be illustrated with the aid of Figure 9.1, which is defined in terms of the asset side of banks' activities. Since credit is defined as all forms of lending to both public and private sectors (less that in the form of reserve assets), and there are assumed to be no other forms of bank liabilities, it is easy to derive the implications for deposits and the money supply.

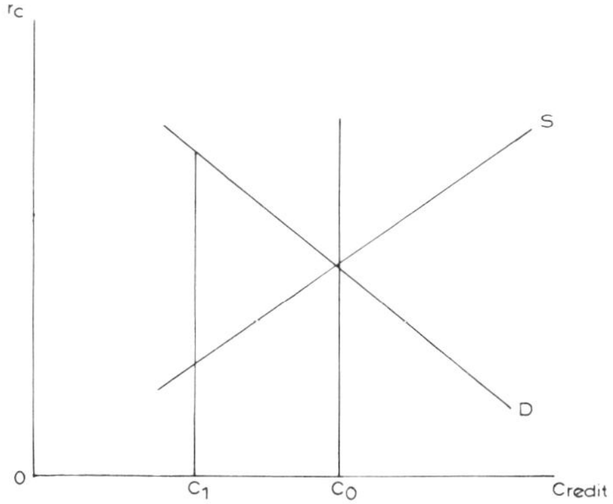

Figure 9.1 Restrictions on Bank Expansion

By setting the quantity of reserves, in combination with a required reserve ratio, sufficient only to support a credit total of OC_1, the banks (and the financial system as a whole) are prevented from achieving the market equilibrium. Starting from this position an increase in reserves will be followed by a multiple expansion of credit and bank deposits. However, if we start from position of OC_0 it would seem that there could be no expansion of deposits.

This is a simple, partial, example which ignores the way in

which excess reserves come into existence and disregards any secondary effects on the rest of the economy. The banks would probably accumulate excess reserves but there would also be repercussions throughout the financial system, with a consequent readjustment of portfolios. At a very minimum the relationship between money and the stock of reserves must be some function of rates of interest (the details of such interrelationships are further considered below). It is clear that there is no simple multiplier relationship between reserves and the money stock; in particular, the demand for bank credit is of crucial significance. The implications of this observation for the determination of the money supply are considered in greater detail in Chapter 10.

(2) Although there are important limitations to the use of simple ratios to explain the money supply, it does not mean that this approach has no value whatsoever. Nor does it mean that the banks are no different from the N.B.F.I.s in their ability to extend credit. These arguments have, however, generally been presented as inseparable elements of the 'new view'. It is therefore necessary to demonstrate the relative importance of the banking sector. The examples also illustrate that the ratios approach cannot be rejected in favour of a structural approach simply because the latter incorporate explicit behavioural assumptions.

Banks versus N.B.F.I.s

In this section the 'new view' argument is considered within a more complete financial system. The discussion is conducted within the context of previously developed comparative-static models, and demonstrates in what way a fully specified behavioural system may prove inferior to a simple ratios approach. Most importantly, it illustrates that, even within this static framework, the banks do possess a relative advantage over the N.B.F.I.s in their ability to expand credit. The discussion is adapted from Coghlan (1977, part II).

Guttentag and Lindsay (1968) examined the question of relative credit-creating potential employing the ratios approach. They set out to show that the conclusion that the banks were unable to expand credit to an extent greater than the

N.B.F.I.s followed from an unrealistic assumption regarding cash reserve holdings, and that by substituting a more realistic assumption the banks could be shown to have greater potential for credit expansion than the N.B.F.I.s. It should be noted that in accordance with the new view attention had turned from the supply of money to the supply of credit.

Their first model is briefly outlined below so that it can then be compared with a structural model developed by Wood (1970). In this way it is possible to provide common ground from which to consider the relative advantages of the two approaches for the analysis of the financial sector.

We begin with the separate simplified balance-sheets:

For the public $L = S + Dp$
For the N.B.F.I.s $S = Da + Ca$
For the banks $Da + Dp = Cb + R$
and $R = \overline{R}$, i.e. is exogenously determined.

where, L = public's total stock of liquid assets, S = public's holdings of N.B.F.I. liabilities, Dp = public's holdings of bank liabilities, Da = N.B.F.I. holdings of bank liabilities, Cb = credit extended by the banks, Ca = credit extended by the N.B.F.I.s, and R = cash reserves of the banks.

The model is of the simplest type with no cash holdings by the N.B.F.I.s or the public, and the following ratios may be defined:

$k = S/Dp$ = public's portfolio preference
$\alpha = Da/S$ = N.B.F.I. reserve ratio
$\beta = R/(Da + Dp)$ = banks' reserve ratio

Employing these ratios it is possible to compute expressions for credit extended, i.e.

$$Ca = \frac{R(1-\alpha)k}{\beta(1+\alpha k)} \text{ and } Cb = \frac{R}{\beta} - R$$

so that

$$Ct = Ca + Cb = \frac{R(1+k)}{\beta(1+\alpha k)} - R \tag{9.16}$$

where Ct is total credit.

In the next stage Guttentag and Lindsay calculate the change in total credit due to either a change in the bank or N.B.F.I. reserve ratios, under the assumption that k is constant:

$$\frac{\partial Ct}{\partial \beta} = -\frac{R(1+k)}{\beta^2(1+\alpha k)} \tag{9.17a}$$

$$\frac{\partial Ct}{\partial \alpha} = -\frac{R(1+k)k}{\beta(1+\alpha k)^2} \tag{9.17b}$$

In order to see the credit expansion potential of one against the other we simply need to compare these two ratios. Thus

$$\frac{\partial Ct/\partial \beta}{\partial Ct/\partial \alpha} = \frac{1+\alpha k}{\beta k} \tag{9.18}$$

Making $\partial Ct/\partial \beta = \partial Ct/\partial \alpha$ reveals the magnitude of k required to equalise the change in total credit resulting from equal changes in bank and non-bank reserve ratios. Using this assumption:

$$k^+ = 1/(\beta - \alpha) \tag{9.19}$$

If $\alpha = \beta$, i.e. the reserve ratios are equal, then k^+ equals infinity. This means that the N.B.F.I.s would only have equal capacity for extending credit if the public holds all its liquid assets in the form of N.B.F.I. liabilities and holds no bank deposits – which are all held as reserves by the N.B.F.I.s. Employing empirical values from U.S. data Guttentag and Lindsay show that, for 1965 values of α and β, k^+ would have had to be 16 for the banks and the N.B.F.I.s to have equal credit expansion capacity, and as it was actually in the region of 2 the banks had a far greater credit-creating capability.

The authors then go on to extend the model to include cash holdings by the public and the N.B.F.I.s, and show that the Tobin 'new view' *conclusion* was a direct result of the assumption made that all financial intermediaries hold their reserves in cash. When Guttentag and Lindsay make this same assumption they obtain the same result.

Wood (1970) attempted to show that the structural approach with endogenous portfolio behaviour (what he was now calling the 'new view') would yield the same result as the multiplier model in the hands of Guttentag and Lindsay. Wood used the simple Guttentag and Lindsay model (which we have presented above) as a starting-point and added explicit behavioural assumptions as follows:

$Dp = Dp(rc, rs)$	Public's demand for bank liabilities
$S = S(rc, rs)$	Public's demand for N.B.F.I. liabilities
$Ct = C(rc, rs)$	Public's demand for credit
$R = R(Dp + Da, rc, \beta)$	Bank demand for reserves
$Cb = Cb(Dp + Da, rc)$	Bank supply of credit
$Da = Da(S, rc, \alpha)$	N.B.F.I. demand for reserves
$Ca = Ca(S, rc)$	N.B.F.I. supply of credit
$rs = rs(rc)$	

where rc and rs are the rates of return on intermediary credit and the liabilities of the N.B.F.I. respectively (serving as prices in the demand and supply functions), and α and β are exogenous shift variables. The yield on demand deposits is assumed to be fixed, and the same rate is available on all credit extended to the private sector. The assumption of a fixed yield on demand deposits will be relaxed later.

In order to determine the effect on total credit of exogenous *ceteris paribus* changes in reserve holding propensities on the part of the financial institutions we need to differentiate the system with respect to the exogenous shift parameters α and β. However, before this can be done, it is necessary to know the specific form of the behavioural relationships assumed. Wood does not in fact supply this information, though it is obvious from his conclusion that he assumed linear relationships throughout. What is not so clear is the fact that there is a considerable degree of linear dependence between variables which, at first sight, appear to be determined by independent behavioural equations. Given the deposits of the institutions and their reserve holdings, the supply of credit (Ca and Cb) is determined. Furthermore, it is impossible to assume that bank deposits are determined by the separate supply from the public and the N.B.F.I.s, while at the same time assuming that both reserve assets and the deposit rate are determined outside the model. If we retain the specific assumptions that have already been made, of an exogenous supply of reserves and an exogenous deposit rate, then it is necessary to assume that the public's demand for deposits is determined residually. We may therefore define the following model:

$Dp = D - Da$	Balance-sheet identity
$S \ = d_3 + d_4 rs$	Behavioural
$Ct \ = d_5 - d_6 rc$	Behavioural
$R \ = b_1 D - b_2 rc + b_3 \beta$	Behavioural
$Cb = Dp + Da - R$	Balance-sheet identity
$Da = a_1 S - a_2 rc + a_3 \alpha$	Behavioural
$Ca = S - Da$	Balance-sheet identity
$rs \ = a_6 rc$	Behavioural

where $Ct = Ca + Cb$.

In terms of exogenous variables only this system reduces to:[3]

$$Ct = Q + \frac{d_6[(1-b_1)R - b_1 a_3 \alpha - b_3 \beta]}{b_1(d_6 + d_4 a_6) + b_2} \tag{9.20}$$

where Q is a constant term.

If we now differentiate Ct by β and α, and write the first partial as a proportion of the second, we obtain:

$$\frac{\partial Ct/\partial B}{\partial Ct/\partial \alpha} = \frac{b_3}{b_1 a_3} = \rho \tag{9.21}$$

In order to obtain this result it is necessary to make the assumption that $d_6 \neq 0$. It must therefore also be true that a necessary condition for Guttentag and Lindsay to obtain their conclusion is that the total demand for credit is not determined by forces entirely independently of the rate of interest. This does not seem to be an unreasonable assumption to make.

Standardising the changes, i.e. making $a_3 - b_3$, gives

$$\rho = \frac{1}{b_1} \tag{9.22}$$

where $b_1 = \partial R/\partial D$, i.e. 'is the derivative of commercial bank demand for reserves with respect to demand deposits'.

Obviously as long as $b_1 < 1$, then $\rho > 1$, and the credit expansion potential of a *ceteris paribus* reduction in reserve ratios is greater for the banks than for the N.B.F.I.s. Wood points out that b_1 is likely to be approximately equal to the required reserve ratio for the banks, i.e. to have an approximate value of 0.10 to 0.15, and so the relative credit expansion potential of the banks exceeds that of the N.B.F.I.s by 7 to 10 times, given an equal change in demand for reserves.

While Wood (1970, pp. 107, 108) does note that 'this result, unlike that of G–L [Guttentag and Lindsay], is independent of k, the size of the banks relative to other intermediaries',[4] he lays stress on the similarities between the results of the two approaches. *This is not correct; they are fundamentally different.* The result obtained by Wood depends only on b_1, i.e. the comparative credit-creating ability of the banks and the N.B.F.I.s as the result of equal changes in reserve ratios is determined only by the banks' reserve ratio. We are back in a world where only the banks are important, and neither the personal sector's portfolio preferences nor the N.B.F.I.s' reserve ratio makes any difference.

To summarise the argument so far, Guttentag and Lindsay produced a traditional ratios-type model which, they argued, refuted the 'new view'. In this model the comparative credit-creating ability of the different financial institutions depended upon the portfolio behaviour of the N.B.F.I.s and the public as well as that of the banks. Wood then produced what he called a 'new view' model in which the comparative credit-creating ability depended solely upon the banks' portfolio behaviour.

This produced a most confusing situation with the true contribution of Gurley and Shaw being lost in a tangle of definitional obscurity. In terms of the 'new view' as originally defined both of these models should be included within this category. To take explicit account of the N.B.F.I.s is, however, not enough; the behaviour of the system has also to be correctly specified. In this respect it is interesting to note that the model set up to oppose the 'new view' provided more intuitively acceptable results from a 'new view' standpoint than the model that actually claimed to represent this view. This indicates that no simple comparison between the ratio and structural approaches is possible; it is necessary also to look closely at the actual behaviour specified.

It is, in fact, necessary to further subdivide the structural approach into linear behaviour, where the asset *level* is determined as a linear function of relative interest rates, wealth and any other behavioural variables, and non-linear or proportional behaviour, where asset *proportions* are a function of the various behavioural determinants. For the present, our particular concern is with the choice between the assumption of linear and proportional behaviour, but that is not to suggest that within these sub-groupings the actual specification is unimportant.

The conclusion that Wood obtains results directly from his employment of *linear* behavioural equations. This may not be immediately apparent since the model incorporates certain assumptions, i.e. a fixed interest rate (zero) on bank deposits together with a fixed quantity of reserves (although the reserve requirement is not in fact fixed), which Tobin had claimed were exactly the conditions required to make the banks *appear* different from the other intermediaries. It needs to be borne in mind that in this model the N.B.F.I.s are already subject to reserve requirements. Another potential difficulty arises because no scale variable enters into the private sector's asset demand functions. Before continuing it is therefore necessary to be sure that it is the linearity assumption that is the cause of the particular conclusion and not these alternative assumptions.

The model has therefore been amended in the following way:

$$\begin{aligned} Dp &= d_1 + d_2 rd - d_7 rs + d_8 S \\ S &= d_3 + d_4 rs - d_9 rd + d_{10} Dp \\ Da &= a_1 S - a_2 rc + a_4 rd + a_3 \alpha \\ rd &= a_7 rc \end{aligned}$$

with all the other assumptions remaining as before, and *rd* being the rate on bank deposits.

Now the demand for bank deposits by the private sector, and the bank deposit rate, are endogenously determined, as also is the level of reserves. In addition some scale variable enters into each of the asset demand functions (in a way that is consistent with the Guttentag and Lindsay model).

Differentiating this new system of equations by α and β, and comparing the partial differentials as before, results in exactly the same conclusion as previously obtained, and given in equations (9.21) and (9.22). So even when the model is generalised to take account of the special restrictive assumptions incorporated in Wood's model, the conclusion, that the comparative credit-creating ability of the banks relative to the N.B.F.I.s depends solely on the banks' reserve ratio, still holds.

In order for the structural model to yield the same result as that obtained by Guttentag and Lindsay it is necessary to amend Wood's model by making the asset demands proportional, i.e.

$$Da = (a_3\alpha - a_2 rc)S = a_1 S$$
$$R = (b_3\beta - b_2 rc)D = b_1 D$$

and

$$S = (d_3 + d_4 rs)Dp = d_1 Dp$$

This results in the following expression for total credit:

$$Ct = \frac{R(1 + d_3 + d_4 rs)}{(b_3\beta - b_2 rc)[1 + (a_3\alpha - a_2 rc)(d_3 + d_4 rs)]} - R \tag{9.23}$$

with

$$rc = \frac{d_5 - Ct}{d_6} \tag{9.24}$$

Partially differentiating (9.23) with respect to α and β, and assuming $a_3 = b_3$, yields:

$$\rho = \frac{1 + a_1 d_1}{b_1 d_1} \tag{9.25}$$

This, then, is apparently identical to the Guttentag and Lindsay result, where $k = S/Dp = d_1$. If $\rho = 1$,

$$k = \frac{1}{b_1 - a_1} \tag{9.26}$$

We have thus obtained a conclusion which depends upon all the portfolio choices specified in the model.

It may possibly be objected that in this case there is an important distinction in that now the various components of the solution, a_1, b_1, Dp and S, are all functions of rc and are therefore endogenous to the model. We are, however, comparing the effect of changes in some economic variables allowing all endogenous variables to change, and the result is independent of the *changes* in interest rates, being only a function of the level. It is therefore possible to conclude that if we are concerned with analysing the effect at equilibrium of small changes in any of the exogenous variables, then *under certain circumstances* the conclusions will be identical whether the model is set up in fixed-ratios form or if *proportional* asset demands are a function of relative interest rates; and what is more, these conclusions will be very different from those obtained from a structural model defining linear portfolio behaviour.

This is an important conclusion since it tells us that there are situations in which simple ratios can be substituted for a complicated set of structural equations without any loss of generality. This should not be too surprising since both are 'new view' models. The structural model specifying proportional behaviour has more in common with the traditional ratios model than with the linear structural model. Often the ratios approach is rejected on the grounds of its lack of realism only to be replaced by (what we have seen to be) the even more unrealistic assumption of a structural model containing only linear behavioural equations.

This conclusion is only possible when comparing the *relative* effects of similar changes to both the banks and the N.B.F.I.s. In the case of a single change, i.e. in available reserves, or the portfolio preferences of the private sector, the effect of any interest-rate changes will not be washed out of the system, but will remain (see Coghlan, 1977). However, the direction of change will be the same as for the multiplier model unless either the demand for credit is unaffected by the rate of interest or the induced interest-rate effects are infinitely large. Although we may be happy to reject these extremes as being unrealistic, these interest-rate effects do substantially qualify the conclusions obtained from the multiplier model, and reduce our ability to identify the exact implications of any policy, or behavioural, change.

Tobin (1963, p. 278) had claimed that the application of the 'new view' automatically led to the conclusion that there was no difference between the credit-creating potential of the banks and the N.B.F.I.s, implying that a transfer of funds from the banks to the N.B.F.I.s simply results in a corresponding reduction in the quantity of bank liabilities and assets. This is, however, contrary to the more usual assumption that a switch of funds from bank deposits to the N.B.F.I.s will always lead to an expansion of credit. For a summary of this alternative position, and references, see Coghlan (1975, pp. 174–81). The apparent 'new view' conclusion referred to above implies a 100 per cent 'direct loss' of bank deposits, whereas an *extreme* monetarist conclusion would presumably be that there would be no 'direct loss' of bank deposits at all, and also no expenditure effects. A more realistic conclusion would lie somewhere between these extremes, with the actual 'loss' depending on the financial system and the economic conditions existing at the time. It should be clear by now that, except in the most extreme and unrealistic of situations, Tobin's 'new view' conclusion requires the N.B.F.I.s to have the same reserve ratio as the banks, *and* that they hold these reserves in the form of government debt, and not as deposits with the banking sector.

For the purpose of analysis a linear structural model is sometimes preferred to the use of ratios on the grounds that some behaviour is better than none, and that the non-linear assumption makes the model too complicated to understand intuitively. As far as this approach is concerned, the arguments presented above would appear to show that this is not so. On the other hand, the ratios approach can, with varying degrees of accuracy, be thought of as a reduced form of the proportional behavioural model, deriving value for expositional purposes from its greater simplicity. The assumption of linearity fails to replicate this latter model, and can, as we have seen above, yield some very misleading results.

The rejection of the linear model for the (static) analysis of financial market behaviour does not leave us with a simple choice between the traditional ratios and non-linear structural models. They are not perfect substitutes, and there is a trade-off in their use between simplicity and accuracy. Furthermore, this trade-off is itself variable, depending on the actual problem being considered. The exact importance of this trade-off and the conditions under which it is least noticeable have been touched upon here but undoubtedly form an important area of future study. Rather than thinking of the two approaches as substitutes, this way of looking at them has tended to emphasise their complementarity.

Before leaving the subject it is necessary to point out some more fundamental weaknesses of this approach. The analysis has not really addressed itself to the *process* through which money is supplied and demanded. In particular there has been no discussion of the income/expenditure side of the economy, and the consequent implications of the credit-creating activities of the financial system. It would, however, seem to be essential to incorporate these interrelationships in order to understand the operation, and significance, of the financial system. As a result of such an approach to the question we are forced to examine the role of credit creation more closely, and to ask whether the operations on the asset side of banks' balance-sheets may not serve to differentiate the banks further from the N.B.F.I.s. This, in fact, is the approach adopted in Chapter 10.

Flexibility of the Financial System

Obviously, the development of the financial institutions has important implications for the economy (as argued in Chapter 8). Such developments have potential significance not only for the velocity of circulation of money, and the supply of money, but also for the definition of money itself. The question we want to consider here is whether the existence of the N.B.F.I.s in any way vitiates monetary control.

To begin with, it is necessary to distinguish two separate types of influence on the velocity of circulation. The first concerns the response to changes in competitive conditions. In general this will be measured by the response of the N.B.F.I.s, and financial markets, to changes in interest rates. Where non-market controls have been imposed there may be credit rationing, and substitutions may occur even though very little movement in relative interest rates is observed. The extent of this substitution will be restricted by the accompanying increase in risk that must surely be a consequence of this enforced adjustment to portfolios. To give an example, the implementation of the Supplementary Special Deposits 'corset' scheme on the banks may well result in an increase in bank acceptance credits[5] held outside the banks. This means that there is an increase in non-bank lending to the company sector, but under a bank guarantee. While there is obviously scope for such expansion, it is hard to imagine there being no limit to such developments. In particular a worsening of company liquidity and profitability, and/or the prospect of sharply rising interest rates, might reverse the process. On the other hand, the longer restrictions are in force, particularly if they are in quantitative form, the greater the chances are that the financial system will be able to adapt to, and thereby partially avoid, these controls. However, before this effect is likely to be very strong the restriction would probably need to be particularly severe and long lasting (this is considered further below).

The second influence will be the natural evolutionary development of the N.B.F.I.s. The N.B.F.I.s develop in order to provide for diversified financial requirements, and tend to specialise in the provision of a particular service. In so doing they may well bring about an increase in the velocity of circulation of money, particularly since we have already identified financial development with economic expansion. All this means is that a given stock of money is employed more efficiently, and supports a greater flow of income and expenditure. It is, however, not necessary that the velocity of circulation should increase, as it is possible that the banking system may also expand *pari passu*. Apart from anything else this will naturally depend on whether additional reserves are made available.

However, such financial developments arise in response to changes in tastes, and in institutional organisation, within society; they are therefore unlikely to be sudden or dramatic. Moreover, there is no reason why these changes should not be explicable, or even, possibly, predictable. A similar increase in velocity could be achieved through industrial integration and the restriction of inter-firm payments, or by other changes affecting the periodicity of payments. In particular there is nothing about such developments which suggests that the existence of N.B.F.I.s will offset the effects of a tight monetary policy. After all, there is no reason why the N.B.F.I.s should not act as rationally as other economic agents. The activities of the N.B.F.I.s are anyway generally quite specific, at least with respect to one side of their business, either borrowing or lending, which suggests that interest-elasticity may be fairly limited in the short term.

These arguments suggest that the introduction of N.B.F.I.s into the analysis does not result in a complete loss of control, though there may be a reduction in the effectiveness of the control instrument. In addition it is worth noting that it is not only the N.B.F.I.s which account for this lack of rigid control but also the ability of individuals and non-financial companies to create substitute credit facilities (trade credit) and to economise on reserve assets. As a result it may be necessary to double the reduction in reserves from what would be necessary if only banks held these assets in order to achieve a particular contraction of demand, offsetting flexibility in the money supply (via the interest-elasticity of reserve assets) and in the velocity of circulation. It is not clear that this reduction in effectiveness is actually a bad thing; after all, another way of looking at it is as an improvement in the flexibility of the financial system. This was the view taken by Tobin and Brainard (1963, p. 384), who argued that 'when a given remedial effect can be achieved either by a small dose of strong medicine or a large dose of weak medicine, it is not obvious that the small dose is preferable. Increasing the responsiveness of the system to instruments of control may also increase its sensitivity to random exogenous shocks.'

Very strong controls which have the effect of severely restricting bank borrowing and lending for a considerable length of time would, however, have implications for the development of new N.B.F.I.s. New financial intermediaries would come into existence in response to the policy measures with the specific aim of filling the gap in financial services that had been created. These institutions will presumably not operate as efficiently as the banks, otherwise they would have evolved naturally within the market environment. This suggests that the offset to policy will be neither immediate nor complete. As already suggested, such developments are only likely in response to persistent and extensive control. However, it is hard to imagine that there would be no development: there is an obvious conflict between rigid controls over the operations of a particular group of financial institutions and the basic role of financial intermediaries to improve the efficiency with which funds are transmitted throughout the economy. Such a development with respect to the activities of the banking sector would indicate the need to reconsider the definition of money. In practice money, at least the broad definition, can only be defined taking account of the institutional and operational structure of the banking sector, and, indeed, that of the financial system as a whole.

It needs to be borne in mind that although we may consider control of the money supply to be an essential prerequisite to control of the rate of inflation, it is inflation and the health of the economy with which we are really concerned. In addition the economy is constantly changing in response to external forces. Over recent years it has proved very difficult to forecast aggregate levels of income and expenditure at all accurately, still less changes within these totals. There is therefore a sense in which some degree of flexibility might be of considerable importance. If there really is a strong relationship between money and the economy, then by setting, and achieving, rigid money-supply targets all exogenous shocks to the economy must naturally be felt by those economic variables which are really the objectives of policy. There is always likely to be a certain amount of flexibility in any advanced financial system, but it is still necessary to weigh up the costs of any attempts to reduce it.

Keynes, in fact, was very clear about the advantages of the flexibility inherent in the operations of the banks. These views are set out in two articles published in 1937, in which Keynes attempted to clarify certain aspects of *The General Theory* in response to criticisms that had been made.

The first thing to note is that in steady-state equilibrium there will be no financial constraints; these will only appear as part of the process of expansion. Corresponding to any planned expansion there is also a necessary financial requirement. Moreover, Keynes was absolutely insistent that such plans could not be financed by planned *ex ante* saving. This is a point worth emphasising since so many macroeconomic models ignore the financial implications of expenditure decisions (see Chapter 2 above):

> The above analysis is useful in exhibiting in what sense a heavy demand for investment can exhaust the market and be held up by lack of financial facilities on reasonable terms. It is, to an important extent, the 'financial' facilities which regulate the *pace* of new investment. Some people find it a paradox that, up to the point of full employment, no amount of actual investment, however great, can exhaust and exceed the supply of savings, which will always exactly keep pace. If this is found paradoxical, it is because it is confused with the fact that too great a press of uncompleted investment decisions is quite capable of exhausting the available finance, if the banking system is unwilling to increase the supply of money and the supply of existing holders is inelastic. It is the supply of available finance which, in practice, holds up from time to time the onrush of 'new issues'. But if the banking system chooses to make the finance available and the investment projected by the new issues actually takes place, the appropriate level of incomes will be generated out of which there will necessarily remain over an amount of saving exactly sufficient to take care of the new investment. The control of finance is, indeed, a potent, though sometimes dangerous, method for regulating the rate of investment (though much more potent when used as a curb than as a stimulus). Yet this is only another way of expressing the power of the banks through their control over the supply of money – i.e. of liquidity (Keynes, 1937a, p. 248).

Keynes clearly places the banks at the centre of the money-supply process, and also stresses the danger of interfering with this process. The importance of the banking system in the generation of expansion does not depend on any special characteristics of that time, and if liquidity constraints are to be kept to a minimum then an overdraft system is likely to be ideal:

> In Great Britain the banks pay great attention to the amount of their outstanding loans and deposits, but not to the amount of their customers' unused overdraft facilities. The aggregate amount of the latter is not known, probably not even to the banks themselves, nor their division between the purely precautionary facilities which are not likely to be used

> in the near future and those which are associated with an impending planned activity. Now, this is an ideal system for mitigating the effects on the banking system of an increased demand for ex-ante finance. For it means that there is no effective pressure on the resources of the banking system until the finance is actually used, i.e. until the phase of planned activity has passed over into the phase of actual activity. Thus to the extent that the overdraft system is employed and unused overdrafts ignored by the banking system, there is no superimposed pressure resulting from planned activity over and above the pressure resulting from actual activity. In this event the transition from a lower to a higher scale of activity may be accomplished with less pressure on the demand for liquidity and the rate of interest (Keynes, 1937b, p. 669).

Keynes could equally well be describing the operation of the banking system as presently constituted. It is a picture of banking behaviour which is consistent with banks operating as 'liability managers', i.e. they adjust their liabilities (predominantly deposits) in order to accommodate the asset side of their portfolios. This is contrary to the more usual approach to bank behaviour which generally takes deposits (and advances) as given and then allocates the remaining assets according to normal portfolio choice (e.g. Parkin, Gray and Barrett, 1970).

The arguments presented by Keynes make a strong case in support of a flexible, responsive, monetary system providing a ready flow of finance in response to industry's needs. In the more inflationary environment of recent years it is likely he would qualify this position to take account of the possible conflict which may exist. The principle, however, remains that while rigid control may contain inflationary pressures it may also restrict the growth potential of the economy.

In addition to justifying a flexible monetary system, the above arguments imply a dynamic model of the economy in which money plays an absolutely crucial role. Changes in investment are the driving-force behind the standard Keynesian model; such changes we now find are crucially dependent upon expansion of the banking system and the money supply. The final chapter develops the outline of just such a model, and discusses its implications for the analysis of the economy as a whole.

Appendix

Derivation of Equation (9.20)

$$Ct = Ca + Cb = Dp + Da - R + S - Da = D - Da - R + S$$

$$D = \left(\frac{R + b_2 rc - b_3\beta}{b_1}\right)$$

$$Ct = \frac{R + b_2 rc - b_3\beta}{b_1} - R + S - Da$$

$$= \frac{R + b_2 rc - b_3\beta}{b_1} - R + d_3 + d_4 a_6 rc - a_1 d_3 - a_1 d_4 a_6 rc - a_3\alpha + a_2 rc$$

$$= R\left(\frac{1 - b_1}{b_1}\right) - \left(\frac{b_3}{b_1}\right)\beta + (d_4 a_6 + \frac{b_2}{b_1} + a_2 - a_1 d_4 a_6) rc - a_3\alpha + Q$$

where Q = a constant term.

$$r = \frac{d_5 - Ct}{d_6}$$

$$Ct = R\left(\frac{1 - b_1}{b_1}\right) - \left(\frac{b_3}{b_1}\right)\beta - \left(\frac{d_4 a_6 b_1 + b_2 + a_2 b_1 - a_1 d_4 a_6 b_1}{b_1}\right)\frac{Ct}{d_6} - a_3\alpha + Q$$

$$Ct\left(\frac{b_1 d_6 + d_4 b_1 + b_2 + a_2 b_1 - a_1 d_4 a_6 b_1}{b_1 d_6}\right)$$

$$= R\left(\frac{1 - b_1}{b_1}\right) - \left(\frac{b_3}{b_1}\right)\beta - a_3\alpha + Q$$

$$Ct = \frac{d_6[(1-b_1)R - b_3\beta - b_1a_3\alpha]}{b_1d_6 + d_4a_6b_1 + b_2 + \underbrace{a_2b_1 - a_1d_4a_6b_1}} + Q$$

$$\frac{\dfrac{\partial Da}{\partial rc}\cdot\dfrac{\partial R}{\partial D} - \dfrac{\partial Da}{\cancel{\partial S}}\cdot\dfrac{\cancel{\partial S}}{\cancel{\partial rs}}\cdot\dfrac{\cancel{\partial rs}}{\partial rc}\cdot\dfrac{\partial R}{\partial D}}{\dfrac{\partial Da}{\partial rc}\cdot\dfrac{\partial R}{\partial D} - \dfrac{\partial Da}{\partial rc}\cdot\dfrac{\partial R}{\partial D}}$$

$$Ct = \frac{d_6[1-b_1)R - b_3\beta - b_1a_3\alpha]}{b_1(d_6 + d_4a_6) + b_2} + Q \tag{9.20}$$

Derivation of equation (9.25)

$$Ct = \frac{R(1 + d_3 + d_4rs)}{(b_3\beta - b_2rc)[1 + (a_3\alpha - a_2rc)(d_3 + d_4rs)]} - R \tag{9.23}$$

$$rc = \frac{d_5 - Ct}{d_6} \tag{9.24}$$

$$Ct = f(rc, \alpha, \beta)$$

$$\frac{\partial Ct}{\partial \alpha} = \frac{\partial f}{\partial rc}\frac{\partial rc}{\partial \alpha} + \frac{\partial f}{\partial \alpha} = \frac{\partial f}{\partial rc}\frac{\partial rc}{\partial Ct}\frac{\partial Ct}{\partial \alpha} + \frac{\partial f}{\partial \alpha}$$

$$\frac{\partial Ct}{\partial \beta} = \frac{\partial f}{\partial rc}\frac{\partial rc}{\partial \beta} + \frac{\partial f}{\partial \beta} = \frac{\partial f}{\partial rc}\frac{\partial rc}{\partial Ct}\frac{\partial Ct}{\partial \beta} + \frac{\partial f}{\partial \beta}$$

$$\frac{\dfrac{\partial f}{\partial \beta}}{\dfrac{\partial f}{\partial \alpha}} = \frac{\dfrac{\partial Ct}{\partial \beta}\left(\cancel{1 - \dfrac{\partial f}{\partial rc}\dfrac{\partial rc}{\partial Ct}}\right)}{\dfrac{\partial Ct}{\partial \alpha}\left(\cancel{1 - \dfrac{\partial f}{\partial rc}\dfrac{\partial rc}{\partial Ct}}\right)}$$

$$\frac{\partial Ct}{\partial \beta} = -\frac{R(1 + d_3 + d_4rs)b_3}{(b_3\beta - b_2rc)^2[1 + (a_3\alpha - a_2rc)(d_3 + d_4rs)]}$$

$$= -\frac{Rb_3(1 + d_1)}{b_1^2(1 + a_1d_1)}$$

$$\frac{\partial Ct}{\partial \alpha} = -\frac{R(1 + d_3 + d_4rs)(d_3 + d_4rs)a_3}{(b_3\beta - b_2rc)[1 + (a_3\alpha - a_2rc)(d_3 + d_4rs)]^2}$$

$$= -\frac{Ra_3(1 + d_1)d_1}{b_1(1 + a_1d_1)^2}$$

$$\frac{\dfrac{\partial Ct}{\partial \beta}}{\dfrac{\partial Ct}{\partial \alpha}} = \frac{\dfrac{-Rb_3(1+d_1)}{b_1^2(1+a_1d_1)}}{\dfrac{-Ra_3(1+d_1)d_1}{b_1(1+a_1d_1)^2}} = \frac{b_3(1+a_1d_1)}{a_3b_1d_1} = \rho$$

and assuming that $a_3 = b_3$,

$$\rho = \frac{1+a_1d_1}{b_1d_1} \tag{9.25}$$

10. THE SUPPLY OF MONEY AND THE DYNAMICS OF ADJUSTMENT

If the monetary base is not controlled by the monetary authorities, it might appear that the stock of money simply responds to the demand for it. This has indeed been the argument that has usually been put forward; it is, however, incorrect. It is a view which depends crucially on the existence of continuous equilibrium in money markets. It is argued in this chapter that the demand for and supply of money are determined independently of each other, even when the monetary base is endogenous, and that we need to take account of the existence of disequilibrium. The idea that there can be disequilibrium in money markets is not a new one, and Friedman and Meiselman's description of money as a residual store of purchasing power can be interpreted in this light. Macroeconomics has, however, been dominated by static-equilibrium models, in particular the *IS/LM* model. This chapter provides the description of an alternative money-supply process which has direct implications for modelling the rest of the economy. The supply mechanism is therefore described within the broad outline of a dynamic model of the economy.

As a starting-point it is useful to recall the main conclusions of the previous chapter. First, it was argued that the banking system stands at the centre of the financial system. Although it is necessary to take account of the rest of the financial system, the operation of the payments mechanism does make the banks importantly different from the N.B.F.I.s. The banks are, however, still subject to the economic forces of supply and demand. This means that an expansion of the monetary base need not result in any simple multiple expansion of the money supply; it is still necessary for a demand for bank credit to exist. Finally, it was argued that the banks play a crucial role in the provision of finance to facilitate an increase in total investment. In particular it was recognised that this was a fundamental part of Keynes's own theory. This is perhaps worth emphasising, since it provides justification for the model outlined here. For example, as Keynes (1937, p. 666) argued:

> In a simplified schematism, designed to elucidate the essence of what is happening, but one which is, in fact, substantially representative of real life, one would assume that finance is wholly supplied during the interregnum [between planning and execution] by the banks; and this is the explanation of why their policy is so important in determining the pace at which new investment can proceed.

The Money Supply and Credit Demand

It has often been argued that the money stock, regardless of definition, has become demand-determined because the monetary authorities have endogenised the reserve supply process. Although there has been considerable movement towards controlling the money stock, the control mechanism has still operated through interest rates rather than variations in the quantity of reserve assets. In 1975 Goodhart was able to write:

> Whereas this [reserve asset control] is often presented in theoretical papers and textbooks as representing reality, or as a desideratum, it is extremely hard to find any attested examples in which central banks – even in countries where most attention is paid to the monetary aggregates, e.g. Germany – actually do behave in this way.

If, in fact, reserves are freely available and/or reserve ratios are infinitely variable, it might be supposed that the money stock becomes demand-determined. That has been the argument usually put forward, at least for the United Kingdom, by both Keynesians and monetarists (e.g. Kaldor, 1970; and Griffiths, 1973). If money is supplied upon demand, as suggested, we then find ourselves in an extreme Keynesian world in which money appears to have no effect on anything. This does not mean that there are no causal links running from money to the rest of the economy, only that the authorities have acted so as to neutralise these effects. Even within this (equilibrium) context it is important to distinguish between an infinitely interest-elastic demand for money and an infinitely elastic supply.

Accepting that the monetary authorities in general have in the past not followed a policy of controlling the monetary base, however defined, but that they have controlled interest rates, does that in fact mean that the stock was necessarily demand-determined? The answer is 'no' – to make such an assumption is to confuse the demand for money with the demand for credit. The distinction is absolutely crucial, for, as will be argued below, the true implication is that the supply of money in fact becomes a function of lending by the banking sector. This process would be constrained if reserve assets were controlled, and the economic implications have been ignored because of the failure to consider the way the authorities actually operate monetary policy.

Given the great scope for substitution between current and deposit accounts at little or no cost in the United Kingdom, it should be clear that any supply instability is nowhere near as likely to show up in a narrow aggregate such as M1, which should therefore be demand-determined. These arguments were made in Chapter 5.

If reserves are freely available, then, assuming fixed portfolio preferences, the money supply will change as a result of changes in the supply of bank advances: that is, interpreting advances broadly to include money lent to both private and public sectors. Moreover, if we accept that advances can be largely exogenous, for example because of such things as business confidence or restrictions on bank lending, then the possibility must exist that bank deposits can grow faster (or slower) than money holdings can be adjusted to their equilibrium values.

If the supply of money is determined independently of demand, then the components of demand must adjust in order to bring demand into line with supply. This adjustment is likely to take some time, depending upon a variety of factors which are discussed below, and in the interim there may exist an excess supply of money. The first question to be answered is to ascertain how the extra money that comes into existence can be thought of as being excessive. The explanation depends critically on the unique characteristics possessed by money. We have already seen that Friedman and Meiselman viewed money as a residual store of generalised purchasing power. Keynes also argued that money cannot be viewed in the same way as any other commodity; it is different in kind. Keynes (1940) put the argument in terms of government borrowing, but, given the financial system in existence, it could easily be extended to include all bank lending:

> There is no difficulty whatever in paying for the cost of the war [or any fiscal deficit] out of voluntary savings – provided that we put up with the consequences [by which Keynes meant inflationary price rises]. That is where the danger lies. A Government, which has control of the banking and currency system, can always find the cash to pay for its purchases of home produced goods. After allowing for the yield of taxation and for the excess of imports over exports, the balance of the Government's expenditure necessarily remains in the hands of the public in the shape of voluntary savings. That is an arithmetical certainty; for the Government having taken the goods, out of which a proportion of the income of the public has been earned, there is nothing on which this proportion of income can be spent. If prices go up, the extra receipts swell someone's income, so that there is just as much left over as before. This argument is of such importance and is so little understood that it is worth our while to follow it out in detail.

In a world in which reserves are freely available, the role of money as a means of payment means that this argument can be translated to the case of borrowing by the private sector. Payments when received are deposited with the banking system to be registered as an increase in the money supply. The money is accepted but it does not necessarily represent an equilibrium demand. While dynamic adjustment is possible, or, rather, inevitable, in the market for any commodity, and while these adjustments will necessarily have implications for other markets, the pervasive influence of money gives it an importance that results in a difference in kind rather than degree. The role of money as a means of payment means that it enters as an intermediary in *all* market transactions. For this reason it is the perfect buffer to soak up any disequilibrium in an uncertain, imperfect, world. Therefore, any disequilibrium in other markets is likely to be reflected in a disequilibrium in the money market. People will accept money, but it would be wrong to suppose that they wish to retain ownership of it. Money is a means to an end, and only to a relatively minor degree (compared with the transactions it facilitates) is it an end in itself. Money is held but this does not mean that it represents an equilibrium demand for money. Current accounts can be kept at the desired level to finance expected transactions, while any temporary disequilibrium balances can be held as interest-bearing deposits in the same bank. Any increase in the supply of money above the equilibrium demand must be followed by an adjustment in the determinants of demand in order to move towards equilibrium. These adjustments can take the form of output, price or interest-rate changes, and the actual response is obviously very important.

The Process of Adjustment

The process of adjustment in response to an increase in the supply of money is likely to depend critically on (i) the uses for which the original advances were made, and on (ii) the responses of the banking sector.

Money can come into existence as a result of bank lending to the public sector or the private sector and as a consequence of net external flows to the private sector. These are not mutually exclusive categories, since changes in any one of these may well be accompanied by offsetting movements in the others. In particular the contribution of the public sector to the money supply can usefully be thought of as the difference between the size of the Public Sector Borrowing Requirement (P.S.B.R.) and the take up of public-sector debt by the private sector. In order to simplify the discussion we shall begin by abstracting from the external account and consider only the uses to which bank lending to the public and private sectors are put. This establishes the framework within which the external side is introduced subsequently.

It seems probable that the actual type of disequilibrium is likely to affect the length of time taken to correct it. The crucial distinction is between credit extended for the purchase of existing assets and credit for direct use in income/expenditure markets. If there is an increase in credit which is used to purchase existing assets, in particular financial assets or dwellings, this will be only the beginning of a process of portfolio adjustment which we might well expect to be mainly concentrated within asset markets. An individual may sell an existing asset because of a change in circumstances, including but not confined to a change in the price of the asset, in order to purchase an alternative asset. If this represents the general case, so that there is some form of market segmentation, the process of adjustment might take a long time. Obviously there will be income effects associated with those transactions, first in terms of payments to intermediaries (brokers of one type or another), and, second, as the asset stock changes in response to any shift in relative prices.

A more general use of borrowed funds, by the private or public sector, would be the purchase of goods and services, either for final use or as inputs to the productive process. This may result in a change in price in a particular market, but it is also possible that, in an economy characterised by imperfect markets, lags in adjustment, fixed contracts, stocks and unemployed resources, these extra demands will, at least initially, be accommodated through non-price adjustments. Money can therefore come into existence which is accepted only as a temporary intermediary between transactions but which is in excess of the quantity desired for retention within existing portfolios. Even if there is some initial price/interest-rate change as a result of a credit expansion, the relevant comparison is not with the return on money particularly but rather with the return on other physical and financial assets. Money is being held only in the process of adjustment, and in this case adjustment might be quite rapid and be concentrated in income/expenditure markets. To take one simple example, if a firm borrows money in order to expand the work-force, there will be an immediate and equivalent rise in income accompanied by an increase in the demand for money. Adjustment will be quick, and there may not be any significant disequilibrium between supply and demand. For other examples income may respond more slowly and an excess supply of money may persist for some time.

We have arrived at an argument suggesting a direct relationship between money and income which does not work through the simple mechanism of a restricted set of nominal yields on financial assets. It does not, however, depend upon the existence of perfectly competitive markets, and derives directly from the Keynesian 'new view' of the financial system incorporating a reasonable approximation of monetary policy as operated by the authorities.

In a market situation where the banks are free to bid for deposits, as exists at present in the United Kingdom, the process of adjustment can be affected markedly by changes in the interest rate paid on deposits relative to the return available on competing assets. By increasing this differential the banks can induce an increase in the demand for money which may at least partially eliminate any potential excess supply. Such a situation may come about if the demand for private-sector advances is growing strongly, and is expected to continue, and the banks are faced with competition for funds from each other or from the public sector. To the extent that the non-bank financial intermediaries (N.B.F.I.s) compete for funds, the effects of any excess supply may be amplified, since the *ceteris paribus* effect of such competition is to increase the velocity of circulation of existing money balances.

To the extent that the banks are effectively competing with the public sector, the supply of money will also be greater, since less will be borrowed by the public sector from the non-bank private sector and consequently more will be borrowed from the banks. Thus changes in bank interest rates can influence both the demand for and the supply of money, and the relative effects will obviously be important in determining the influence of money on the economy. It may be that the money supply is growing very rapidly but that this will have little immediate effect on the rest of the economy. As long as the banking sector is bidding strongly for deposits, thereby closing the gap between public-sector and bank deposit interest rates, then part of the increase in the money supply will be matched by an increase in the demand for money, as the private sector switches between public-sector debt and bank deposits. To this extent there will be no implications for output or prices, since it is the supply of money relative to equilibrium demand that is crucial.

On the other hand, if the bank deposit/public-sector debt interest differential goes the other way, the money supply can fall but without fully closing the gap between the demand for and supply of money. Looking at only the total quantity of money in existence may therefore be extremely misleading. The stock of money is only important relative to the demand for it. This has obvious implications for the interpretation and conduct of monetary policy.

Monetary Disequilibrium and the Balance of Payments

The argument so far has been developed within the context of a closed economy, and this is further complicated when the analysis is extended to an open economy. Extending the model in this way reveals the same problems for the international monetary approach that the closed-economy model exposed in the high-powered money multiplier supply mechanism. These centre on the failure to take account of the distinction between the demand for money and the demand for credit. If anything, this distinction is even more crucial for the international monetary argument. There is no disagreement that the balance of payments is a monetary phenomenon, and the equilibrium conditions remain the same, but it is not possible to describe disequilibrium situations, and the process of adjustment, simply in terms of the gap between the demand for and supply of money.

The monetary approach to the balance of payments (M.A.B.P.) emphasises the relationship between the balance of payments,[1] and/or the exchange rate, and divergences between the supply of and demand for money (see Chapter 2). If the exchange rate is fixed, the authorities can only control domestic credit, and the quantity of foreign reserves and the supply of money become endogenous. In the case of floating exchange rates reserves are given, the money supply becomes a potential control variable, and the exchange rate changes in order to restore equilibrium. The argument that follows is conducted in terms of fixed exchange rates, as is normally the case, but it can easily be turned around to apply to a situation where exchange rates are allowed to find their own level. It should also be pointed out, and as will become clear below, that although the disequilibrium mechanism mentioned above is rejected as a general description of the process involved, the conclusions regarding potential control remain unaltered.

Main attention is centred on the suggestion that balance-of-payments disequilibrium is associated with disequilibrium between the demand for and supply of money. This contention is found embedded in the very foundations of the monetary approach. There are many references to this effect in an essay written by Frenkel and Johnson (1976) introducing some of the major papers that have been written in this area. For example, 'a surplus in the money account reflects an excess domestic flow demand for money', so that naturally 'the monetary approach focuses on the determinants of the excess domestic flow demand for, or supply of, money' (Frenkel and Johnson, 1976, p. 21). The following description of the adjustment process comes from one of Johnson's contributions to that volume (Johnson, 1976, p. 273):

> Disequilibrium between the demand for money and the initial stock will be corrected through a divergence of expenditure from income and a balance of payments surplus continuing until its cumulative effect has been to make the stock of money held by domestic residents equal to the quantity demanded, as determined by real income and the price level. . . . Balance of payments policies will not produce an inflow of international reserves unless they increase the quantity of money demanded, and unless domestic credit policy forces the resident population to acquire the extra money wanted through the balance of payments via an excess of receipts over out-payments; the balance of payments surplus will continue only until its cumulative effect in

increasing domestic money holdings satisfies the domestic demand for money.

There would therefore seem to be no room for ambiguity about the suggested process: disequilibrium in the balance of payments will be related to inequality between the demand for and supply of money. This argument can be easily summarised as

$$\Delta R = f(M^d - M^s) \qquad (10.1)$$

The change in foreign reserves, ΔR, is related to the gap between the demand for and supply of money ($M^d - M^s$). (The exact definition of foreign reserves is important to the argument and this is considered further below.)

Moreover, 'the essential foundation of the monetary approach is the assumption that the demand for money is a stable function of a few macroeconomic variables' (Frenkel and Johnson, 1976, p. 25) – for example, real income, Y, prices, P, and interest rates, r:

$$M^d = g(Y, P, r) \qquad (10.2)$$

Therefore, real disturbances which change any of these behavioural determinants will also create a monetary disequilibrium. In addition, of course, any monetary disequilibrium originating in the rest of the world (R.O.W.) will feed back to the domestic economy. This implies that we may observe a balance-of-payments disequilibrium without there being any apparent imbalance between the demand for and supply of money. For example, if the result of excess money balances (that is, excess to equilibrium) in R.O.W. is to increase the exports of the domestic economy, then domestic incomes will rise along with the money supply, and the *demand* for money may also rise by an equivalent amount. However, even if the supply of and demand for money increase simultaneously, this does not rule out subsequent adjustment to restore equilibrium on the balance of payments. Tsiang (1977) has pointed out the inconsistency of the monetary argument in apparently ignoring the income-elasticity of the demand for money, thereby requiring the demand for money not to vary with income during the process of adjustment.

One area in which the M.A.B.P. is deficient is in its neglect of the process through which the money supply actually comes into existence. Once this is taken into account, the analysis needs to be further qualified. This does not deny that the balance of payments is a monetary phenomenon, nor that the equilibrium conclusions of the international monetarists still hold; what it does do is substantially qualify the adjustment mechanism that has been widely referred to in the literature. This is important because if the monetary approach is to have practical value, it must be capable of describing disequilibrium situations, and the path and timing of any return towards equilibrium.

Given the present organisation of the monetary system in the United Kingdom, and in most other countries, the money supply is not controlled directly by restricting the availability of bank reserve assets, but through changing the price at which bank reserves will be supplied. This approach, combined with the political sensitivity of interest-rate movements, means that the supply of money will be determined by the quantity of credit (to all customers) provided by the banks. This process was described above for a closed economy. It was emphasised that there is no necessary requirement for the equilibrium demand for money to change by the same amount as the demand for bank credit, and therefore the supply of money, though the motives for demanding bank credit should also result in expenditures (on goods and securities) which will have the effect of raising the demand for money. The speed with which equilibrium is achieved depends critically on the form the expenditures take. This model now needs to be extended to allow for external currency flows influencing the money supply, and adjustment through the balance of payments.

The idea that there can be disequilibrium between the demand for and supply of money is not new, and, of course, underlies the monetary approach to the balance of payments. However, there are important implications for this model once we recognise the significance of the demand for credit in determining the money supply, and that there is no need for this to be matched, in the short term, by an equilibrium demand for money, or if it is, only because of the expenditures facilitated by the credit creation. It should be helpful to consider one or two examples. In all cases we start from a position of universal equilibrium, and assume there are no exogenous shifts in real variables (apart from an increase in credit demand).

First, suppose that there is an increase in the demand for bank credit but that it cannot be provided domestically, perhaps because of quantitative restrictions on bank credit expansion to the private sector. There is no reason why the additional credit cannot be provided from overseas. In this case there will be an increase in reserves, and the money stock, not caused by any prior excess demand for money, which will result in an excess supply. The M.A.B.P. would suggest that a surplus on the balance of payments should be associated with an excess of money demand over money supply. Given a stable demand for money as a function of a few variables (e.g. equation (10.2)) the M.A.B.P. requires one of these behavioural determinants of the demand for money to change, with a fixed money supply, in order to create a balance-of-payments disequilibrium. We now find, however, that the determinants of credit demand are also capable of creating such a situation. Moreover, the M.A.B.P. provides support for this process, once the money-supply mechanism is recognised, for if the behavioural determinants of the demand for bank credit and the demand for money were the same, there could be no disequilibrium between the supply of and demand for money. The process and speed of adjustment will depend on the uses to which the credit is put, and this is considered below. It is, however, unlikely to depend on disequilibrium between the demand for and supply of money.

One obvious example where an inflow from abroad in response to a demand for credit will not result in automatic monetary disequilibrium, or compensating outflows, is when the borrowing is undertaken by the public sector. If the balance of payments is defined as the 'balance for official financing', or confined to the current account and long-term capital account, the so-called 'basic balance', then the purchase of public-sector debt from abroad will lead to a balance-of-payments surplus, but will have no direct effect on the money supply. An indirect effect is possible if the inflows stimulate confidence in the economy. However, in this case the effect is likely to be a *reduction* in the money supply, as sales of public-sector debt to the non-bank private sector will be encouraged. The process is explained in detail below, where it is also suggested that the correct application of the monetary approach requires a redefinition of the external component of the money supply.

Even if we restrict our attention to the private sector, it is still possible for there to be a direct substitution of borrowing from abroad for domestic credit. In this case there will be inflows across exchanges but no necessary monetary disequilibrium. The possibility of such substitution is made more likely by the existence of large multinational companies operating in the United Kingdom. It should therefore be clear that one implication of this suggested approach to money-supply determination is that there are likely to be substitutions between the various sources of credit, and in particular that domestic credit expansion (D.C.E.) is unlikely to be exogenously determined by the authorities; or even if it is directly controlled, inflows can occur because of credit demands without any prior change in the determinants of the demand for money.

We turn now to consider increases in the money supply resulting from an expansion of domestic credit. One possible use of new credit is the purchase of existing assets. In that case disequilibrium between the demand for and supply of money could persist for some time but without resulting in substantial external flows. For example, if the new credit is demanded because of an increase in the demand for housing, relative returns and income/expenditure may be slow to change. Because of uncertainty and imperfect information and markets, an excess supply of money may exist under such circumstances without causing a balance-of-payments outflow. In fact the balance of payments may only respond as the disequilibrium is transmitted to other markets.

Suppose, on the other hand, that new money is spent in such a way that it leads to an increase in the demand for money. It is even possible that if the money, the new credit, is spent on increasing wage payments, for example, then demand might actually increase to the same extent as supply. But that does not mean there will be no repercussions on the balance of payments. As the increase in income is spent some will flow abroad, thereby reducing the supply of money, income and consequently the demand for money. All will be moving together – the fact that balance-of-payments equilibrium requires money market equilibrium is irrelevant to the process of adjustment. (We are back with Tsiang's observation of simultaneous adjustment.) It should be clear from these examples that there is no necessary connection between balance-of-payments disequilibrium and inequality between the demand for and supply of money.

Before proceeding to consider how we are to define the various components of the money supply in practice, it is of interest to consider the attempts that have been made to verify empirically the validity of the monetary approach. Two criteria are generally thought to be fundamental: first, domestic credit expansion must be exogenous (see below); and second the demand for money must be a stable function of a few variables. The first is usually taken as datum (explicitly or implicitly), and empirical testing has concentrated on the latter. These studies have in general been successful, within their own terms of reference, in that they have been able to conclude that a stable demand for money can be identified (see, for example, the evidence and references contained in the volume edited by Frenkel and Johnson, 1976).

It is obviously true that the monetary approach depends crucially on the existence of a stable demand for money function. However, as was pointed out in Chapter 5, it is quite another thing to be able to measure it directly employing non-simultaneous-equation techniques. Within the monetarist framework the supply of money is always adjusting towards demand (i.e. demand and supply are not equal), with, it would seem, quite long lags – which are reflected in balance-of-payments disequilibrium. In consequence, single-equation techniques should be incapable of identifying a stable demand for money schedule – even though such a stable relationship may actually exist. Thus the claims that stable demand functions have been estimated, far from providing strong support for the monetarist cause, are more suggestive that that particular approach is invalid. The introduction of the further complications discussed above only serves to make it even more unlikely that a stable demand relationship can be identified in this way.

Defining Foreign Reserves

Adherents of the monetary approach to the balance of payments write the supply of money as

$$M \equiv D + R \tag{10.3}$$

Where M = the stock of money, D = the stock of domestic credit, R = the stock of foreign reserves, the external counterpart of the money supply, and ΔR reflects any balance-of-payments disequilibrium.

The monetarist description of the endogeneity of foreign reserves (and money) obviously requires reserves and domestic credit to be statistically independent. It would not be much use if a change in foreign reserves automatically implied an identical change in domestic credit in the opposite direction. The normal assumption, in fact, is that domestic credit is exogenous, determined by the authorities, and therefore totally independent of any change in reserves. There is, of course, always the possibility of a behavioural relationship existing, at least in the short run, through the 'reactions' of the authorities to sterilise reserve changes. This is, however, very different from the existence of a direct statistical dependence between the two series.

Any use of this approach for the analysis of the U.K. economy naturally requires an empirical interpretation of identity (10.3). Changes in foreign reserves are usually assumed to be the 'balance for official financing' (B.O.F.). This is, however, not the case, and such an assumption is misleading. Because of the importance now given to money-supply statistics and to the balance of payments it is essential that the interrelationships existing between these two aggregates are fully understood. The best way of doing this is to identify as closely as possible those flows having an independent influence on the domestic money supply.

To begin with we need to establish three basic identities for money, the Public Sector Borrowing Requirement (P.S.B.R.) and B.O.F.

The central definition of the money supply employed in the United Kingdom is Sterling M3(£M3), and it is this we shall concentrate attention on.

$$\Delta\pounds M3 \equiv \Delta NC + \Delta\pounds Lg + \Delta\pounds Lp - (\Delta Df - \Delta Lf) - (\Delta\$Dp - \Delta\$Lp) - (\Delta\$Dg - \Delta\$Lg) - \Delta NDL \quad (10.4)$$

The change in £M3 is equal to the changes in notes and coins, ΔNC, bank lending in sterling to the private and public sectors, Δ£Lp and Δ£Lg, the net overseas indebtedness of the banking sector (ΔDf – ΔLf), the net foreign currency position of the private and public sectors with the banks (Δ$Dp – Δ$Lp) and (Δ$Dg – Δ$Lg), and the change in the non-deposit liabilities of the banking sector, ΔNDL.

$$\text{P.S.B.R.} \equiv \Delta NC + \Delta Bp + \Delta Bf + \Delta\pounds Lg + \Delta\$Lg - \text{B.O.F.} \quad (10.5)$$

The P.S.B.R. plus B.O.F. is financed by issues of notes and coins, and net lending by the private, overseas[2] and banking sectors to the public sector, ΔBp, ΔBf, Δ£Lg and Δ$Lg.

$$\text{B.O.F.} \equiv CA + \Delta Nf + \Delta Bf + (\Delta Df - \Delta Lf) \quad (10.6)$$

B.O.F. is equal to the current account plus the change in net overseas lending from abroad to the private and public sectors, ΔNf and ΔBf, plus the banking sector's net overseas indebtedness.

In order to obtain B.O.F. on the right-hand side of the money-supply identity we need to substitute for Δ£Lg in (10.4) from (10.5):

$$\Delta\pounds M3 \equiv \text{P.S.B.R.} - \Delta Bp + \Delta\pounds Lp + \text{B.O.F.} - \Delta Bf - (\Delta Df - \Delta Lf) - (\Delta\$Dp - \Delta\$Lp) - \Delta\$Dg - \Delta NDL \quad (10.7)$$

Comparing this expression with identity (10.3) we can see that if B.O.F. is equal to the change in the external counterparts of the money supply, the remaining terms on the right-hand side must be equal to the change in domestic credit. This, however, is a most unsatisfactory set of definitions, as should be clear from an inspection of the components making up B.O.F., identity (10.6). To take just one example, an increase in public-sector borrowing from abroad will increase B.O.F. *and* Bf, in identity (10.7), by an exactly equal and offsetting amount. To the extent that B.O.F. can be interpreted as a change in the external counterpart to the money supply, this means that there is an exactly equal and opposite change in domestic credit and foreign reserves. A change in B.O.F. tells us absolutely nothing about the money supply, past, present or future. This is hardly consistent with the monetary approach, which at a very minimum requires the definition of domestic credit to be independent of the definition of the external counterparts. Moreover, it should be clear that any attempt to employ these definitions to determine empirically the causal relationship between D.C.E. and foreign reserves will be biased by the inclusion of common elements in both variables.

In order to concentrate attention on those elements of the external account that have an independent effect on the money supply, it is necessary to substitute for B.O.F. from identity (10.6). This gives

$$\Delta £M3 \equiv [(\text{P.S.B.R} - \Delta \$Dg) - \Delta Bp + \Delta £Lp] + CA + \Delta Nf - (\Delta \$Dp - \Delta \$Lp) - \Delta NDL \quad (10.8)$$

However, even this fails to identify separate components of the money supply which are statistically independent of one another. This is because there are components of the current account of the balance of payments which represent flows to, or from, the public sector. These in turn represent income or expenditure items which enter into the P.S.B.R. For example, government purchases of aircraft from abroad would represent an outflow on the current account and an equal, offsetting, increase in the P.S.B.R. (expenditure minus income). It is therefore possible conceptually, though not in practice, to split the P.S.B.R. into that part which results from domestic expenditure exceeding domestic income, the domestic P.S.B.R.(D.P.S.B.R.) and that part resulting from foreign expenditure exceeding foreign income, the foreign P.S.B.R.(F.P.S.B.R.), i.e.

$$\text{P.S.B.R.} \equiv \text{D.P.S.B.R.} + \text{F.P.S.B.R.} \quad (10.9)$$

In order to eliminate the common elements from the analysis, it is necessary to subtract F.P.S.B.R. from both the P.S.B.R. and the current account. That leaves the domestic borrowing requirement and the current-account transactions of the private sector, CAPR. The new identity we end up with is

$$\begin{aligned}\Delta \pounds M3 \equiv &\ [(\text{D.P.S.B.R.} - \Delta \$Dg) - \Delta Bp + \Delta \pounds Lp] \\ &+ \text{CAPR} + \Delta Nf - (\Delta \$Dp - \Delta \$Lp) - \Delta NDL\end{aligned} \tag{10.10}$$

where each of the components are statistically (although not necessarily behaviourally) independent of the others. By defining those flows contained within the square brackets as 'domestic credit expansion' we can see that the external influences are restricted to the current-account transactions of the private sector, net foreign lending to the U.K. non-bank private sector, and the change in the private sector's net foreign currency position with the banks. A more convenient categorisation, however, is to aggregate these flows together and define those external transactions affecting £M3 as the current account of, and net overseas capital flows to, the private sector, *as long as they are converted to sterling*. The change in public-sector foreign currency deposits, Δ$Dg, has been subtracted from the D.P.S.B.R. in order to eliminate any statistical dependence between D.C.E. and external flows. Otherwise, if these flows were included among the external counterparts, the P.S.B.R. would increase by the same extent, Δ$Dg, that external flows fall; and there would be no net effect on the money supply. This procedure is anyway more consistent with the idea of taking the public sector's borrowing needs as predetermined.

It may help to clarify the position if we compare this exposition with the official definitions as contained in table 11.3 of the *Bank of England Quarterly Bulletin*. The first thing to notice is that, officially, domestic credit expansion is defined to include sterling lending to overseas, as well as the F.P.S.B.R. and foreign currency deposits of the public sector. If we are to follow suit and add these items to domestic credit expansion, we must necessarily subtract them from the external counterpart, giving

$$\begin{aligned}\Delta \pounds M3 \equiv &\ [\text{P.S.B.R.} - \Delta Bp + \Delta \pounds Lp + \Delta \pounds Lf] + CA \\ &+ \Delta Nf - (\Delta \$Dp - \Delta \$Lp) - \Delta \$Dg - \Delta \pounds Lf - \Delta NDL\end{aligned} \tag{10.11}$$

Domestic credit is now as officially defined, so it remains only to see if the external influences defined here are reconcilable with external and foreign currency finance (E.F.C.F.) as defined in table 11.3 of the *Bulletin*. E.F.C.F. is broken down in terms of flows to:

(1) Public sector = B.O.F. $- \Delta$Bf $- \Delta$\$Lg, i.e. official financing of the balance of payments, B.O.F., less market-related flows to the public sector from abroad, ΔBf, and foreign currency lending by the banks to the public sector, Δ\$Lg.
(2) Overseas sterling deposits = $-\Delta$£Df.
(3) Banks foreign currency deposits (net) = $-(\Delta$\$Dp $- \Delta$\$Lp) $-$ (Δ\$Dg $- \Delta$\$Lg) $-$ (Δ\$Df $- \Delta$\$Lf). This is quite straightforward and defines the banks' switched position.

Putting these together we get:

$$\text{E.F.C.F.} = \text{B.O.F.} - \Delta\text{Bf} - \Delta\$\text{Lg} - \Delta£\text{Df} - (\Delta\$\text{Dp} - \Delta\$\text{Lp}) - (\Delta\$\text{Dg} - \Delta\$\text{Lg}) - (\Delta\$\text{Df} - \Delta\$\text{Df}) \quad (10.12)$$

This certainly reinforces our previous argument that B.O.F. is a totally inadequate measure of the external influences on the money supply (and, of course, changes in the level of official reserves would be even less useful in this role). However, it remains necessary to reconcile this definition with that previously obtained in identity (10.11). At first sight this may seem difficult to do since they might appear to be very different and totally unrelated. If they are indeed equal, only different definitions of the same total, then the result of setting them equal to each other would be the definition of B.O.F. given in identity (10.6). And that, in fact, is what happens, i.e.

$$\text{B.O.F.} - \Delta\text{Bf} - \Delta\$\text{Lg} - \Delta£\text{Df} - (\Delta\$\text{Dp} - \Delta\$\text{Lp}) - (\Delta\$\text{Dg} - \Delta\$\text{Lg}) - (\Delta\$\text{Df} - \Delta\$\text{Lp}) \equiv \text{CA} + \Delta\text{Nf} - (\Delta\$\text{Dp} - \Delta\$\text{Lp}) - \Delta\$\text{Dg} - \Delta£\text{Lf}$$

reduces to

$$\text{B.O.F.} \equiv \text{CA} + \Delta\text{Nf} + \Delta\text{Bf} + (\Delta\text{Df} - \Delta\text{Lf}) \qquad (10.6)$$

It is interesting to note that the way D.C.E. and external influences have been officially defined introduces a direct statistical relationship between the two supposedly independent influences. E.F.C.F. as defined in identity (10.12) may on the face of it appear to be independent of D.C.E. in that it contains no items automatically identifiable with the components of D.C.E. However, since E.F.C.F. is also equal to the external counterparts identified in (10.11), we can easily see that the public sector's current-account transactions, banks' sterling lending overseas and any change in the public sector's foreign currency bank deposits are all included in D.C.E. *and*, with an opposite sign, in the external counterpart. The inclusion of these common elements would obviously bias the results of any statistical attempts to verify the monetarist hypothesis. Such a test would first require the cancellation of these offsetting items, and this would return us to identify (10.10), which would therefore seem the most logical starting-point for any empirical test. There is a problem, however, in that it is not possible to identify separately many, if not most, of the public sector's current-account transactions. In practice there will always remain certain common elements which will bias any statistical test in favour of confirming the monetarist hypothesis, which is not to deny that such a behavioural relationship may actually exist. After all, the objective is only to illustrate the problems to be faced in trying to obtain reliable evidence and to identify in the real world the practical counterparts of the abstract theory.

This example demonstrates the care that must be taken in defining the concepts implied by the abstract theory of the monetary approach. As is so often the case, the correspondence between theory and reality is not as close as might superficially be supposed. It is, in fact, quite easy for us all to give different meanings to the same words. In addition the obvious importance of credit flows in the supply function we have ended up with illustrates the danger of ignoring the demands for credit in any analysis of monetary adjustment mechanisms.

Sterilisation of External Currency Flows

Reference was made above to the possibility that the authorities may adopt a policy of deliberately offsetting any external currency flows. It is quite easy to see from identity (10.10) that if, for example, the current account of the private sector were in deficit, thereby tending to reduce the money supply, this could be offset by deliberate action by the authorities either to reduce sales of debt to the non-bank private sector or to increase the D.P.S.B.R. Alternatively, the private sector could offset this tendency by borrowing more from the banks or overseas; and, of course, the opposite reactions would serve to sterilise a current-account surplus.

The monetarists would naturally protest that the ability to sterilise a balance-of-payments deficit is strictly limited by the finiteness of foreign reserves and the limited ability of the government to borrow from abroad. This is obviously true and should be taken into account. However, no such constraint limits the authorities' ability to neutralise a foreign currency inflow; and furthermore, this asymmetry in the practicalities of sterilisation has important implications for the adjustment towards balance-of-payments equilibrium.

The old Gold Standard system, to which the monetarist approach is often compared, is generally described in terms of symmetrical adjustment. Deficit countries experience a contraction of the money supply and a deflation of the economy, while in surplus countries the money supply automatically increases, and with it the level of demand. In this way the surplus and deficit countries are working together in order to resolve the underlying disequilibrium. With the introduction of the possibility of sterilising inflows but not outflows (except temporarily) this international harmony is no longer guaranteed. Now the whole burden of adjustment is placed on the deficit countries, regardless of the underlying causes of the initial disequilibrium.

We should add that this argument is only concerned with the practical possibilities of sterilisation, and not with any value judgements concerning the desirability of such actions. It may be the case that certain countries are following excessively inflationary policies, so that the surplus countries may view any ability to neutralise these forces as a necessary means of restraining the inflationary tendencies of the expansionary economies. The justice of the situation need not concern us here, but it should be clear that there are quite likely to exist circumstances in which placing the weight of adjustment upon the deficit countries is inappropriate as a means of resolving the imbalance that may have arisen.

Controlling the Money Supply

The discussion so far illustrates the problems facing the monetary authorities in employing rates of interest as the main instrument of monetary policy. In the first place, faced with a strong demand for loans by the private sector, the banks will compete strongly for deposits. Under these circumstances moderate increases in the rate of interest on public-sector debt may not succeed in curtailing the credit expansion and a temporarily unstable situation may develop. This will be only temporary because the cost of borrowing will also be increasing, even if the banks reduce their borrowing–lending differential. A persistent rise in interest rates must eventually succeed in stopping the expansion, with the likelihood of an evaporation of the previous high level of credit demand. Allowing for lags in response it is probable that a gap will then open up between bank deposit rates and alternative interest rates, so that the demand for money will actually fall. In this case, although the supply of money may appear to be under control, there may still be an excess supply which will continue to have effects on the rest of the economy. The monetary authorities can therefore succeed in reducing the stock of money, but without resolving the underlying disequilibrium. Even if they succeed in changing expectations, it is not clear, given the adjustment process outlined above, that this will reduce the existing excess supply of money, or cancel out its effects on the economy. To the extent that the authorities can control only the level of particular interest rates, rather than being able to 'fine tune' interest-rate differentials, there is the possibility that short-term control may be difficult to achieve. The control solution in such a case requires a reduction of borrowing from the banking sector, and/or a reduction in the net sterling receipts of the private sector from abroad. Attempting to achieve such control through the banking sector requires a reduction in bank credit to either the public or private sectors, and some rational criteria should be employed in determining which should go short.

An increase in public-sector interest rates may also succeed in attracting additional funds from abroad into public-sector debt. It is sometimes suggested that this inflow will actually lead to an increase in the money supply. In fact, as should be clear from the discussion above, such *additional* flows make no difference at all – unless, that is, it increases confidence in the performance of the economy, and/or the public sector's funding programme, resulting in increased domestic purchases of gilts and a *reduction* in the money supply. Also, if the external inflow into public-sector debt has been diverted from the private sector, there will be a reduction in the money supply. So again it will be relative interest rates that will be important, and if all rates move up together it may only succeed in increasing the supply of money.

These control problems are made worse by the possibility that a monetary expansion may reflect only a reallocation of private-sector portfolios towards the banks. In this situation, when the demand for and supply of money are changing at the same rate, there may be no immediate problem. It will, however, be difficult to identify exactly what is happening, and the monetary authorities may be forced to try to sell even more public-sector debt in response to unfavourable comment at a time when such action is inappropriate. Such action is anyway unlikely to achieve its objective easily, and may prove unduly disruptive to the private sector of the economy. This is of some importance, since control of monetary conditions generally is only a means to an end and is not an ultimate objective in itself.

An Interpretation of the 1970s

In order to assist our understanding of the money-supply process described above, we shall turn to an explanation of recent economic events, particularly for the period following 1971. The 1960s were characterised by financial controls that worked through direct instructions imposing quantitative and qualitative restrictions on the advances the banks were permitted to make to the private sector. As soon as there was any sign that advances might show any appreciable increase, very tight restrictions were immediately imposed. As a consequence the money stock grew only gradually, roughly in line with the rest of the economy. It might even be argued that the growth in the money supply over this period corresponded closely to the equilibrium demand.

The suggestion that these quantitative credit controls were successful in achieving their objective implies that there was not perfect substitution for bank credit. It requires that the operation of the N.B.F.I.s, and therefore the velocity of circulation of money, was not sufficiently flexible to satisfy the excess demands for credit that were created. It also means that external sources of money and finance were not capable of alleviating these credit demands. This should not be particularly surprising given the importance of expected exchange-rate changes in determining external currency flows.

In 1970 and 1971 came the first signs of some relaxation in the tight control over advances, and advances grew as permitted. This movement was completed in September 1971, with the introduction of 'Competition and Credit Control' (C.C.C.). All restrictions on bank lending were removed, while at the same time a number of important structural changes were made – all intended to improve the competitiveness and efficiency of the banking system. In particular the clearing banks were permitted, and encouraged, to compete for deposits, and were allowed to bid for 'wholesale' deposits for the first time. The outcome was an explosive increase in lending to the private sector accompanied by rapid growth in the money stock broadly defined (M3). Figures 10.1 and 10.2 summarise this information. This increase in money failed to leak abroad because the money supply in the other main industrialised countries was also rising very fast at this time, because of lags in perception and adjustment, because domestic and foreign financial markets are not perfect substitutes for most individuals, and because of restrictions on international transactions imposed by exchange control regulations. Anyway, to expect instantaneous substitution ignores the role money plays as a buffer stock absorbing temporal disequilibrium in the economy.

The introduction of C.C.C. was accompanied by a fall in the rate on certificates of deposit (as proxy for a wholesale deposit rate), though by the third quarter of 1972 it had started to rise and actually doubled between 1971(1) and 1973(1); this increase continued during 1973. The increase in the C.D. rate was accompanied by a general rise in competing interest rates, e.g. the Consol rate, but the movement was much less pro-

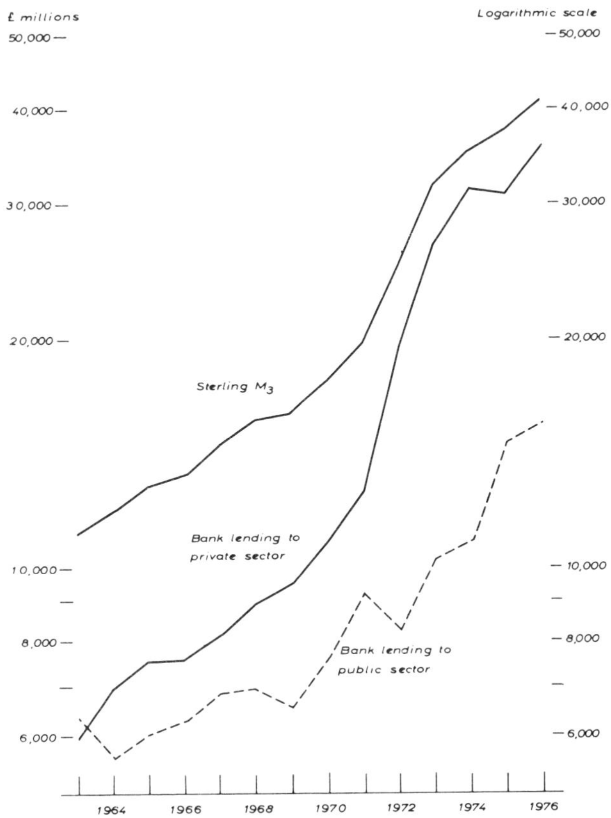

Figure 10.1 Movement of Sterling M3, Bank Lending to the Public Sector and Bank Lending to the Private Sector

nounced with the result that the Consol – C.D. differential narrowed substantially. This trend was reversed during 1974. In addition the Supplementary Special Deposit Scheme was introduced in December 1973 which imposed severe penalties on the banks if their interest-bearing eligible liabilities exceeded some stipulated growth rate. This coincided with a rapid rise in oil prices which had a severely depressing effect on business confidence. From this point on, the growth in M3 declined considerably, but inflation accelerated.

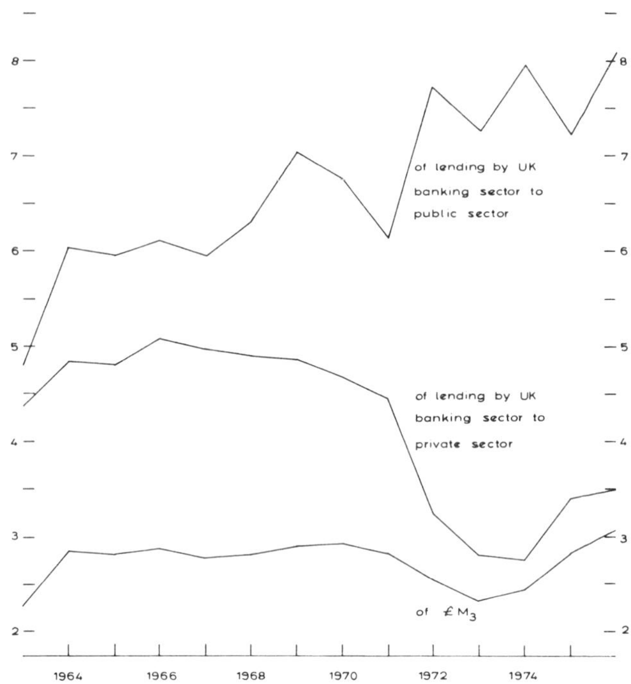

Figure 10.2 Velocity of Circulation

The model sketched out above would suggest that the rapid rise in advances to the private sector after 1971 contributed a substantial 'exogenous' influence on the money supply – by which it is meant that the supply of money was determined by factors independent of demand. Although the increased competition from the banking system probably expanded the demand for deposits, as argued above, it is hard to imagine a narrowing of bank borrowing and lending rates accounting for the substantial expansion in advances that took place. If we accept that the pre-1971 money stock closely followed an equilibrium demand relationship, then it is difficult to argue that supply did not exceed the equilibrium demand to quite a considerable degree. This would seem to be inevitable even if we allow for a stock-adjustment effect in response to the new competitive environment in which the banks found themselves, which anyway might be expected to change the composition of deposits held.

The inflationary effects of this increase in the supply of money were damped down by the real growth potential of the economy resulting from the existence of substantial unemployment and the competitive behaviour of the banks in bidding up interest rates on deposits. At the same time, the successful competition for funds away from the public sector, particularly in 1973, resulted in the growth of M3 being misleadingly fast. The argument is that the creation of new bank finance is likely to be associated with any significant expansion of the economy. To the extent that the first-round expansionary effects are insufficient to equate demand completely with this supply, then this potential excess supply may be reduced by a relative increase in bank deposit rates. Therefore, the subsequent increase in public-sector interest rates resulted in a reduction in the growth rate of M3, but may not have reduced the inflationary consequences resulting from the previously generated supply of money. It is not impossible that the excess supply could actually have increased following the fall in the rate of return offered on deposits. Furthermore, the inflationary consequences of this excess supply would have become amplified by the fact that much of the slack in the economy had by now been absorbed, and that the deterioration in business confidence, and the current account of the balance of payments, following the substantial deterioration in the terms of trade, reduced the possibility of a continued real growth of output. This illustrates an important point that the *speed of adjustment* will depend on many factors external to the supply of money; it is in this way that the announcement effect of monetary targets on expectations is likely to have an effect. What followed was an unprecedented and unexpected combination of high and rising rates of inflation and high and rising levels of unemployment. Far from being incompatible, as sometimes suggested, these developments were virtually inevitable given the model presented above. And, of course, the current account of the balance of payments deteriorated substantially. At the same time, reasonable capital flows to the private sector were maintained as the result of foreign investment in the North Sea oil fields.

The monetary authorities have often been blamed for the explosion in the money stock after the introduction of C.C.C. in 1971, and for the following rapid inflation. This criticism has generally concentrated attention on the size of public-sector borrowing from the banking sector, related to, and dependent upon, the size of the Public Sector Borrowing Requirement. Figures 10.1 and 10.2 show that this is largely unfounded, and the expansion of the money supply in this period was predominantly determined by lending to the private sector. This possibility for the private sector to create its own disequilibrium has been overlooked because of the failure to consider the asset side of banking sector activities and the way in which monetary policy is actually operated. To the extent that there was a problem this was really created by the non-market controls placed on the banking system prior to C.C.C. Taking into account the extensive nature of these controls the problems of transition might have been less if the transition had been more gradual, but it is difficult to criticise the movement towards a more competitive, market-orientated, system. The main problem, as has been argued before (e.g. by Coghlan, 1975), was not the removal of controls on bank lending and the movement towards a more competitive environment, but rather the restrictions and controls imposed upon the banking sector throughout the 1960s.

Faced with this new system, and the rapid increase in the money stock, what should the monetary authorities have done? The increase in the money stock was generally viewed as being demand-determined, so that there therefore seemed to be no particular cause for concern for the future, assuming that the expansion of activity that could be observed to be taking place was acceptable to the authorities. Even if the problem of a supply-determined money stock had been recognised, it is not clear that there were effective short-term options other than reversion to the use of the non-market controls from which it was the objective to break away.

Conclusion

The model outlined above was based on *Keynesian* foundations, with the money supply changing in response to movements in bank credit (broadly defined) and external flows to the private sector. When combined with a stable demand function this supply mechanism suggests a direct relationship between money and output and prices. The speed of adjustment will depend on, among other things, the use to which the credit is put, and the reaction of the banking sector in bidding for deposits. The discussion has therefore been in terms of a disequilibrium framework, with the supply of money being accommodated via channels very similar to those underlying a monetarist explanation, but with the quantity of money not being determined in response to an exogenously determined monetary base.

It was also shown that it is not possible to argue that balance-of-payments disequilibrium is necessarily related to the non-equality of the domestic demand for money with its supply. Moreover, neither the balance for official financing, nor the implied official definition of 'external and foreign currency finance', provide unambiguous measures of the external influences on the money supply which are independent of domestic credit expansion. The net effects of the foreign account are restricted to the current account of, and net overseas lending by, the non-bank private sector, less the net change in the foreign currency position of the U.K. private sector with the banks. It is important to understand these relationships if money and the balance of payments are to be reconciled.

An important implication of the general argument is that there are circumstances under which the private sector of the economy is capable of generating its own expansion without the need for an 'exogenous' fiscal stimulus. It does, however, require that the banking system is permitted to meet the increased demands for credit made by the private sector.

NOTES

Chapter 1

1. Given a binomial distribution the selection of any two from n can simply be obtained through the combinatorial rule, i.e.

$$n_{C_2} = \frac{n!}{2!\,(n-2)!} = \frac{1}{2}n\ (n-1)$$

For an explanation see any elementary statistical textbook.

2. There is also an efficiency gain from adopting a monetary unit that is cheap to produce, and therefore does not tie up a scarce resource. This gain accrues to the producer of the means of payment (see the later discussion on *seignorage*).

Chapter 2

1. The comparison of eventual long-run equilibrium positions after all consequences of a *ceteris paribus* change have worked themselves out.

2. The *IS/LM* model is derived diagrammatically in the Appendix to this chapter.

3. There is no implied presumption here about relative productivity as between sectors, though some (e.g. Bacon and Eltis 1976) would argue that productivity is much higher in the private sector.

4. It is of course necessary to assume, for the purposes of this simplified example, that resources are perfectly adaptable.

5. The exchange rate is defined as the number of units of foreign currency that can be purchased for one unit of the domestic currency; it is therefore the ratio of the former to the latter. Consequently a devaluation would reduce e and increase exports. e is included explicitly in the equation to allow for non-price benefits of a devaluation. This, however, is not necessary to the following arguments, but does reinforce the relative price effect.

6. The *IS* schedule is now slightly different. The income idently has become,

$$Y \equiv C + I + G + X - Z \qquad (2.4a)$$

substituting for $X - Z$ from equation (2.17) the new *IS* schedule is

$$r = \frac{1}{a}\,[A + c_0 - (1 - c_1 - f_4)Y - c_1 T + G - f_1 e - f_2 FD + f_3(P - Pf)] \qquad (2.9a)$$

7. This, as will be argued below, is an extreme simplification, but it is convenient for present purposes. The monetary authorities do have the

ability to control the money supply, though not in the way normally supposed, so it may not be too unrealistic.

Chapter 3

1. Friedman (1953) initially developed the argument in order to establish a platform from which to attack the analysis of 'imperfect competition' (Chamberlin, 1933; Robinson, 1933). He starts by distinguishing positive economics from normative economics as the difference between 'what is' and 'what ought to be', but continues by defining the former much more narrowly. Accordingly, 'hypotheses should be judged by the conformity of their predictions to events, rather than the conformity of their assumptions, in some descriptive sense, to reality'. The choice between alternative hypotheses is to be decided by their relative 'simplicity' and 'fruitfulness'. The simplest is the one embodying the least initial knowledge, and the most fruitful, the one yielding the most precise prediction over the widest area, and the most suggestive of additional lines of research. Logical completeness and consistency are relevant, but play an essentially subsidiary role.

2. Correlation coefficients simply show the degree of linear correlation, relatedness, between two series, e.g. r_{CA} would be the correlation between C and A, or $r_{CA.M}$ the partial correlation between C and A holding M constant.

3. For example, compare the following two equations with (2.11) and (2.12).

4. Obtained by substituting the income identity into (3.7).

5. It is worth noting, however, as an example of the *ad hoc* nature of this study, that the substitution of the income identity into (3.8) in fact results in

$$C = a + VM - A \tag{3.8b}$$

6. V and k cannot possibly have the same interpretation as before.

7. We can, of course, define different multipliers for different measures of fiscal policy; essentially this requires different assumptions about the endogenous elements of policy (for example, see Hansen, 1973). However, the multipliers still only apply to actual magnitudes.

8. Named after Shirley Almon (1965). It is not clear how reliable this method is in approximating an unknown lag distribution. For example, when Cargill and Meyer (1974) compared various methods for estimating lag patterns, they found that the Almon technique performed relatively poorly and concluded that it is an unreliable method of approximating an unknown lag distribution.

9. In addition to the attempts to explain the behaviour of the economy, albeit within very basic models, there have also been attempts to obtain purely statistical evidence of the association between money and income. This is surveyed briefly in the Appendix to this chapter.

10. A second article the same year by Crockett (1970) examined the statistical relationship between money and income, and this is referred to in the Appendix to this chapter.

11. A reaction function defines the 'reactions' of the authorities in response to changes in economic variables they wish to control (for example, see Coghlan, 1975).

Chapter 4

1. This category will include any short-term, capital-safe assets not included in the money supply.

2. The cost could, however, be substantially increased if there were a variable cost associated with such transactions, since the size is practically doubled by the need to switch out of, and then into, money.

3. Instead of denoting average money holding by M we could, of course, write $k/2$, as before.

4. A capital-uncertain asset is a marketable security whose price is determined by the market; this is usually taken to be a bond with a coupon fixed in money terms.

5. The important characteristic is that the whole distribution can be explained in terms of two of its 'moments' (see p. 104). The normal distribution can be explained in terms of the mean and the standard deviation, which is exactly what is required for the analysis.

6. Strictly speaking, that is not quite correct, since the analysis employs the first moment about the origin and the second moment about the mean.

7. Arbitrage means the purchase of securities in one market for immediate resale on another in order to profit from a discrepancy in yields.

Chapter 5

1. The problem with statistics is admirably illustrated by this quotation from Sir Joshia Stamp (1929, pp. 258–9): 'Harold Cox, when a young man in India, quoted some Indian statistics to a Judge. The Judge replied: "Cox, when you are a bit older, you will not quote Indian statistics with that assurance. The government are very keen on amassing statistics – they collect them, add them, raise them to the Nth power, take the cube root and prepare wonderful diagrams. But what you must never forget is that every one of those figures comes in the first instance from the *chowty bar* (village watchman) who just puts down what he damn pleases."'

2. Without taking logarithms these equations would be written as:

$$M^* = \frac{A_0 Y^{a_1} P^{a_2}}{R^{a_3}} \quad \text{and} \quad \frac{M}{M_{-1}} = \left[\frac{M^*}{M_{-1}}\right]^{\lambda} U$$

3. Unlike most other demand for money studies either in the United Kingdom or the United States, estimation at the Bank of England has generally included the rate of interest in the form $(100 + R)$. This is quite the opposite of the more normal Keynesian assumption when employed in the demand for money broadly defined, since it implies that the interest-elasticity increases with the rate of interest, and approaches zero as the rate of interest becomes very small, i.e.

$$\frac{\partial M}{\partial R}\frac{R}{M} = \frac{-a_3 R}{1+R}.$$

It is, however, not an unreasonable assumption when applied to narrow money balances, and illustrates the importance of the actual definition of money employed.

4. An argument that is often employed to support this assumption is that a change in the scale of measurement, e.g. a conversion of pounds to dollars, would not change real expenditures or the demand for real balances. This is certainly true, but it is not strictly relevant to this argument. What we are concerned with is a continous updating of uncertain information, not a single discrete change that is universally accepted. Moreover, even if there is some theoretically correct concept of the price level which would display a unitary elasticity, it is unlikely to correspond to any of the actual data series available.

5. This study was estimated in first differences, and it has subsequently been shown (Courakis, 1978; and Hendry and Mizon, 1978) that this particular formulation was not a good description of the data generating process.

6. Before taking logarithms, and for a single variable, X, this equation would be written as

$$X^e = \Pi(X)^{\alpha(1-\alpha)_i}$$

Again, a geometrically declining distributed lag is being implicitly assumed, therefore resulting in the familiar Koyck lag pattern.

7. See also Hendry and Mizon (1978).

8. The erratic adjustment of money to price changes seems to be associated with the seasonal adjustment of the variables; when unseasonally adjusted data were employed, the long-run value remained the same but full adjustment took place after a one-quarter lag.

9. Sterling M3 consists of notes and coins held outside the banks plus total sterling-denominated deposits of U.K. residents with the banking sector.

10. Notes and coins held outside the banks plus the current accounts of the banking sector.

Chapter 6

1. For example, substituting -1 for R_{ij} into (6.33) yields

$$\frac{\sigma_1^2 + \sigma_1\sigma_2}{\sigma_1^2 + \sigma_2^2 + 2\sigma_1\sigma_2}$$

This in turn simplifies to

$$\frac{\sigma_1(\sigma_1 + \sigma_2)}{(\sigma_1 + \sigma_2)^2}$$

which reduces to the expression given in (6.41).

Chapter 7

1. A valuable check for consistency is to see if investment, A_1D_1, plus present consumption, OF_1, equals income, OA_1, plus borrowing, D_1F_1. This

is obviously true in this case since $OA_1 = OD_1 + A_1D_1$, and $OD_1 + D_1F_1 = OF_1$; therefore, $A_1D_1 + OF_1 = OA_1 + D_1F_1$.

2. An examination of Figures 7.9, 7.10 and 7.12 also indicates that a fall in the rate of interest will invariably result in an increase in the level of investment.

3. For the purposes of this illustration the only financial liability issued by the government is assumed to be cash, and that the government acquires real assets of equivalent value, so that net worth is zero.

4. The central control and planning of financial flows does not eliminate the need for saving and investment to be separated. The difference is that under such a system it is directly controlled from the centre instead of being left to the operation of free-market forces.

Chapter 8

1. Questions of efficiency in the movement of funds will of course also be important and these are considered in more detail later in the chapter.

2. At the time when small regional banks existed in the United Kingdom the London discount market developed in order to facilitate the transfer of funds between banks. In recent years the development of the inter-bank market has further improved this process.

3. As outlined in 'Competition and Credit Control', *Bank of England Quarterly Bulletin*, September 1971.

4. Holdings of private-sector debt, plus public-sector debt of over five years to maturity, must not exceed twenty times their own capital and reserves, and total assets must not exceed thirty times capital and reserves.

5. These are deposits at the Bank of England, money at call and short notice, Treasury bills, British government securities with less than a year to maturity, and local authority and commercial bills eligible for rediscount at the Bank of England.

6. These are the banks that were previously defined as 'accepting houses, overseas banks and other banks'. The present more detailed breakdown is between 'accepting houses, other British banks, American banks, Japanese banks, other overseas banks and consortium banks'.

7. Building society shares are not equivalent to the equity issue of a normal company, and are usually highly liquid. Shareholders are members of the society while depositors are creditors.

8. The only other asset held by the intermediaries is a liquid reserve in the form of currency.

9. The supply curve of an industry composed of perfectly competitive firms is given by the horizontal summation of the marginal cost curves of each individual firm (above minimum average cost).

Chapter 9

1. It is assumed that the public sector do not hold any bank deposits.

2. It may be the case that the reserve ratios of the banks and the N.B.F.I.s have been imposed by the monetary authorities.

3. The derivations of all final equations are contained in the appendix to this chapter.

4. In fact this is not quite correct since k is really the public's preference ratio, the ratio of S to Dp, not D. It is, however, a convenient approximation and is retained in the text.

5. These are bills accepted by banks and are thereby discountable at preferential terms. The accepting bank (any of the listed banks) becomes guarantor of the debt and accepts a contingent liability in the event of default by the original debtor.

Chapter 10

1. That is, the balance of payments broadly defined to include current- and capital-account flows.

2. Obviously this does not include that overseas lending which is a counterpart of the official financing requirement, but it does include all other public-sector flows entering the capital account of the balance of payments.

REFERENCES

Additional references have been included which were not mentioned in the text when they are relevant to the arguments presented. These are distinguished by an asterisk (*).

Chapter 1

C. Bresciani-Turroni, *The Economics of Inflation* (Northampton: Dickens & Co., 1937; first published in Italian by Università Bocconi, 1931).

K. Brunner and A. H. Meltzer, 'The Uses of Money: Money in the Theory of an Exchange Economy', *American Economic Review*, vol. 61, no. 4, Dec 1971.

R. Cameron, *Banking in the Early Stages of Industrialisation* (London: Oxford University Press, 1967).

R. W. Clower, 'Introduction', in *Monetary Theory*, ed. R. W. Clower (Harmondsworth: Penguin Books, 1969).

F. H. Hahn, 'On the Foundations of Monetary Theory', in *Essays in Modern Economics*, ed. M. Parkin (London: Longman, 1973).

J. R. Hicks, *Critical Essays in Monetary Theory* (Oxford: Clarendon Press, 1967).

E. V. Morgan, *A History of Money* (Harmondsworth: Penguin Books, 1965).

G. L. Shackle, 'Comments on R. L. Clower's paper on Theoretical Foundations of Monetary Policy', in *Monetary Theory and Monetary Policy in the 1970s: Proceedings of the 1970 Sheffield Money Seminar*, ed. G. Clayton, J. C. Gilbert and R. Sedgwick (London: Oxford University Press, 1971).

Chapter 2

R. Bacon and W. Eltis, *Britain's Economic Problem: Too Few Producers* (London: Macmillan, 1976).

M. J. Bailey, 'The Welfare Effects of Inflationary Finance', *Journal of Political Economy*, vol. 64, 1956.

*R. J. Barro and H. I. Grossman, 'A General Disequilibrium Model of Income and Employment', *American Economic Review*, vol. 61, Mar 1971.

K. Brunner and A. H. Meltzer, 'Government, the Private Sector and "Crowding Out"', *Banker*, vol. 126, no. 605, July 1976.

V. Chick, 'Financial Counterparts of Saving and Investment and Inconsistency in Some Simple Macro Models', *Weltwirtschaftliches Archiv*, vol. 109, no. 2, 1973.

*C. F. Christ, 'A Short-run Aggregative-demand Model of the Interdependence and Effects of Monetary and Fiscal Policies with

Keynesian and Classical Interest Elasticities', *American Economic Review*, Papers and Proceedings, vol. 57, no. 2, May 1967.

R. L. Clower, 'The Keynesian Counterrevolution: A Theoretical Appraisal', in *The Theory of Interest Rates*, ed. F. H. Hahn and F. P. R. Brechling (London: Macmillan, 1965).

R. T. Coghlan, 'Alternative Portfolio Approaches to Balance of Payments Adjustment', *Scottish Journal of Political Economy*, vol. 25, no. 1, Feb 1978.

J. M. Culbertson, *Macroeconomic Theory and Stabilization Policy* (New York: McGraw-Hill, 1968).

R. Dornbusch, 'Notes on Growth and the Balance of Payments', *Canadian Journal of Economics*, vol. 4, no. 3, Aug 1971.

I. Fisher, *The Purchasing Power of Money*, 2nd ed. (New York: Macmillan, 1913).

J. A. Frenkel and H. G. Johnson, *The Monetary Approach to the Balance of Payments* (London: Allen & Unwin, 1976).

M. Friedman, 'The Role of Monetary Policy', *American Economic Review*, vol. 58, Mar 1968.

A. H. Hansen, *A Guide to Keynes* (New York: McGraw-Hill, 1953).

J. R. Hicks, 'Mr. Keynes and the "Classics"', *Econometrica*, vol. 5, no. 2, Apr 1937; reprinted in J. R. Hicks, *Critical Essays in Monetary Theory* (London: Oxford University Press, 1967).

D. Hume, 'Of Money', in *Political Discourses* (Edinburgh: Fleming, 1752); Reprinted in *Money and Banking*, ed. A. A. Walters (Harmondsworth: Penguin Books, 1973).

J. M. Keynes, *The General Theory of Employment, Interest and Money* (London: Macmillan, 1936).

J. M. Keynes, 'Alternative Theories of the Rate of Interest', *Economic Journal*, vol. 47, no. 2, June 1937a.

J. M. Keynes, 'The "Ex-Ante" Theory of the Rate of Interest', *Economic Journal*, vol. 47, no. 4, p. 668, Dec 1937b.

A. Leijonhufvud, *On Keynesian Economics and the Economics of Keynes* (New York: Oxford University Press, 1968).

*A. Leijonhufvud, *Keynes and the Classics*, Occasional Paper No. 30 (London: Institute of Economic Affairs, 1969).

J. Locke, *Some Considerations of the Consequences of the Lowering of Interest and Raising the Value of Money* (printed for Awnsham and John Churchill at the Black Swan in Paternoster Row, 1691).

R. A. Mundell, 'The Monetary Dynamics of International Adjustment Under Fixed and Flexible Exchange Rates', *Quarterly Journal of Economics*, May 1960.

R. A. Mundell, 'The Appropriate Use of Monetary and Fiscal Policy for Internal and External Stability', *International Monetary Fund Staff Papers*, vol. 9, Mar 1962; reprinted in *Monetary Theory and Policy*, ed. R. S. Thorn (New York: Random House, 1966).

*D. Patinkin, 'Price Flexibility and Full Employment', *American Economic Review*, vol. 38, no. 4, Sep 1948; revised version in *Readings in Monetary Theory*, American Economic Association (New York: Blackistone, 1962).

*J. J. Polak, 'Monetary Analysis of Income Formation and Payments Problems', *International Monetary Fund Staff Papers*, vol. 6, no. 1, Nov 1957.
Radcliffe Report on the Working of the Monetary System, Cmnd 827 (London: H.M.S.O., 1959).
*J. Robinson, 'The Rate of Interest', *Econometrica*, vol. 19, no. 1, Jan 1951.
W. L. Silber, 'Fiscal Policy in *IS–LM* Analysis: A Correction', *Journal of Money, Credit and Banking*, vol. 2, no. 4, Nov 1970.
*R. W. Spencer and W. P. Yohe, 'The "Crowding Out" of Private Expenditures by Fiscal Policy Actions', *Federal Reserve Bank of St Louis Monthly Review*, vol. 52, no. 10, Oct 1970.
J. Tinbergen, *On the Theory of Economic Policy* (Amsterdam: North-Holland, 1952).

Chapter 3

S. Almon, 'The Distributed Lag between Capital Appropriations and Expenditures', *Econometrica*, Jan 1965.
L. C. Andersen and K. M. Carlson, 'A Monetarist Model for Economic Stabilization', *Federal Reserve Bank of St Louis Monthly Review*, vol. 52, no. 4, Apr 1970.
L. C. Andersen and J. L. Jordan, 'Monetary and Fiscal Actions: A Test of their Relative Importance in Economic Stabilization', *Federal Reserve Bank of St Louis Monthly Review*, vol. 50, no. 11, Nov 1968.
A. Ando and F. Modigliani, 'The Relative Stability of Monetary Velocity and the Investment Multiplier', *American Economic Review*, vol. 55.
M. Artis and R. Nobay, 'Two Aspects of the Monetary Debate' *National Institute Economic Review*, no. 49, Aug 1969.
C. R. Barrett and A. A. Walters, 'The Stability of Keynesian and Monetary Multipliers', *Review of Economics and Statistics*, vol. 48, no. 4, Nov 1966.
T. F. Cargill and R. A. Meyer, 'Some Time and Frequency Domain Distributed Lag Estimators: A Comparative Monte Carlo Study', *Econometrica*, Nov 1974.
E. H. Chamberlin, *The Theory of Monopolistic Competition* (London: Oxford University Press, 1933).
R. T. Coghlan, 'Bank Competition and Bank Size', *Manchester School*, vol. XLII, no. 2, June 1975.
F. Cripps, W. Godley and M. Fetherston, 'Public Expenditure and the Management of the Economy', Memorandum submitted to the House of Commons Expenditure Committee, and published in their Ninth Report on *Public Expenditure, Inflation and the Balance of Payments* (London: H.M.S.O., 13 Aug 1974).
A. D. Crockett, 'Timing Relationships between Movements of Monetary and National Income Variables', *Bank of England Quarterly Bulletin*, vol. 10, no. 4, Dec 1970.
S. K. Edge, 'The Relative Stability of Monetary Velocity and the Investment Multiplier', *Australian Economic Papers*, Dec 1967.
G. R. Fisher and D. K. Sheppard, *Effects of Monetary Policy on the United*

States Economy: A Survey of Econometric Evidence (Paris: O.E.C.D., Dec 1972).

M. Friedman, 'The Methodology of Positive Economics', in *Essays in Positive Economics* (University of Chicago Press, 1953).

M. Friedman and D. Meiselman, 'The Relative Stability of Monetary Velocity and the Investment Multiplier in the United States, 1897–1958', *Research Study Two in Stabilization Policies*, prepared by E. Cary Brown *et al.* for the Commission on Money and Credit (Englewood Cliffs, N.J.: Prentice-Hall, 1963).

W. Godley and F. Cripps, 'Demand Inflation and Economic Policy', *London and Cambridge Economic Bulletin*, no. 84; reprinted from *The Times*, 22 and 23 Jan 1974.

S. M. Goldfeld and A. S. Blinder, 'Some Implications of Endogenous Stabilization Policy', *Brookings Papers on Economic Activity*, no. 3, 1972.

C. A. E. Goodhart, 'Monetary Relationships: A View from Threadneedle Street', in *Papers in Monetary Economics*, vol. 1 (Reserve Bank of Australia, 1975).

C. A. E. Goodhart and A. Crockett, 'The Importance of Money', *Bank of England Quarterly Bulletin*, vol. 10, no. 2, June 1970.

C. W. J. Granger, 'Investigating Causal Relations by Econometric Models and Cross-Spectral Methods', *Econometrica*, vol. 37, July 1969.

B. Hansen, 'On the Effects of Fiscal and Monetary Policy: A Taxonomic Discussion', *American Economic Review*, vol. 63, no. 4, Sep 1973.

J. R. Hicks, 'A Suggestion for Simplifying the Theory of Money, *Economica*, Feb 1935; reprinted in J. R. Hicks *Critical Essays in Monetary Theory* (London: Oxford University Press, 1967).

N. Kaldor, 'The "New" Monetarism', *Lloyds Bank Review*, no. 97, July 1970.

London Business School Centre for Economic Forecasting, *Economic Outlook 1977–80*, 1977.

F. Modigliani, 'The Monetarist Controversy, or Should we Foresake Stabilization Policies?', *American Economic Review*, vol. 67, no. 2, 1977.

*W. Poole and E. B. F. Kornblith, 'The Friedman–Meiselman C.M.C. Paper: New Evidence on an Old Controversy', *American Economic Review*, vol. 63, Dec 1973.

W. Rees–Mogg, 'How a 9.4 % Excess Money Supply gave Britain 9.4 % inflation', *The Times*, 13 July 1976; see also 'Programme for Economic Stability', leader in *The Times*, 20 Sep 1976.

J. Robinson, *Economics of Imperfect Competition* (London: Macmillan, 1933).

C. A. Sims, 'Money, Income and Causality', *American Economic Review*, vol. 62, no. 4, Sep 1972.

R. Tarling and F. Wilkinson, 'Inflation and Money Supply', in *Economic Policy Review*, no. 3, Department of Applied Economics, University of Cambridge, Mar 1977.

D. Williams, C. A. E. Goodhart and D. H. Gowland, 'Money, Income, and Causality: The U.K. Experience', *American Economic Review*, vol. 66, no. 3, June 1976.

Chapter 4

W. J. Baumol, 'The Transactions Demand for Cash: An Inventory Theoretic Approach', *Quarterly Journal of Economics*, vol. 66, Nov 1952.

K. Brunner and A. H. Meltzer, 'Economies of Scale in Cash Balances Reconsidered', *Quarterly Journal of Economics*, vol. 81, no. 3, 1967.

*O. E. Covick, 'The Quantity Theory of Drink – A Restatement', *Australian Economic Papers*, Dec 1974.

F. Y. Edgeworth, 'The Mathematical Theory of Banking', *Journal of the Royal Statistical Society*, vol. 51, 1888.

M. Friedman, 'The Role of Monetary Policy', *American Economic Review*, vol. 58, Mar 1968.

M. Friedman, 'The Quantity Theory of Money – A Restatement', in *Studies in the Quantity Theory of Money*, ed. M. Friedman (University of Chicago Press, 1956); reprinted in *The Optimum Quantity of Money and Other Essays* (London: Macmillan, 1969).

M. Friedman and D. Meiselman, 'The Relative Stability of Monetary Velocity and the Investment Multiplier in the United States, 1897–1958', *Research Study Two in Stabilization Policies*, prepared by E. Cary Brown *et al.* for the Commission on Money and Credit (Englewood Cliffs, N.J.: Prentice-Hall, 1963).

J. R. Hicks, 'A Suggestion for Simplifying the Theory of Money', *Economica*, Feb 1935; reprinted in J. R. Hicks, *Critical Essays in Monetary Theory* (London: Oxford University Press, 1967).

J. R. Hicks, *Critical Essays in Monetary Theory* (Oxford: Clarendon Press, 1967).

*H. G. Johnson, 'Notes on the Theory of Transactions Demand for Cash', in *Essays in Monetary Economics*, ed. H. G. Johnson (London: Allen & Unwin, 1967); reprinted from *Indian Journal of Economics*, vol. 44, part 1, no. 172, 1963.

J. M. Keynes, *The General Theory of Employment, Interest and Money* (London: Macmillan, 1936).

H. M. Markovitz, 'Portfolio Selection', *Journal of Finance*, vol. 7, no. 1, Mar 1952.

H. M. Markovitz, *Portfolio Selection* (Yale University Press, 1959).

D. Orr, *Cash Management and the Demand for Money* (New York: Praeger, 1970).

D. Patinkin, *Money, Interest and Prices* (New York: Harper & Row, 1965).

D. Patinkin, 'The Chicago Tradition, the Quantity Theory, and Friedman', *Journal of Money, Credit and Banking*, vol. 1, no. 1, 1969; reprinted in *Studies in Monetary Economics*, ed. D. Patinkin (New York: Harper & Row, 1972).

J. Tobin, 'The Interest–Elasticity of Transactions Demand for Cash', *Review of Economics and Statistics*, vol. 38, no. 3, 1956.

J. Tobin, 'Liquidity Preference as Behavior Towards Risk', *Review of Economic Studies*, vol. 25, Feb 1958.

J. Tobin, 'The Theory of Portfolio Selection', in *The Theory of Interest Rates*, ed. F. Hahn and F. Brechling (London: Macmillan, 1965).

E. L. Whalen, 'A Rationalization of the Precautionary Demand for Cash', *Quarterly Journal of Economics*, vol. 80, no. 2, 1966.

Chapter 5

M. J. Artis and M. K. Lewis, 'The Demand for Money: Stable or Unstable?', *Banker*, vol. 124, no. 577, Mar 1974.
M. J. Artis and M. K. Lewis, 'The Demand for Money in the United Kingdom: 1963–1973', *Manchester School*, June 1976.
P. Cagan and A. J. Schwartz, 'Has the Growth of Money Substitutes Hindered Monetary Policy?' *Journal of Money, Credit and Banking*, vol. 7, no. 2, 1977.
R. T. Coghlan, 'A Transactions Demand for Money', *Bank of England Quarterly Bulletin*, vol. 18, no. 1, Mar 1978.
A. S. Courakis, 'Serial Correlation and a Bank of England Study of the Demand for Money: An Exercise in Measurement Without Theory', *Economic Journal*, vol. 88, no. 351, Sep 1978.
M. Friedman, 'The Role of Monetary Policy', *American Economic Review*, vol. 58, Mar 1968.
C. A. E. Goodhart and A. Crockett, 'The Importance of Money', *Bank of England Quarterly Bulletin*, vol. 10, no. 2, June 1970.
Z. Griliches, 'Distributed Lags: A Survey', *Econometrica*, Jan 1967.
G. Hacche, 'A Review of Demand for Money Relationships', *Bank of England Quarterly Bulletin*, vol. 14, no. 3, Sep 1974.
M. J. Hamburger, 'The Demand for Money in an Open Economy: Germany and the United Kingdom', *Journal of Monetary Economics*, Jan 1977.
D. F. Hendry and G. E. Mizon, 'Serial Correlation as a Convenient Simplification, Not a Nuisance: A Comment on a Study of the Demand for Money by the Bank of England', *Economic Journal*, vol. 88, no. 351, Sep 1978.
D. W. Jorgenson, 'Rational Distributed Lag Functions', *Econometrica*, vol. 32, no. 1, Jan 1966.
N. Kaldor, 'The "New" Monetarism', *Lloyds Bank Review*, no. 97, July 1970.
L. M. Koyck, *Distributed Lags and Investment Analysis* (Amsterdam: North-Holland, 1954).
D. E. W. Laidler, 'The Influence of Money on Economic Activity: A Survey of Some Current Problems', in *Monetary Theory and Monetary Policy in the 1970s*, ed. G. Clayton, J. C. Gilbert and R. Sedgwick (London: Oxford University Press, 1971).
D. E. W. Laidler and J. M. Parkin 'The Demand for Money in the U.K., 1955–67: Preliminary Estimates', *Manchester School*, vol. 38, no. 3, Sep 1970.
L. D. D. Price, 'The Demand for Money in the United Kingdom: A Further Investigation', *Bank of England Quarterly Bulletin*, vol. 12, no. 1, Mar 1972.
J. Stamp, *Some Economic Factors in Modern Life* (Westminster: P. S. King & Son, 1929).

K. F. Wallis, 'Seasonal Adjustment and Relations between Variables', *Journal of the American Statistical Association*, vol. 69, no. 345, Mar 1974.

Chapter 6

*A. D. Bain, 'Flow of Funds Analysis: A Survey', *Economic Journal*, Dec 1973.
Bank of England, *United Kingdom Flow of Funds Accounts 1963–1976* (May 1978).
S. Brittan, *Steering the Economy* (Harmondsworth: Penguin Books, 1971).
*J. Cohen, 'Copeland's Money flows After Twenty-five Years: A Survey', *Journal of Economic Literature*, 1972.
*G. S. Dorrance, *National Monetary and Financial Analysis* (London: Macmillan Press, 1978).
J. C. Francis and S. H. Archer, *Portfolio Analysis* (Englewood Cliffs, N.J.: Prentice-Hall, 1971).
H. Levey and M. Sarnat, *Investments and Portfolio Analysis* (New York: Wiley, 1972).
J. Revell, *The Wealth of the Nation* (Cambridge University Press, 1967).
J. Revell and A. R. Roe, 'National Balance Sheets and National Accounting – A Progress Report', *Economics Trends*, 1971.
A. R. Roe, *The Financial Interdependence of the Economy, 1957–1966* (Department of Applied Economics, University of Cambridge/Chapman & Hall, Nov 1971).

Chapter 7

*I. Fisher, *The Theory of Interest* (London: Macmillan, 1930).
*J. Hirshleifer, 'On the Theory of Optimal Investment Decision', *Journal of Political Economy*, Aug 1958.
*J. Hirshleifer, *Investment, Interest and Capital* (Englewood Cliffs, N.J.: Prentice-Hall, 1970).

Chapter 8

*G. Clayton, 'British Financial Intermediaries in Theory and Practice', *Economic Journal*, Dec 1962.
*H. G. Johnson, *Readings in British Monetary Economics* (London: Oxford University Press, 1972), section v.
J. M. Keynes, *The General Theory of Employment, Interest and Money* (London: Macmillan, 1936).
J. Revell, *The British Financial System* (London: Macmillan, 1973).
G. L. S. Shackle, *Expectations in Economics* (Cambridge University Press, 1955).
*E. R. Shaw, *The London Money Market* (London: Heinemann, 1975).
*D. K. Sheppard, *The Growth and Role of UK Financial Institutions* (London: Methuen, 1971).

*J. Tobin and W. C. Brainard, 'Financial Intermediaries and the Effectiveness of Monetary Controls', *American Economic Review*, May 1963.

Chapter 9

R. T. Coghlan, 'Bank Competition and Bank Size', *Manchester School*, June 1975.
R. T. Coghlan, 'Analysis Within the "New View"', *Journal of Money, Credit and Banking*, Aug 1977.
M. Friedman and A. J. Schwartz, *A Monetary History of the United States, 1867–1960* (Princeton University Press, 1963).
J. G. Gurley and E. S. Shaw, 'Financial Aspects of Economic Development', *American Economic Review*, Sep 1955.
*J. G. Gurley and E. S. Shaw, *Money in a Theory of Finance* (Washington, D.C.: Brookings Institution, 1960).
J. M. Guttentag and R. Lindsay, 'The Uniqueness of Commercial Banks', *Journal of Political Economy*, Oct 1968.
J. M. Keynes, 'Alternative Theories of the Rate of Interest', *Economic Journal*, June 1937a.
J. M. Keynes, 'The "Ex-Ante" Theory of the Rate of Interest', *Economic Journal*, Dec 1937b.
J. Tobin 'Commercial Banks as Creators of Money', in *Banking and Monetary Studies*, ed. D. Carson, for Comptroller of the Currency, U.S. Treasury (Homewood, Ill.: Irwin, 1963); reprinted in *Essays in Economics: Macroeconomics*, ed. J. Tobin (Chicago: Markham Publishing Co., 1971), from which references have been taken.
J. Tobin and W. C. Brainard, 'Financial Intermediaries and the Effectiveness of Monetary Controls', *American Economic Review*, May 1963.
J. M. Parkin, M. R. Gray and R. J. Barrett, 'The Portfolio Behaviour of Commercial Banks', in *The Econometric Study of the United Kingdom*, ed. K. Hilton and D. F. Heathfield (London: Macmillan, 1970).
J. H. Wood, 'Two Notes on the Uniqueness of Commercial Banks', *Journal of Finance*, Mar 1970.

Chapter 10

R. T. Coghlan, 'Bank Competition and Bank Size', *Manchester School*, June 1975.
*R. T. Coghlan, 'A New View of Money', *Lloyds Bank Review*, July 1978.
J. A. Frenkel and H. G. Johnson, 'The Monetary Approach to the Balance of Payments: Essential Concepts and Historical Origins', in *The Monetary Approach to the Balance of Payments*, ed. J. A. Frenkel and H. G. Johnson (London: Allen & Unwin, 1976).
C. A. E. Goodhart, 'Monetary Relationships: A View from Threadneedle Street', paper presented at the Reserve Bank of Australia Conference in Monetary Economics, July 1975.
B. Griffiths, 'Resource and Efficiency, Monetary Policy and the Reform of

the U.K. Banking System', *Journal of Money, Credit and Banking*, Feb 1973.

H. G. Johnson, 'The Monetary Theory of Balance of Payments Policies', in *The Monetary Approach to the Balance of Payments*, ed. J. A. Frenkel and H. G. Johnson (London: Allen & Unwin, 1976).

J. M. Keynes, 'The "Ex-Ante" Theory of the Rate of Interest', *Economic Journal*, Dec 1937.

J. M. Keynes, *How to Pay for the War: A Radical Plan for the Chancellor of the Exchequer* (London: Macmillan, 1940); first published as three articles in *The Times* in Nov 1939.

N. Kaldor, 'The "New" Monetarism', *Lloyds Bank Review*, no. 97, July 1970.

S. C. Tsiang, 'The Monetary Theoretic Foundation of the Modern Monetary Approach to the Balance of Payments', *Oxford Economic Papers*, Nov 1977.

AUTHOR INDEX

SUBJECT INDEX